Ulysses' Sail

Ulysses' Sail

AN ETHNOGRAPHIC ODYSSEY
OF POWER, KNOWLEDGE, AND
GEOGRAPHICAL DISTANCE

Mary W. Helms

PRINCETON UNIVERSITY PRESS
PRINCETON, NEW JERSEY

Copyright © 1988 by Princeton University Press

Published by Princeton University Press, 41 William Street,
Princeton, New Jersey 08540
In the United Kingdom. Princeton University Press, Guildford, Surrey

All Rights Reserved

Library of Congress Cataloging in Publication Data will be found
on the last printed page of this book

ISBN 0-691-02840-0

Publication of this book has been aided by the Whitney Darrow
Fund of Princeton University Press

This book has been composed in Linotron Bembo type

Clothbound editions of Princeton University Press books are printed
on acid-free paper, and binding materials are chosen for strength
and durability. Paperbacks, although satisfactory for personal
collections, are not usually suitable for library rebinding

Printed in the United States of America
by Princeton University Press,
Princeton, New Jersey

Many shall run to and fro, and knowledge shall be increased
Book of Daniel 12:4, King James Version

Contents

vii

List of Illustrations

ix

LIST OF ILLUSTRATIONS

Preface

~~~~~~

Several years ago, as part of an ethnohistoric reconstruction of the structure and functioning of the native chiefdoms of Panama at the time of initial European contact, I postulated that Panamanian chiefs and neighboring elites in Colombia and Central America engaged in mutual long-distance activities that were of a political-ideological rather than strictly economic nature. More specifically, I proposed that, for elites of the pre-Columbian Intermediate Area, there was "common ground . . . between the chiefly pursuit of esoteric contacts with geographically distant peoples and the development . . . of esoteric contacts with cosmologically and cosmographically 'distant' supernatural forces" (Helms 1979:3).

Unfortunately the ethnohistoric and archaeological data directly pertinent to the pre-Columbian Intermediate Area do not allow for clear substantiation of this hypothesis. Yet this proposal, if it can be shown to be ethnographically valid, contains important implications for our understanding both of the nature of long-distance contacts among traditional societies and of the significance of such contacts in processes of cultural change. The purpose of the present volume is to redress the ethnographic limitations of my earlier work by exploring the ideological nature and political significance of geographical distance and long-distance contacts with data taken from the general ethnographic record. We may then be in a better position to gain new insights into the meaning of activities directed toward such realms, particularly where these involve elites of traditional societies.

In the several years that it has taken to pursue this subject I have enjoyed the support particularly of the University of North Carolina at Greensboro. I offer my sincere thanks for the research leave-of-absence granted to me for the spring semester of 1985, for the research grant-in-aid that financed much of the preparation of the final manuscript, and for the unflagging assistance of the library staff, particularly the interlibrary loan division. I also wish to acknowledge the assistance of skilled typists Carole Greene, Connie Prater, and Pattie Simpson, and photographer David Conner.

January 1987
Greensboro, North Carolina

Ulysses' Sail

I

Positions and Problems

Basic Hypotheses

In European literature the noble wanderer Ulysses pursues conflicting goals. In Homer's epic, after adventuring into unexplored regions of mystery and magic he simply wants to go home, to return to Penelope and the domestic bliss of a quiet life in Ithaca. In Dante Alighieri's *Commedia*, however, the hero forever abjures such creature comforts and turns away to sail west, in company with a valiant crew, beyond the portals of the known world, out through the pillars of Hercules into the starry darkness of the unknown Western Sea, driven by restless curiosity to a fatal search for wisdom and experience.[1]

THE SECURITY of home or the challenge of adventure; the centrality of the *axis mundi* or the lure of the distant horizon where the arching sky dips down to touch the earth. Both have their appeal and both have drawn men to them. Although many, indeed most, have stayed at home, an inquiring few, like Ulysses, have ventured forth to distant perils, riches, and adventures. This essay is concerned with the symbolic construction of geographical space and particularly geographical distance, with travel and knowledge of distant lands, with long-distance specialists of various sorts who make it their business to go away, perhaps for many months or years, and then, hopefully, return with tangible or intangible rewards, with gems and spices, fine cloth, or glistening feathers, with wondrous tales or closely guarded secrets of the legendary regions they have seen. Finally, this essay considers

---

[1] "O brothers, do not forbid your senses . . . the adventure of the world without human beings that lies beyond the sun. Consider the nature of your origin. You were not made to live like beasts, but for the pursuit of virtue and of knowledge" (Dante 1966:108).

the widespread association of political "elites" with foreign or distant goods and information. I am especially concerned with the political and ideological contexts or auras within which long-distance interests and activities may be conducted. Not only exotic materials but also intangible knowledge of distant realms and regions can be politically valuable "goods" both for those who have endured the perils of travel and for those sedentary homebodies who are able to acquire such knowledge by indirect means and use it for political advantage.

In discussing these general topics as they relate to nonindustrial societies I am building on several basic assumptions or hypotheses. The first concerns perceptions of geographical space and, more importantly, geographical distance. The second concerns the role played by political-religious elites in exploring and exploiting this distance. The third concerns our anthropological perceptions of the significance and activities of travelers to distant, or at least foreign, lands.

In considering geographical space and distance I am assuming that in traditional societies space and distance are not neutral concepts, but are accorded sociological, political, and especially ideological significance. More specifically, I argue that geographical distance from a given cultural heartland may correspond with supernatural distance from that center; that as one moves away from the *axis mundi* one moves toward places and people that are increasingly "different" and, therefore, may be regarded as increasingly supernatural, mythical, and powerful, the more distant they are from the heartland. As a corollary I argue that in traditional societies horizontal space and distance may be perceived in sacred or supernatural cosmological terms in much the same way that vertical space and distance from a given sacred center is often perceived in supernatural dimensions and accorded varying degrees of cosmological significance, perhaps being seen as ascending (or descending) and increasingly mystical levels of the universe, perhaps identified as the home of gods, of ancestors, or of good or evil spirits or powers. I posit that just as the sky (heavens) above may seem to curve around and touch, even merge with, the land or sea at the far horizon, so geographically distant places and peoples may be included with celestially distant "locales" and beings in the overall cosmology of a traditional society.

To the extent (and it varies greatly among societies) that geographically distant places, peoples, and experiences are perceived (either at first hand or by some manner of extrapolation) within essentially supernatural or cosmological contexts, then knowledge of, or acquaintance with, geographically distant places, peoples, and things rightfully falls within the domain of political-religious specialists whose job it is to deal with "mysteries." Knowledge of geographically distant phenomena, whether acquired directly or indirectly, may be expected to form part of the corpus of esoteric knowledge controlled by these traditional specialists, even as esoteric knowledge of "vertical" or "other" dimensions of the sacred falls within their domain. Stated somewhat differently, the select few who are either able or expected to become familiar with geographically distant phenomena may be accorded an aura of prestige and awe approaching the same order, if not always the same magnitude, as that accorded political-religious specialists or elites in general. In fact, those with direct experience of such distant matters are themselves likely either to be political-religious specialists or elites (or their agents) or, if derived from other sectors of society, may be accorded comparable honors, though to be sure these rewards may vary in accordance with the nature and context of their foreign experience.

The traditional anthropological approach to distant contacts frequently has been subsumed under the rubrics of long-distance "trade" and "traders." In this study trade is considered as only one of several possible motives for long-distance activities, and long-distance traders are subsumed under the more general concept of "long-distance specialists." In fact, while fully acknowledging the very great importance of long-distance trade and exchange in the political and economic systems of pre-industrial societies great and small, in this study I have chosen to be concerned primarily with political-ideological aspects of long-distance contacts in traditional societies and do not discuss trade per se except as long-distance trade and traders are associated with, or possibly subsumed under, political-ideological matters. In so doing I certainly do not intend to imply as a general tenet that the material dividends or economic contexts of long-distance contacts are in any way secondary or unimportant to cultural processes. I do wish, however, to approach the study of long-distance contacts from a different perspective and, in so doing, to sharpen our awareness of the diversity of underlying contexts, motives, and activities involved in traditional long-distance associations and, therefore, directly relevant to our understanding of the tangible and intangible results of such contacts.

It is important to emphasize that the assumptions outlined above are offered as general guidelines for the ensuing discussion rather than as scientific dictums to be proven or disproven by rigorous method. The ethnographic and ethnohistoric data on which this study rests are rarely so complete for any given society that all of the above "hypotheses" can be examined within a single setting. Rather, bits and pieces of information have been assembled from a wide range of cultures and will be examined and interpreted within the paradigms offered above. In effect, in the following chapters I present a series of essays on several topics that can be generally related in the final perspective, though not often within a single well-documented framework. Using ethnographic illustrations from many areas, I draw attention to various elements or characteristics associated with concepts and activities involving geographical distance under various circumstances. Ultimately, it is hoped, the accumulated weight of diverse pieces of evidence will support the general tenets outlined above.

The incompleteness of the data presented reflect the fact that the questions I am exploring usually have not been directly addressed in ethnographic reports (happily there are a few notable exceptions, e.g., Thornton 1980; Gossen 1974; Overing-Kaplan 1977; Sahlins 1981). Consequently, many data have been accumulated piecemeal from a range of book and journal articles originally written for other reasons. Which is to say that "fieldwork" for this study was conducted in the library stacks, and my information was obtained primarily from the wealth of ethnographic and ethnohistoric data that has accumulated over the last century. Presentation of this material, however, has necessitated its removal from the larger contexts of village studies, regional analyses, or topical reports in which I found it, and in some cases I

6

have undoubtedly introduced distortions or interpretations that the original authors did not include or did not intend. Yet, just as there have yet to be completely adequate solutions to the problem of retaining appropriate context in recording data from geographically located fieldwork, so I see no reason to ignore this body of library material because of problems of quality control. In spite of their incompleteness, the data are rich and fascinating, and presumably were originally compiled and published with the hope that they would be of some future value. The challenge lies not in the data per se, but in our interpretation of them.

In this respect I have chosen to range widely, using illustrative material from any and all ethnographic regions, juxtaposing examples from the Tlingit with evidence from Timbuktu. This approach again may be questioned. Suffice to say that it is my intent to discuss some general points which require ethnographic verification, and that the emphasis is intended to fall primarily on the topics considered rather than on the completeness of the ethnographic record. Here again, although problems of "apples and oranges" undoubtedly will appear to some, I am attempting to seek the middle ground between pure speculation and the extreme rigidity that would be enforced by strict acquiescence to the limitations of the data per se. Such problems are inherent in any attempts to discuss issues cross-culturally or when data are sought from already existing ethnographies.

Finally, I do not intend to imply that peoples in all traditional societies necessarily view geographical distance and long-distance contacts in the cosmological and political-ideological contexts discussed below. Anthropological common sense and the ethnographic record both suggest that there is a great range of relative emphases on the cross-cultural spectrum. Given the uneven nature of available data to date, it seems best to suspend explicit judgment on the degree of universality of this characteristic, at least for the moment.

Distance and Knowledge

Underlying the discussion in the following chapters are certain assumptions concerning the political significance of knowledge and the conceptualization of space and especially of distance that should be briefly reviewed by way of introduction. Let us begin with space and distance. Fundamental to my argument are two assumptions regarding space and distance in traditional society: that space and distance are neither neutral nor homogeneous concepts, and that they are not static concepts. Basically, following Durkheim's recognition of the importance of socially differentiated space,[2] I would concur with Giddens (1979:198–225; see also Pinxten et al. 1983:15–16, 159–60) that space (like time) is a dynamic factor in many aspects of social life and, accordingly, should be considered more seriously in our formulations of social theory. As Thornton discusses at some length (1980:8–13), space is not culturally relevant to only some societies (e.g., *civitas*) but not to others (e.g., *societas*); rather "concepts of differentiated space" (e.g., we–they; here–there) underlie many forms of social-territorial relationships. Nor is space simply an aspect of the "environment" in which social activity occurs. On the contrary, space often is an integral element in the nature of that activity and should be considered as such.

In this study, in which geographical aspects of space, particularly geographical distance, receive considerable attention, space is not considered just as an attribute of the physical landscape. Rather, to appreciate the symbolic significance accorded geographical space and distance it is necessary to recognize cognitive concepts of cosmic space, qualities of space as it is perceived to exist in all directions, above, below, and inclusive of the horizontal plane of the earth's surface. Space, in short, is a cultural con-

---

[2] "Space is not the vague and indetermined medium which Kant imagined; if purely and absolutely homogeneous, it would be of no use, and could not be grasped by the mind. Spatial representation consists essentially in a primary coordination of the data of sensuous experience. But this co-ordination would be impossible if the parts of space were qualitatively equivalent and if they were really interchangeable. To dispose things spatially there must be a possibility of placing them differently, of putting some at the right, others at the left, these above, those below, at the north of or at the south of, east or west, etc., etc., just as to dispose of states of consciousness temporally there must be a possibility of localizing them at determined dates. This is to say that space could not be what it is if it were not, like time, divided and differentiated . . . all these distinctions evidently come from the fact that different sympathetic values have been attributed to various regions" (Durkheim 1915:11).

ceptualization the nature or content of which may vary greatly depending on cultural context. Though definable in many dimensions, space in traditional society is nonetheless rarely considered to be as "vast," as infinite, or seemingly as neutral as are our concepts of the cosmos today. Space as an aspect of traditional "worlds" instead is finite in extent and is socially and cognitively differentiated into qualitatively different aspects, "identified" and filled with points and locations, with social interactions and paths of activity. Space is charged with meaning and differentiations, with mundane familiarities, and with cosmic mysteries. It changes shape and form. Its attributed powers and values, its intimacy or its expanse *give* significance to actions, people, places, things; make them accessible or render them "distant," make them mundanely commonplace or instill them with foreign exoticism.

This perspective, of course, derives largely not only from Durkheim but also from the seminal work of Mircea Eliade, who, in a series of volumes, explores the symbolic significance of space in considerable detail.[3] As is well known, much of Eliade's focus has been on the concept of the "Center" as the heartland of social and religious models of organized cosmic space and of social and ideological life, and as the focal point for communication with the sacred (Eliade 1969, especially pp. 39–56; see also Smith 1972 for a succinct survey of Eliade's contributions on the subjects of sacred space and also time). Consideration of the Center has also led to questions of accessibility or of "distance." As Eliade has shown, distance as one aspect or quality of space (and of time) is an important variable in actions and attitudes. At its simplest, distance means an interval of separation and the quality of the "not near" or "not here." Beyond that, "distance" and "distant" can convey a range of spatial, temporal, or relational associations. Since, in Eliade's work, "distance" is generally explored within

[3] The very diverse cultural conceptualizations and designations of space also have been recognized and analyzed by many other scholars representing several disciplines whose studies are of the utmost importance for those interested in pursuing any dimension of the subject. Further familiarity with this field of inquiry can be found in works by (among others) van Gennep (1960:15–18), Tuan (1977), Carlstein et al. (1978), Isaac (1965), Hallowell (1955), Watson (1970), Downs and Stea (1973), Kolaja (1969), Sorokin (1943), Turner (1972).

the context of the functions and meaning of the Center, it seems most appropriate to broaden the perspective by also considering the nature of distance as it relates to the "Periphery." Consequently, in this study distance in the context of peripheries of geographical space is the major concern.

Again, as we shall see in more detail, and as a moment's reflection readily suggests, the characteristics that constitute "distance" in such settings are extremely variable; fixed measurement of segmented units, of meters or of miles, is only one of many attributes for determining geographical "distance" (see Deutsch and Isard 1961). Subjective impressions ("it didn't seem far") or amount of time or degree of effort (type of communication or transportation) expended in reaching one's destination, whether "near" or "far," define or qualify even measured units of distance. Nonetheless, though distance may be a relative concept, the qualities attributed to geographical "distance" and to the "overcoming" of distance by time or effort, as well as specific locational attributes of distant phenomena, can confer distinct characteristics on people, things, and experiences associated with geographical distance. The perspectives emphasized in this study rest on the argued assumption that the significance of interchanges of peoples and material goods across geographical distances can be better understood if we know something of the qualities attributed to space and distance in particular situations, or at least appreciate that symbolic qualities of some sort are likely to be attached to concepts of geographical distance and by extension to tangible expressions of experiences with distance.

As Eliade has again shown, discussion of space and distance also implies discussion of time, for time (as fixed points of the past and the future or as periods of duration) is an aspect of both, and vice versa. In the analysis of geographical aspects of essentially cosmological space and distance with which I am concerned cerned, the relevant temporal associations are primarily with cosmological time. Cosmological space-time is most obvious in the association of geographical distance with a range of concepts concerning things and events that, like geographical distance itself, are "not immediately here," are "outside" and "out of sight" and, therefore, more or less unknown, concepts involving past origins (creations, ancestors, beginnings) or future prospects (utopias, afterlives, underworlds), and the ties between the present and the temporally/spatially distant (see Eliade 1963, especially pp. 34–38).

Insights and understandings that derive from comprehension of the space-time significance accorded to geographical distance and the things derived therefrom become part of the corpus of esoteric knowledge controlled by political-religious specialists as an attribute and legitimation of their status, power, and authority. The importance of knowledge as an attribute of leadership and as the ultimate expression of the concept (quality) of humanness can hardly be overemphasized. In the mythologies and cosmologies of a great many (perhaps all) societies, the capacity for wisdom, knowledge, and understanding identifies people as distinct from animals, while the attainment and expression of knowledge and understanding separates, refines, and elevates the condition of human existence from those attending animal existence. Within human society itself, the further elaboration of wisdom and knowledge identifies additional human qualities and social differentiations, separating some persons from the wider group, elevating them to higher positions of power and influence, sacralizing and even sanctifying them, as wisdom becomes a veritable "gift of the gods." Thus Lienhardt says that traditions of the Skilluk kings "give details of their duplicity and cunning, their military prowess, and their cruelty and caprice. In this way they are approximated to God for these, *and particularly intelligence and knowledge*, are qualities by which a man manifests the power of God in him" (Lienhardt 1954:159, my emphasis). In a more pragmatic vein a comment by de Laguna concerning the qualifications of chiefs among the Yakutat Tlingit neatly summarizes the political significance of knowledge: "The higher the rank of the individual and the greater the consequent responsibilities, the more stress was set upon wisdom, judgment, and education. . . . [The sib chief's] word alone could command respect . . . because he was known to be well educated and therefore wise" (1972:465).

A Tlingit chief's education included the development of a range of abilities: curing, artistic skills, knowledge of weather patterns and animal behavior, but especially knowledge of traditional songs, histories, stories, language, and ceremonial details *not only of his own people but of as many outside groups as he could learn about or personally visit* (ibid., pp. 465–66; my emphasis). This list is a familiar one. Proper conduct of rituals and performances, expertise in chants, stories, dances and myths, divination, curing, and (as Chapters 3 and 4 explore in more detail) knowledge of the ways of foreigners and other "external" conditions form the "stock in trade" of many honored elders, shamans, clan leaders, chiefs and kings—all those who "really know," whose voices, like the voices of the old men of the Aranda, are "invested with the authority of knowledge . . ." (Strehlow 1947:159).

Other categories of esoteric knowledge involving domains that are foreign or "outside" in one way or another have also legitimated authority and underwritten expressions of power in many societies. The art of scribing—of that which is "written on bamboo and silk, . . . engraved on metal and stone, . . . cut on vessels to be handed down to posterity" (Chang 1983:89), or otherwise recorded in sacred texts, both the magic of the written word itself and the ability to read and write—has often been interpreted as a mystical craft that reveals divinations, opens the secrets of sacred writings, provides the efficacy of amulets and holy talismans, and preserves ancestral knowledge. Literacy has been the main qualification of many holy men and learned scholars who have sought procurement as diviners and advisers to noble princes, kings, and emperors. As we shall see, their magical talent has been particularly appreciated by chiefs of foreign tribes where literacy was not a native art, and where the seemingly superhuman capacities of learned stranger-scribes was enhanced by their derivation from a foreign land.

Literacy is only one of a number of esoteric crafts and skills that attest to the exceptional abilities and powers of those who have mastered them. Master navigators in Polynesia, smiths in Africa, metallurgists in the Americas, astronomers and astrologers in imperial China or among the Maya have all evidenced control of special forms of knowledge that granted them exceptional status. The ultimate exemplar of the sacred craftsman with high standing, however, is the "wise stranger" or "culture hero" who not only commands exceptional abilities but also comes from a distant place, who introduces heretofore unknown skills, and then, like the Ngonde chief who long ago arrived as a stranger bringing agriculture and the art of smelting iron to unsettled hunters and gatherers, "[becomes] their chief because he knew much that they did not" (Wilson 1958:21, 48–49).

Esoteric knowledge is knowledge of the unusual, the exceptional, the extraordinary; knowledge of things that in some way or another lie beyond the familiar everyday world. It should not be surprising, then, to find that many domains of esoteric knowledge include "foreign" elements from geographically distant places, whether it be knowledge of the customs or sacred texts of foreign peoples, recognition of the contributions of foreign scholars and culture heroes, or the acquisition of rare and powerful wonders from legendary or cosmologically potent distances.

In all modes of exceptional intellectual endeavor where knowledge and, therefore, power is seen to derive at least in part from familiarity with "outside" phenomena (whether terrestrial or nonterrestrial), those who wish to acquire or manifest such power must, ipso facto, become experts on things and places "outside." In so doing they will unavoidably be paralleling knowledge of geographically and/or ideologically distant domains with supporting concepts regarding the social and political "distance" that rightfully accrues to those specialists who delve into esoteric matters removed from the much more localized (geographically and ideologically) world of mundane everyday life. Of course, it is not only the peculiar nature of esoteric knowledge that creates political "distance" but the politics involved in dealing with such information. Indeed, it is the political usefulness of the control of knowledge per se that creates discriminating categories of knowledge and identifies "esotericism" in knowledge in the first place. Controlling access to esoteric knowledge, in turn, becomes a major means of effecting political and ideological "distancing" in society. The means both of producing this type of knowledge and of controlling access to it are diverse, but very often they involve some means or expression of secrecy (see Lindstrom 1984).

Secrecy can connote many things, but common to all is the implication of concealment or reticence and the production of mystique. Within the context of esoteric knowledge, concealment or reticence or mystique can be used in an intriguing number and variety of ways to effect "distance" or separation of one sort or another. Some manifestations of secrecy in regard to knowledge serve to keep both information and the expression of power and authority hidden from the uninitiated. Biernoff describes such a situation among aborigines in eastern Arnhem Land in which individuals pass through a series of levels of intellectual development in which each successive level provides a different and distinctive world view unknown to (kept secret from) initiates in lower levels. Only the elders have passed through all levels, have access to *all* types of knowledge, know all the variant world views, and therefore have all the power that such knowledge can provide. Yet, in keeping with the secrecy and hiddenness associated with learning, these elders keep a low public profile; they, too, stay "hidden" from public view. "Power and authority are often almost unrecognizable as such, when viewed from outside, as they are so frequently successfully hidden by secrecy, with an absence of overt, public action" (Biernoff 1978:103, 104).

In marked contrast to these retiring Australian elders are the many situations in which secrecy is used to protect or limit the distribution of powerful knowledge to a small number of individuals in order that those few, armed with potent insights and powers, can then properly distinguish themselves in public (see Bird and Kendall 1980:17). So, for example, a Maori orator, knowing that one of the qualities of a good speech is erudition, may conceal the real extent of the chants, songs, proverbs, genealogies he knows so that he can constantly produce a "fresh" and seeming endless supply of material for future audiences and also protect the power inherent in chants by limiting their currency and familiarity (Salmond 1975:55).

In these and other examples,[4] a social-ideological hierarchy or

---

[4] Sometimes image management is the proper approach for ritual leaders to use. According to Murphy, among the Kpelle "more important than the actual secret content . . . is the skill with which one can convey the impression of having dangerous secret knowledge. . . ." Impression is managed by a brief, taciturn, guarded speech style: "A [ritual specialist] does not make long conversations"

set of specialist statuses is identified and "separated" from the common body politic by the mutual recognition of asymmetry of knowledge by ritual and political leaders and audience. Such asymmetry can be taken to considerable extremes, to the point where knowledge specialists may literally withdraw from participation in active daily life and enter a life of seclusion—another type of "distancing" or "hiddenness" or secrecy. Such was the expected behavior of the high prince of the Kinga of East Africa (Park 1966:232), and such is the atmosphere often surrounding hermits and mystic recluses, such as the "saints" in Swat Pathan society, where, according to Barth, the awe in which saints are held by Pathan villagers (and the political influence gained thereby) derives from their knowledge and mystic powers enhanced by the asocial isolation of most saints, who avoid usual village socializing (Barth 1965:101). A different type of secretness and "hiddenness" can be associated with high-level policy in situations like that evidenced by Peruvian Incas where the necessary uncertainties, vacillations, discussions, disputations involved in decision making might be aired only between the Inca and his private secretary so that only a firmly resolved conclusion was presented to the outside world (Zuidema 1982:426).

Perhaps the ultimate expression of the extreme to which secret knowledge (knowledge of "distant" things/places) can separate or distance the specialist from society (and one which leads us back to the subject of geographical distance and foreign knowledge) is expressed in the concept of heroic behavior as defined by the Mande of West Africa and presented in various texts discussed by Bird and Kendall (1980). The content of Mande heroic literature focuses on the quest for strange or esoteric knowledge, for the secrets that underlie the mystical powers or forces that human actions unleash. The hero in these epics is viewed as someone with very special powers whose actions stand in considerable

(1981:670, 673). Another strategy, exemplified by the Mambai of East Timor, allows for outward demonstration of the possession of knowledge while simultaneously withholding content—a technique again managed by skillful speech or by keeping ritual performances deliberately obscure (Traube 1984). Alternatively, the deliberate introduction of complications that can enhance obscurity can achieve a comparable goal, as Malagasy astrologers well know (Bloch 1968:294). For a general discussion of secrecy see Tefft (1980).

contrast to more mundane behavior and who, as an individual pursuing his own interests, tends to have a disrupting influence on social, group life. Since the hero wishes to distinguish himself with great deeds made possible by his exceptional abilities, he takes pains to keep his affairs and abilities highly secret so that other, ordinary men will not learn his powers or know how to perform heroic acts. In the text of one of the epics, however, the *hero's* secret power and extraordinary abilities are contrasted with the esoteric, unknown qualities of the *stranger*, which is to say, with someone who not only does not respond to the pull of social conformity but also severs bonds of social affiliation and actually stands outside society (Bird and Kendall 1980:18).

Bird and Kendall point out that, in contrast to Western epics, Mande epics and Mande heroes focus more on the acquisition and display of mystical magical power than on physical heroic action. Yet in some ways the Mande hero's individualistic quest for esoteric knowledge suggests the Dantean figure of Ulysses, who physically turned away from society to travel and explore unknown regions in search of exceptional knowledge. This point is not lost on Mande young people. Although raised in large, close-knit families, youths learn that "their culture lavishes esteem and adulation on its rebels. The figures preserved in history are those who broke with the traditions of their village, severed the bonds of the [social collectivity], traveled to foreign lands searching for special powers and material rewards, but just as importantly, they are also the ones who returned to the villages and elevated them to higher stations" (ibid., p. 22). The effect of this important literary tradition is "to spin the headstrong youth out into the world of adventure," to convince him he is a person of destiny. Whether he is simply attending school outside the village or enduring the miserable life of a migrant worker abroad, at home he is a hero whose experiences and exploits return glory to his people.

The equation of travel with individuality and sedentariness with group conformity will emerge in Chapter 3 in discussion of both real and perceived characteristics of long-distance travelers. The value of distant lands and peoples as sources of esoteric knowledge and exotic material wealth of more or less restricted access will also be a recurrent theme in following chapters. Indeed, the relative inaccessibility of geographically distant realms, the difficulties and dangers inherent in traveling to or otherwise contacting distant places, and the relatively few long-distance specialists in most societies would seem readily to pre-adapt such contacts (and the resulting goods and information) as "esoteric" phenomena, and thereby as fit subject matter for political-religious leaders.

The reverse side of secrecy in acquisition of knowledge (and often paired with an emphasis on secrecy) is open competitive display of knowledge gained, when learned men vie with each other in exhibition of their esoteric repertoires (Ong 1982:43–44). Here, too, knowledge of geographically distant places and things may be encountered, even highlighted, among the esoterica displayed. Nowhere is this form of "heroic challenge" better expressed than in the Finnish national epic, the Kalevala, where not only is esoteric knowledge conspicuously displayed, but the competition, fittingly enough, takes place in a legendary distant place, Kalevala, the Land of Heroes, whose learned men are unexcelled. In one episode, the fame of Väinämöinen, the great culture hero, patriarch, and wise minstrel of the north, spread far and wide until it reached another learned singer, Joukahainen, a "meager youth" of Lapland to the south, who enviously made the long journey to Kalevala and challenged Väinämöinen to a song duel. Unfortunately for Joukahainen, his own not insubstantial learning was branded as mere childish tales and "woman's wisdom" by the older singer, who knew much more about hidden truths fit for "bearded heroes" who lived in legendary places. After a lengthy competition involving understanding of the "origins" of things (i.e., basic knowledge of the creation of the universe), Joukahainen lost, and by a magical song of Väinämöinen's was himself sunk chin-deep into a muddy swamp, where he stayed until he had promised sufficient recompence to Väinämöinen for his brash challenge (Kirby 1907: Runa III).

Fortunately for more contemporary contenders of the ethnographic present, knowledge competitions generally do not end in such extreme conditions, although the participants undoubtedly take such challenges with equal seriousness and debate the "origins of things" with equal intensity. Such challengers may also find that knowledge derived from distant places (as Väinämöinen exemplifies) is highly prestigious and particularly difficult to challenge. Such, at least, is the experience of San Blas Kuna (Panama) chanters and shamans who prefer to acquire esoteric knowledge from instructors outside their home regions in no small measure because the greater prestige and authority associated with knowledge derived from prestigious teachers in a distant place stand them in good stead in the rivalrous status challenges that arise, particularly in public ceremonies, when one learned man casts doubt on the extent or accuracy of another's learning (see Chapter 4). Indeed, during public ceremonies, when liberal supplies of chicha encourage self-assertiveness among a usually restrained people, knowledge displays, including expertise in foreign experiences and languages, erupt dramatically even among otherwise ordinary men. "Ex-sailors brag of their voyages, and those who know foreign languages speak them ostentatiously and expound at length about language-learning: young educated men who otherwise speak Cuna insist on Spanish, and those who claim to know English show off their few words . . ." (Howe 1974:256–57; see also 160–65, 232–33, 252–60; 1986:59). Jivaro shamans of South America, who have come to value the superior magical powers that derive from neighboring Canelos shamans, who acquire even more superior powers, in turn, from contact with Europeans (missionaries), are equally competitive, a practice that has further encouraged acquisition of new techniques and knowledge from afar (Harner 1973:202; see also Chapter 3 below). "Competitive creativity" in ritual proceedings among ritual specialists of the Iraqw of Tanzania, who have great faith in powers deriving from the "outside," has had a similar effect (Thornton 1980:210; see also Gladwin 1970:132).

In short, as I illustrate in more detail below, knowledge of distant places, peoples, things, and events may be considered a significant part of the overall body of esoteric understanding that informs political-religious specialists and their activities. That this can be so derives, in turn, from perceptions of geographical space and distance that accord cosmologically symbolic significance to such realms and thereby identifies them as appropriate subjects for specialists in matters of sacred or at least supernatural distance; matters that, regardless of (or inclusive of) the type of distance involved, are by definition esoteric and exceptional and not within the purview of ordinary men.

2

The Cultural Creation of Space
and Distance

Left to itself, the physical landscape "has no form." Replete though it may seem to be with mountains and valleys, rivers and forests, islands, oceans, and continental expanses, a landscape has no meaningful shape and significance until it is accorded place and identity in the social and cognitive worlds of human experience. Human experience, in turn, invests territory and landscape with a most remarkable diversity of properties and interpretations which have in common the faculty of ordering and organizing what otherwise appears to be a very chaotic world.

Given the peculiarities of the human perspective, order and organization are required in both micro and macro dimensions; on the one hand, the organization of individual, family, and village life within the rhythms of the days, months, and years; on the other, nothing less than the investigation and interpretation not only of the earth but of the cosmos, of everything in the heavens above, the earth below, and the waters under the earth. The greatest intellectual challenge (and grandest human conceit) lies in combining the two; in seeking to interpret and embed social continuity and harmony at home within the "natural" or cosmological order, and seeking to interpret the nature and significance of the universe within the perspectives of the social order at home.[1]

Either way, the ordering of home and the ordering of the universe involve constant concern with the known and the un-

[1] Becker's comment on "microcosmization" and "macrocosmization," though focusing on celestial phenomena versus man and his earthly living space, is appropriate: ". . . by means of micro- and macrocosmization man humanized the heavens and spiritualized the earth and so melted sky and earth together in an inextricable unity" (Becker 1975:18).

known, for each identifies the other. Generally, the known is likely to be more immediate or closer at hand, while the unknown lies at a distance, often invisible or "out of sight," up above in levels of the heavens or down below in the netherworlds beneath the earth, in the future or in the ancestral past, or beyond terrestrial horizons in geographically distant lands. The unknown, in other words, is situated toward the extremes of a temporal plane or dimension (past and future) or of spatial planes or dimensions, either vertical (the above and the below) or horizontal (geographical distance in any direction).

These locational planes may be combined in cosmological schemata, and generally are. Associations between time and space, either vertical or horizontal, have been frequently recorded in ethnographic descriptions of native cosmologies. Associations between the two spatial dimensions, the vertical and the horizontal, though attested to ethnographically, seem somewhat more problematical, possibly either because there is more cultural variation (e.g., emphasis can be placed either on the horizontal or the vertical, or on both, but to varying degrees) or because this aspect of native cosmology has not yet been rigorously investigated.

Particularly in nonliterate societies, concern with the spatially or temporally unknown and with the ordering of cosmic (natural) and social forces must be expressed by tangible celestial or terrestrial manifestations. Thus close study is accorded and cosmological (or sociological) interpretations are applied to constellations and the movements of heavenly bodies, to oceans, rivers, forests, mountains, caves, and to numerous other landforms, flora, and fauna. In this chapter emphasis is placed primarily on conceptualizations of terrestrial phenomena and particularly on the values accorded to geographical distance. In so doing, of course, I am putting paradigmatic emphasis on only *part* of a cosmological unity that for most traditional societies includes terrestrial and celestial space, operational (ecological) and epochal (historical) time, and strongly defined cosmic centers or *axis mundis*, as well as cosmic peripheries or frontiers.

21

Spatial Zones

The ethnographic record shows that terrestrial space and landscape phenomena often have been defined in a variety of ways to illustrate or make tangible basic contrasts between normative or moral orders. Sometimes the contrast highlights the safe, civilized, cultural life of home with the dangerous, uncivilized, "natural" world "outside." Sometimes the contrast distinguishes between the "near" and known and the "far" and unknown or, perhaps better said, between the directly known and the "known about," where what is "known about" parts of the outside world can be adjusted as needed to communicate particular moral states of great good or great evil or particular cosmological conditions of great powers and potencies.

Perhaps the most common (and ethnographically familiar) means of marking such contrasts by territorial differentiation is achieved by recognizing socioterritorial dichotomies or a series of zones, often concentric, to which are attributed a range of sociological or ideological values and characteristics. Within the Western tradition, for example, such a contrast is stated in the dichotomy between the ancient Hebrew concept of the wild or the wilderness as a place or condition of desolation (desert, wasteland) devoid of God's blessing, and recognition of the settled community or countryside as a place of fruitfulness, filled with such blessings (e.g., White 1972:12–14; Smith 1969:108). Other examples of dichotomies and of zoning (or some aspect thereof, e.g., emphasis on boundaries or thresholds between zones) appear virtually worldwide. Let us briefly consider a few to get a sense of the contrasts expressed.

The Bashu of eastern Zaire offer a typical example of dichotomized zoning from Africa. The Bashu view the homestead and the bush as separate and conflicting worlds. The bush is an extremely dangerous place associated with "disorder, wild animals, ritual pollution, and malevolent spirits." All ritually dangerous things, activities, and beings are kept there, away from the homestead which, in contrast, is associated with "order, domestic animals, ritual purity, and benevolent spirits." When, and if, the world of the bush intrudes into the world of the homestead, misfortune results (Packard 1980:244).

The Lugbara of Uganda and the Congo, in turn, recognize a range of sociospatial categories. Each family cluster, with its neighboring lineages—"normal" people at the center of society— considers itself surrounded by a fringe of societal quasi-members or "closer strangers" who are thought to be not quite normal, to possess superhuman powers, and whose territories, distantly visible in the smoke of their field burning, are filled with sorcery and magic. Still farther away, and totally outside the Lugbara social system, is the rest of the world, peopled with inverted and asocial beings who are hardly human in appearance, walk on their heads, and somehow manage to exist in thick forests rather than on the open plateau that the Lugbara inhabit (Middleton 1960:236–37).

In an intriguing study of the sociopolitical use of space among the Iraqw of Tanzania, Thornton describes another variation on the zoning theme. Beyond the cleared, sacred, ritually pure inhabited area of households lies a frontier region and, beyond that, the dangerous wilderness. The frontier is an "outside" realm traditionally inhabited by Iraqw who had been exiled for antisocial activities or, more recently, settled by emigrants led by ritual specialists into this rather unwholesome territory. The more distant wilderness includes uninhabited bush (typified by trees) and lands populated by hostile outsiders, some of whom are viewed as part of the natural disasters of the wilderness, where, for example, one may expect to encounter either Masai raiders or rampaging buffalo (Thornton 1980:73–83, 88, 125).[2]

Good examples of spatial zoning can also be found in lowland South America. The simplest are again dichotomies between two zones separating man and nature, the public and the private, the safe and the dangerous. A frequent expression of such contrasts in the great river systems of the Amazon basin compares the inhabited river region as a safe and "socialized" space, where every river bend and local place is named, and therefore known, with the forest beyond, a dangerous, mysterious and undifferentiated

[2] See also Fernandez (1982.106–9) for detailed discussion of a diverse range of "zone-worlds" from village to deep forest among the Fang of Gabon.

wilderness of spirits and monsters (e.g., Goldman 1940; 1977 regarding the Cubeo).

Variations on this pattern contrast not only river with forest but also downstream with upstream. The Barasana of southeastern Colombia and northwestern Brazil, for example, identify the river mouth and downstream portion of their domain with properly socialized and "respectable" agricultural life, and view as distinctly marginal the upstream and sidestream reaches, where agriculture and fishing are difficult and hunters and gatherers must rely on forest products. Upstream hunters and gatherers, however, are also seen as mediating between good and proper downstream life and the evil forces of the still more distant headwater forest, the habitat of forest animals and cannibalistic evil spirits (Hugh-Jones 1977:192–94; see also Hugh-Jones 1979).[3] Comparable zoning is described by Roe for the Shipibo of the Peruvian montaña, who associate "true" people, civilization, and light with an inner ring of village life, and see spirits, hostile tribes, and foreigners in the surrounding green wall of the dark, dangerous tropical forest. At the farthest reaches, in the most distant mountains, are the most exceptional beings; ogres, Amazons, and culture heroes (Roe 1982:136, 138).

Island life, with its natural zones of dry land, littoral, and sea, would also seem to offer obvious material for cosmological zoning. Indeed, symbolic spatial zoning can even extend overseas beyond the horizon to include distant islands or even the sky.[4] The Gawa Islanders in the northeast Massim region of Papua New

[3] The Gê-speaking groups of central Brazil are famous in the ethnographic literature for their use of physical space, particularly circles, to express the dynamic and mysterious qualities of life and the cyclical unity of time and space (Posey 1979:3–4). Seeger describes a set of six concentric zones recognized by the Suya, who consider the plaza ritual center, surrounding houses and wasteland, and even the more distant garden zones to be reasonably safe, domestic, "named" regions which are surrounded, in turn, by distinctly antisocial, though still "named," forest containing both useful products and wild animals and enemies. Still farther away lies the unnamed, powerfully dangerous, distant forest inhabited by monsters and mythical beasts (Seeger 1977:342–47, 353, 355; 1981:66–70, 77–79, 210–11; Posey 1979:3–4).
[4] The examples briefly considered here refer to several islands or island clusters associated with the kula trade ring, and are derived from studies concerned with the ideology of kula activities.

Guinea discussed by Munn (1977) distinguish four broad spatial zones: inhabited hamlets on top of the island, the bush extending down the cliffs, the beaches, and the sea. It is more meaningful, though, to consider these zones as two broad divisions separated by a liminal threshold. The land zones, or land as a whole, is contrasted with the sea in qualities of motion and weight. Land is stable and heavy, weighted down, while the sea is associated with lightness, slipperiness, speed, and upwardness. The intermediate beach, in contrast, is somewhat anomalous. It is a contact point both for overseas visitors and for foreign-derived evil and sickness, and is a site for Gawan purification rites (Munn 1977:40–41).

Other investigators have viewed the ocean itself as a sort of immense bridge or threshold between contrasting zones of near and far. Montague, discussing Trobriand concepts of spatial reality, identifies a pair of land zones, the Trobriand earth and distant foreign lands of kula contacts, respectively, bridged by the ocean. This reality, however, also symbolizes contrasting categories of outer and inner "experience." Outer experience is that which, like stone, is substantial, solid, directly perceivable through vision, and includes living people of the Trobriands, while inner experience is amorphous, like wind, indirectly perceptible (as noise, hearing, smell), full of movement and instability, and includes other-worldly ancestral ghosts. Foreign lands across the sea, being out of sight, invisible from home, are conceptually associated with the qualities of inner experience, and foreigners, though seemingly "solid," are in reality amorphous beings and are correlated with inner category beings. The ocean, which appears solid from a distance but dissolves into movement on closer view, is a conveyance between these realms, allowing movement back and forth between them (Montague 1980:74–78, 83–86).

The ocean not only contacts distant lands but also contacts the sky, and allows us to consider the sky as the outermost zone of a series of spatial differentiations that begin at a home base. Tambiah presents just such a scheme also derived from Trobriand categories and expressed in myths and fantasies in which canoe travels are compared with magical trips through the sky. Land, again, signifies "anchoring," stability, and traditional agricultural life, while the sea, separated from the land by the beach and its spiritual powers, is characterized by unanchored movement, turbulence, speed, up and down motion, and, by virtue of contacting kula islands, as a route to possible fame or failure. The ocean is also the "middle domain" between land and sky. Sky, which arches above the sea, contains an intensified set of the same values associated with the sea—speed, motion, buoyance, expanse of vision. Yet sky and sea also meet, and when they do they create power-filled contact or boundary points, just as sea and land conjoin at the beach, which then becomes charged with procreative power. If sea and sky conjoin badly, shipwreck will result. Sea and sky conjoined properly, however, identify points of positive contact, as at the horizon or at islands on the horizon where ritually charged exchanges of kula valuables may be conducted (Tambiah 1983:192–98).

The conjunction of ocean and sky or at least (in more continental settings) of water and sky, generally at the horizon, extends horizontal terrestrial space into what is often a more encompassing vertical or celestial space. As such it would seem to go beyond the intentions of this review, which is focused on concepts accorded geographically distant earthly places. But it is also a tenet of this essay that geographically distant places may partake of the same or comparable values accorded to symbolically charged vertical planes or levels that are also "distant" from the home center. It is logically satisfying, therefore, to find considerable ethnographic evidence for the symbolic recognition of the conjunction of earth and sky, of horizontal distance and vertical distance, at a distant point or boundary. (Conjunction with the underworld at the horizon or world's end is not irrelevant in this context and is also amply attested to ethnographically, but will be set aside in this overview in favor of the more visually obvious celestial realm).

In general, earthly or terrestrial conjunctions with the sky are interpreted as contact points or as a boundary between these two domains, as exemplified by the Trobriand concepts elucidated by Tambiah. The celestial realm is frequently viewed either as a hemispheric or bowl-shaped dome arching over the earth or encircling ocean and touching at the horizon, or as a flat plane (or series of planes) suspended above the earth but "connected" through pillars or earth-bearers or points of some sort (e.g., constellations of stars, pillars of precious stones, waterfalls, high mountain peaks, or tall trees) located either at or toward the world's end or at (what we define as) cardinal points. Specific examples are numerous and show much individual variation. The Yakutat Tlingit, for one, believed that the sky touched the water at the horizon, yet the end of the earth lay even farther beyond. From behind or beyond the horizon strange things could come as "from the edge of the world, perhaps from islands out of sight of land, or from the mysterious realm beyond the barrier of the horizon" (de Laguna 1972:794). In the case of the Yakutat villagers, these strange, foreign things included drift iron, bamboo, and all manner of exciting flotsam carried by the Japanese current and strewn along the ocean beach. There are stories of men who tried in vain to visit the places from which these treasures came. "One man from Sitka . . . drifted out to sea, beyond sight of land. He came to an island where he lived among the sea otters. After a year he was able to return. . . . Presumably he came close to the edge of the world" (ibid.).

In many cosmological schemes the junctions of earth and sky also effected exchange between these two realms. Many of these interactions involve widespread beliefs in a great circulation of water that flows down streams and rivers to the ocean, then moves up to celestial levels, where it may flow back along celestial "rivers," like the Milky Way (thought to mirror earthly streams), to return to earth eventually as rain or in river form in cosmologies where the Milky Way is believed to meet earthly rivers at the horizon (see Hugh-Jones 1982:195; Urton 1981:37–38, 64, 56–60). The contact points or boundaries between the celestial and the terrestrial also allow culture heroes or ancestors to move between these two dimensions by traveling to a horizontal or world's end contact point and then moving up into the celestial plane (or down to the underworld), reversing the process on the return trip. "There was a widespread belief in Polynesia that [the earth and sea] was simply a flat surface terminating at the horizon and over which the dome-shaped sky spread as a lid; . . . souls of the dead, traveling across the sea to the horizon, could pass hence downwards into mythical subterranean regions . . . or upwards into the skies" (Williamson 1933a:77; see also 1933b:305–10). In some cases the dead simply stayed at a place that extended beyond or behind the base of the horizon (1933a:307–9). Consequently, foreigners were those who "came from behind the sky": "in the Marquesas the firmament was regarded as the lid or cover of the earth. The people believed that the blue shade of the atmosphere was solid matter, and that the sky touched the horizon, and that was why they took for gods the strangers who first arrived at their islands" (ibid., p. 91; see also Goodenough 1986:558–59).

Emphasis on boundaries or transformational thresholds between spatial zones, rather than on zones themselves, may present sharper symbolic contrasts. Boundaries, even if shifting and movable, can emphasize a more exclusive sense of "us" versus "not us." Boundaries can make the *edge* as important as the *center*. Whereas zones, particularly of the concentric variety, can give a sense of graduated change from the center out toward the periphery, boundaries or thresholds mark the point *within* which proper life is expected to exist, and separate it more definitively from that which lies without. Boundaries keep (or try to keep) the "good" inside and the "evil" outside. Boundaries keep all eyes turned back, inward toward the center, or, for those who must venture forth, mark the point where ritual protection must begin to safeguard travelers and where purification must take place on their return before they may safely re-enter society.

Perhaps the most elaborate or demonstrative examples of cosmological boundary marking occur in highly ranked chiefdoms and in states, where sacred images or the sanctified ruler himself ceremonially circumscribe the realm. Thus, in Hawaii, images of the gods were carried each year on a ceremonial procession around each major island to signify possession or retention of the land (kingdom) (Sahlins 1981:18–19). Similarly, newly crowned Southeast Asian kings marched around their capitals or toured principal shrines to define and symbolize the protected sacredness of their realms (Wheatley 1971:433). On a grander scale, the Chinese Emperor Shun inaugurated the practice of making a ceremonial circuit of the four sacred mountains on the borders of his kingdom every five years (in the intervening years the emperor remained in his capital, symbolizing the axis of his domain) (ibid., p. 434).[5]

The contrasting perceptions of sacred versus profane space created by such boundaries is also nicely expressed by several examples from less complex societies in southwestern North America. Navajo concepts of space and the structure of the world illustrate the point. The Navajo universe is defined by four sacred mountains, located roughly to the east, west, south and north, which delimit the territory composing the Navajo world. Even though the actual boundaries of this world are somewhat "fuzzy" and unstable, moving with expansions of population or territory and not visibly marked, its exclusiveness is apparent in the very clear, often emphatic distinction between Navajos and non-Navajos and in the assertion that all really important phenomena are concerned with the Navajo world and Navajo deeds.[6] Everything else, being non-Navajo, is considered to cause trouble or chaos and to be potentially dangerous to the Navajo people (Pinxten et al. 1983:22). Non-Navajo persons are regarded as bad influences and as sources of "noise" who will take away Navajo knowledge and weaken those possessing such knowledge (ibid., p. 26; Reichard 1963:158). The outside world itself is undefinable because it is indefinite and uncontrollable. The circumscribed space of the

---

[5] In actuality the borders, or better said, frontiers of the kingdom varied considerably in character, that of the north more clearly delineating Chinese from steppe and forest dwellers while that of the south was much more unstable and far less clear-cut (cf. Schafer 1967:34).

[6] For Navajos there can be no real sense of spatiality or worldliness in the outside world; only "distant places linked through voyages," as exemplified by an account by a Navajo woman of two trips away from the Navajo reservation to Chicago and to San Francisco, in which she provided detailed information on traveling through the Navajo reservation, passing the Sacred Mountains, and being at her place of destination, but gave no attention to the vast territories between the Navajo lands and Chicago and San Francisco, respectively (Pinxten et al. 1983:24, 147).

Tewa concepts of the sacredness of their bounded world, where all good and desirable things should stay, and the dangers of the land outside the four sacred mountains are very similar to Navajo beliefs. Those who had to venture into the outer world, such as buffalo hunters, sought ritual assistance prior to departure, for they were leaving the Tewa world and would be among people (Plains Indians) whom the Tewa did not recognize as such. On their return the hunters were again subjected to ritual precautions and purifications in order to be safely reintegrated into Tewa society (Ortiz 1969:172–73).

Navajo world is to be filled as much as possible with controllable good, while uncontrollable evil is to be dispersed beyond, the farther the better, so as to diminish its power. Consequently, foreign things, being distributed over large areas and not under Navajo control, are very dangerous (ibid.).

These examples of boundaries and zones serve as reminders that in traditional societies the recognized extent of the political-religious cosmos may be geographically limited—a very different concept from that of the all-inclusive, global cosmos held by members of Western societies today.[7] Other physical territories, including those that may be the setting for necessary activities such as subsistence hunting (see note 6) or long-distance traveling or trading, may be located geographically outside the sacred precepts. Existence beyond the borders of the cosmically blessed and protected, however, does not necessarily (though it may) render such territory devoid of symbolic status or of mystical significance and contexts. On the contrary, although (or rather, since) the region and its inhabitants may lie beyond the realm of the safe and the known, considerable attention to ritual procedures and protection may be required of travelers or resource seekers before it can be safely traversed or exploited (see Chapter 3). In this very important respect, therefore, contact with the geographically distant "unknown" may be considered comparable to contact with distant spiritual levels and unknowns.

Similarly, to the extent that lands outside sacred boundaries are not only unknown but "unknowable" (as in the case of the "void" beyond the Navajo world) or that people, things, and events at a geographical distance are considered uncontrollable (as are rampaging buffalo and Massai raiders in the view of the Iraqw), distant lands may again require ritual attentions comparable to those directed to other dimensions of the universe. Thus it is that oracle bone inscriptions of the Shang dynasty of China note that the emperor made prognostications pertaining "to weather, *the border regions*, or misfortunes and diseases" (Chang 1983:45–46; my em-

---

[7] The term cosmos is used here in the dictionary sense of signifying "the universe conceived as an orderly and harmonious system" or "any self-inclusive system characterized by order and harmony" (Webster's New Collegiate Dictionary, 1953).

phasis). All these subjects presumably fell into a more or less common category of things "distant," invisible, powerful, and potentially dangerous, and all, apparently, were subject to "investigation" by the same royal ritual specialist (see Chapter 4).

There is yet a third aspect of geographically delimited zoning that is pertinent to the symbolism of geographical distance. Whereas concentric or dichotomous zoning may establish a set of gradations between "us," "not quite us," and "others," and boundaries may emphasize an exclusive sense of "us" versus "not us," under certain circumstances we may identify a type of zoning involving what might be better described as "levels of inclusiveness." Such "levels" incorporate a range of territories scaled from smaller or more restricted locales to larger or more inclusive regions. At the same time the symbolic significance accorded these realms ranges from the more "immediate" to the more "rarified." "Inclusive" zoning seems to be particularly obvious in contexts of moral *communitas* and attendant religious symbolism such as religious pilgrimage; thus both examples summarized here deal with what has also been termed pilgrimage "fields" or "catchment areas" associated with particular levels of shrines.

In Theravada Buddhist societies of Southeast Asia there are a number of holy places containing relics or otherwise associated with the Buddha's lifetime which are deemed to be pilgrimage centers. Keyes (1975) has discussed a pilgrimage tradition of northern Thailand (in the area associated with the Yuan tradition of Theravada Buddhism) involving a series of twelve such shrines whose locations constitute a sort of "sacred or ritual topography." Four of the shrines are situated within a particular valley (Ping River) and constitute the first "moral community." (In this example the levels of each of the moral communities are to be viewed from the perspective of Ping Valley residents.) Four more shrines outside the valley are associated with the major northern Thai principalities. In conjunction with those in the valley, these four constitute a second moral community. The third, and next larger, moral community includes the shrine most sacred to followers of Lao Buddhism, and, therefore, includes all adherents of Yuan and Lao Buddhism. The fourth moral community is defined by the addition of a still more sacred shrine in Rangoon,

CHAPTER 2

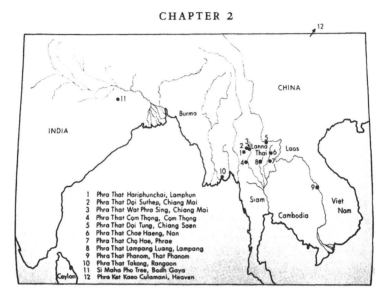

1 Phra That Hariphunchai, Lamphun
2 Phra That Doi Suthep, Chiang Mai
3 Phra That Wat Phra Sing, Chiang Mai
4 Phra That Com Thong, Com Thong
5 Phra That Doi Tung, Chiang Saen
6 Phra That Chae Haeng, Nan
7 Phra That Cho Hae, Phrae
8 Phra That Lampang Luang, Lampang
9 Phra That Phanom, That Phanom
10 Phra That Takong, Rangoon
11 Si Maha Pho Tree, Bodh Gaya
12 Phra Ket Kaeo Culamani, Heaven

FIGURE 2.1

Geographical location of northern Thai Buddhist shrines. From C. F. Keyes, Buddhist pilgrimage centers and the twelve-year cycle: Northern Thai moral orders in space and time. *History of Religions* 15 (1975), p. 84, figure 1. By permission of the University of Chicago, publisher. © by The University of Chicago. All rights reserved.

Burma, and the fifth by the addition of the Bodhi tree at Bodh Gaya, the famous shrine in distant India sacred to all Buddhists. (Although Keyes feels that the number of pilgrims from northern Thailand who actually traveled to India probably was never very great, the sense of inclusion in an "all Buddhist" world was probably significant, even though vague.) The final shrine is the Culamani shrine in heaven, which defines a community of Buddhists including "all sentient beings." The set of six "levels" of sacred shrines "defines successively more inclusive communities of seekers after merit, with boundaries that are spatially described . . ." (ibid., pp. 87–88). Figures 2.1 and 2.2 illustrate the geographical locations and the sacred topography defined by these shrines.

A similar system of sacred places has been described for Hindu India by Bhardwaj (1973), who views the innumerable sacred

32

places of the Hindus as a system of nodes with varying degrees of religious significance. Within this system some pan-Hindu and supraregional shrines (Badrinath, Hardwar) may be focal points for spatially wide and culturally diverse fields of pilgrims from the entire Indian subcontinent. The "catchment area" for these shrines defines the limits of Hindu religious space. At the other extreme, distinctly local shrines may serve as centers for congregations of devotees from the immediate vicinity. Between these two extremes are regional and subregional sacred places serving corresponding pilgrim "fields" (1973:6–7, 158–59, 173; see also Turner 1972:201–3).

Directionality, Distance, and Time

Patterns of spatial zoning, as described above, utilize terrestrial locations and landscape characteristics in a "flat," two-dimensional, synchronic manner that emphasizes contrasts between "here" and "there" or between a central or internal area and a peripheral or outside area. Cosmological interpretations of space and distance, however, rarely settle for such shallow perspectives. On the contrary, it is probably safe to assume that members of virtually all societies recognize some conjunction of space and time in their ideological paradigms, although societies may show significant variation in the extent to which temporal dimensions are emphasized in their particular sociological and cosmological formats (e.g., discussion of descent-ordered societies versus spatially ordered societies in Overing-Kaplan 1977:9–10). Conceptions of time may vary, too, appearing in some circumstances as another dimension for the expression of social or moral contrasts (such as when the past or the future is compared with the present), while in other settings serving as sequential units that record the oscillating or cyclical passage of ecological or celestial phenomena (annual growth cycles and seasons, the repeated movements of heavenly bodies, the stages of human life) or the historical-mythological traditions of forebears leading into the present (Leach 1961). Be that as it may, it is undoubtedly true for many traditional societies that "the horizontal universe does not of itself achieve its fullest meaning. Its existence is explained by the un-

33

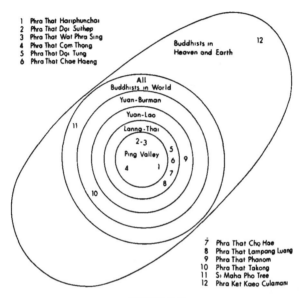

1 Phra That Hariphunchai
2 Phra That Doi Suthep
3 Phra That Wat Phra Sing
4 Phra That Com Thong
5 Phra That Doi Tung
6 Phra That Chae Haeng

Buddhists in Heaven and Earth   12

All Buddhists in World

Yuan-Burman

Yuan-Lao

Lanna-Thai

2-3

Ping Valley   5 6 9

4   1

7

8

11

10

7 Phra That Cho Hae
8 Phra That Lampang Luang
9 Phra That Phanom
10 Phra That Takong
11 Si Maha Pho Tree
12 Phra Ket Kaeo Culamani

FIGURE 2.2

Northern Thai (Ping Valley) Buddhist shrines as sacred topography. From C. F. Keyes, Buddhist pilgrimage centers and the twelve-year cycle: Northern Thai moral orders in space and time *History of Religions* 15 (1975), p. 86, figure 2. By permission of the University of Chicago, publisher. © by The University of Chicago. All rights reserved.

ceasing flow of time . . ." (León-Portilla 1973:70). Indeed, in the absence of time there could be no life and no universe at all.

Time can be expressed geographically in a number of ways that often involve spatial location or directional progressions. The ancient Maya and Mexicans, whose recognition of time was the most all-encompassing aspect of their cosmological systems, interpreted time as an accumulated series of journeys over space; journeys made by deities, each of whom bore the burden of a temporal period of days or months or years on his back held fast by a tumpline (even as earthly travelers carried their burdens) until, wearied and in need of rest, at the completion of a time journey, another god assumed the burden and the temporal cycle continued. Time itself was especially associated with the sun as a divine reality of solar time, and the movement of the sun in daily cycles and in annual cycles around the four grand quarters of the universe from east to north (up) to west to south (below) constituted the major temporal marker (León-Portilla 1973; Hunt 1977:70–72).

The identification of temporal cycles or periods with spatial locations can be expressed by people, too, as well as by celestial bodies and deities. For example, the "levels of inclusion" defined by the twelve Buddhist shrines in northern Thailand also contained a cyclical temporal aspect. Each shrine was associated with a given year in a recurrent twelve-year period, and pilgrims ideally visited the particular shrine designated by the position of the year of their birth within the cycle. (Those whose birth year associated them with the most distant shrines in India or with the shrine in heaven were assigned substitute holy places; see Keyes 1975:74–75, 81.) Temporal cycles and spatial locations can also be conjoined by marking successive points along the circumference of zonal borders to correspond to time sequences. When the Chinese Emperor Shun circumambulated his domain every fifth year he began his passage at the eastern mountain in the second month and, following the path of the sun, moved on to the southern mountain in the fifth month, the western in the eighth, and the northern in the eleventh month, thereby "integrat[ing] space and time and coordinat[ing] the dispositions of his sanctified territory and the ordering of the calendar" (Wheatley 1971:434).

As some of these examples suggest, delineation of the dimensions and qualities of space-time may involve not only spatial location but also concepts of directionality. The ethnographic literature is replete with examples identifying particularly the use of "cardinal points," "cardinal directions," or "cardinal quadrants" as directional markers (the four sacred mountains visited by Emperor Shun are obviously a case in point), and specifying associated colors, motifs, seasonal characteristics, and moral qualities.[8] For our purposes, one of the more fascinating of these cardinal di-

[8] Not infrequently the four directions are seen in association with two more, up and down, all emanating from the center point, the *axis mundi*.

rectional associations is that of the Iraqw (Thornton 1980), whose spatial zones were summarized above.

According to Thornton, the Iraqw apply stereotypes to foreign groups, and adjust their behavior in accordance not only with economic or political experiences but also with the qualities currently associated with particular directions. Regardless of actual political and territorial divisions, "foreigners" are divided into four groups: the Masai, always spoken of as being in the north; the Tatoga, always said to be in the south; the Bantu-of-the-West (Iramba, Wanyaturu, Isanyu), associated with the west; and the Bantu-of-the-East (Wambugwe), associated with the east. East and west are considered the dominant directions, with east being "bad" and west "good." Since the east is considered ritually dangerous, a place of witches, so the eastern Bantu are believed to have especially strong medicines and magic, and Iraqw generally keep a distance from them. The western Bantu groups, on the other hand, are associated with a "good" direction and enjoy a "good" reputation expressed in substantial trade with the Iraqw, who also attend western Bantu rituals. North and south are not as strongly valued as east and west in terms of good and bad, but represent instead expected "future" events and remembered "past" events, respectively; events associated with Iraqw territorial expansion and with conditions of deceit and trickery (negative reciprocity). The south and the past include lands forcefully usurped by the Iraqw from the Tatoga with whom relations are now somewhat ambivalent. The north, the direction of the future for the Iraqw, who hope eventually to expand territorially in that direction, too, holds the constant menace of Masai raiders with whom the Iraqw maintain only very formal, distant, and sometimes quarrelsome contacts (Thornton 1980:119–29, 131, 256).[9]

It is useful, too, to bear in mind several caveats concerning cardinal directions. The symbolism of cardinal directions is a topic that at times holds more relevance for Western investigators than for those being investigated. Consider, for example, the follow-

[9] In a comparable manner, Rosaldo (1978) discusses how stereotypical inferences about bad social character were assigned to the Ilongots by Spanish missionaries in accordance with the negative qualities associated by the Spaniards with the territory inhabited by them

ing statement: "Of the four quarters of the sky, the north and the south are treated with indifference, whereas the east is in various ways identified with life, health and wealth, and the west with illness, evil magic, misfortune and death" (Wagner 1954:33). When carefully read, what is presented as a description of "cardinal quarters" appears in fact to be an account, not of a four-directional cosmological system, but of a two-directional one in which east and west are significant.

This description, relating to the Abaluyia of Kavirondo, Kenya, goes on admirably to indicate how the symbolic meanings attached to east and west can receive support from the local environment. "In Kavirondo not only does the sun rise in the east bringing 'milk and health' with it, but the rain, too, comes from that direction, and all major streams flow from the east or northeast" (ibid.). The west, in turn, is the direction in which illness should be sent, the location of the country of the dead (in the west and below the earth), and the direction (note) where the Luo, their principal enemies, "happen to live."

On the other hand, and as a second caveat, consider the cautionary statement by Fraser concerning the south Nias Islanders off the coast of Sumatra where "Nias cosmology, like that of many regions, is less concerned with actual directions than with symbolic ones." "Space in Nias is plotted relative to the aristocracy of the village rather than, as in our world, by reference to fixed, geodetic coordinates" (Fraser 1968:37, 38). Specifically, for the Nias the essential cosmic directions are sunrise and sunset and upriver and downriver (an axis independent of the actual course of the river usually located nearby). "Upriver" also indicates chiefship, and the end of the village street where the chief's house stands is considered the upriver direction (also associated with life, aerial creatures, "east," "south," and the sun). This end is opposite, and opposed to, the "downstream" direction, where the entrance to the village is located (and which is correlated with death, commoners, water animals, "west," and "north") (see also Fernandez 1982:103–4). Facing "downstream," on the right of the chief is the region of sunrise (identified with light and life) and on his left the region of sunset (identified with the dead). Sunrise and sunset, however, are oriented toward the conventional east and west, so that the nobility is generally synonymous with south, even if the actual location of the chief's end of the village should be to the conventional north of the commoners (ibid.).

In brief, judging from the contrastive examples presented by the Abaluyia and the Nias, the nature of "directional reality" and its cultural focus cannot be automatically assumed but at least to some extent are empirical questions to be answered in the field. Following Thornton, the qualities associated with distance and directionality may then also influence the nature and conduct of foreign affairs (see also Rosaldo 1978; note 9).

Among the Iraqw, as described by Thornton, two of the directional qualities influencing foreign relations with outsiders involve temporal associations either with the past or with the future. This is by no means an isolated case. Many groups attribute to distant domains and the peoples or other creatures resident there qualities reflecting not only spatial distance from the homeland but temporal distance from the present as well. In other words, the differentiation of beings and behaviors according to spatial zones, such as were described above, may also be representative of temporal zones.

A richly detailed example of spatial distance corresponding with temporal distance has been documented by Gossen (1974) for the Mayan *municipio* (community) of San Juan Chamula located in the Chiapas highlands in southern Mexico. (A greatly simplified chart of the spatial and temporal zones as presented by Gossen is shown in Figure 2.3.) For the Chamulas, time and space form a single structural reality focusing on their home community, which they believe is the center of the earth, and extending outward to encompass the rest of the known and also the unknown world. In Chamula cosmology their community, by virtue of its high elevation in the Chiapas highlands, is considered the locale closest to the sun and, therefore, is the only truly safe and virtuous place on earth. Chamulas living here represent fully civilized, morally proper behavior. As one leaves the secure confines of the municipio, however, and moves away in physical space, one is also moving back in time, so that creatures, things, and events in geographically more and more distant places are believed to exist in conditions of increasing moral danger and chaos

Characters involved	Levels of social and physical proximity	Time level	Condition of universe	Ritual and symbolic significance
Monkeys, demons, witches, Jews	Amorphous places, outside universe	Before sun and moon; darkness	No order of any kind	Negative and ambiguous, therefore dangerous
Major deities, early people, inanimate and anthropomorphic objects, wild and anthropomorphic animals, people from other countries	Unknown places, whole earth, sky, sea, Guatemala	First creation	Creation of order from chaos	High symbolic significance for ritual and cosmology; statements of symbolic primacy: light, right hand, up, etc.; higher metaphorical heat
		Second creation		
Early people, unspecified people, anthropomorphic animals, major and minor deities, Mexican government	Underworld, elsewhere in Mexico, woods of Chamula and lowlands	Third creation		
	Lowlands, unspecified highland places, other Indian municipios	Fourth creation		
Lowland ladinos, other highland Indians, minor supernaturals, wild and domestic animals, witches, ladinos, Chamulas	Unspecified Chamula places, San Cristobal, Zinacantán	150–500 years	Order established, but ever threatened, instability	Low symbolic significance for ritual and cosmology; lower metaphorical heat
		80–150 years, maximum genealogical memory		
	Specific Chamula places	1–80 years, lifetimes of living people		

FIGURE 2.3

An outline of Chamula cosmology. Adapted from G. H. Gossen, *Chamulas in the World of the Sun*, 1974, p. 233, figure 5. By permission of Gary H. Gossen.

such as existed in earlier epochs of this creation and in preceding creational eras even longer ago. Ultimately, if one traveled far enough, one could reach the edge of the universe and could see the sun and moon (as deities) plunging into and emerging from the encircling sea.

The immediate reality of this cohesive view of the conjunction of space and time is evidenced by Chamulas questioning Gossen whether people bit and ate one another in his country. Since in

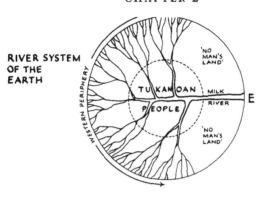

RIVER SYSTEM
OF THE
EARTH

FIGURE 2.4

River system of the earth as conceptualized by the Tukanoan Pira-Parana (Barasana). From C. Hugh-Jones (1979), *From the Milk River· Spatial and Temporal Processes in Northwest Amazonia*, p. 242, figure 37. Cambridge University Press, publisher. Copyright by and reprinted with the permission of Cambridge University
Press.

Chamula cosmography the United States is located in practically
the outermost zone of distance at the edge of the earth (see Figure
2.3), it follows that asocial behavior such as cannibalism, which
was eliminated long ago in Chamula, might still occur at this distant place. On the other hand, being fair-skinned and blue-eyed,
Gossen was also frequently asked if he had earth gods or saints as
relatives. The most distant confines of the earth, therefore, can
harbor both great sacredness and severely asocial behavior, both
being associated with distant time as well as with distant space
(Gossen 1974:18–30, 233, 236).

The Barasana of the Vaupes region of southeastern Colombia
and northwestern Brazil, whose river-centered spatial zones were
described above, also include a temporal element in their cosmological schema. Unlike the Chamulas, the Barasana territorially
separate the asocial from the sacred aspects of distance, relegating
the asocial to geographical distance (upstream headwater regions)
"beyond" in space, and the sacred (presocial) to geographical distance (downstream, river mouth) considered as "before" in time
(see Figure 2.4). In Barasana space-time the source of good, human society derives from the east, the river mouth, the starting

point for journeys of anaconda ancestors who originally traveled up the river, following the path of the sun from east to west, bringing useful cultural traits and stopping at various points along the way to "create," "name," and establish human groups and settlements. The east and downstream direction, therefore, connotes the ancestral origins of cultural life, and as one proceeds upstream, following the anaconda journeys, the temporal dimension becomes "younger," relatively more recent. The extreme headwaters, where evil spirits still dwell in the forests, is, in a sense, not yet within time, since it lies beyond or outside of the domain of anaconda journeys and, therefore, of proper social control (Hugh-Jones 1977:192–93).

Forests, though often considered distant and usually imbued with exceptional powers, are not always evil and not always "beyond the pale." In describing the cognitive worlds of Quichua-speaking residents of "an aboriginal fringe" of settlements around the highland urban center of Quito, Ecuador, Salomon tells of the strong association these city dwellers maintained during the colonial era, and probably since Incaic or even pre-Incaic times, with the forests of the Amazonian montaña. Although historically ties between the forests and the highlands have been complex, the forest has long been, and continues to be, a refuge for ancient, traditional, ancestral knowledge. Particularly since the indigenous highland societies experienced repeated conquests by foreign peoples who introduced their own knowledge and power, the forests were viewed by the survivors as a repository for the ancient aboriginal knowledge that was repeatedly expelled from the highlands. The forest thus became the ideological tie with the native state of being that existed before Christianity was established and that continues to exist "beyond" and "behind" the foreign religion currently expressed in the capital. Consequently, Quichua residents of Quito who live, as it were, between the traditionality of the outer forest and the currency of the central city, are located "in time as well as in space" (Salomon 1981:195).[10]

[10] Another excellent example of spatial-temporal ethno-political zones is recorded by Roe in *The Cosmic Zygote* (1982) which concerns the Shipibo of the Peruvian montaña. In oral traditions the Shipibo, who live on the Ucayali river, regard nearby forest peoples like the Cashibo in negative terms as stupid, amoral,

These few ethnographic examples have not only emphasized time relative to location and to direction but have also associated the temporal aspect of distant space-time with the past, with ancestors or ancestral conditions. They illustrate, too, how distant space and time can be imbued with a dynamic quality or context, as times/places where things can happen. Generally, in traditional society ancestor-associated space-time not only commemorates historical events of a now gone past but also retains a sense of currency and immediacy; mythical ancestral situations and activities continue to condition the present in a "real," immediate, and cumulative manner that can involve known contemporary actors or influence interpretation of current events (see also Chapter 5). The currency of the ancestral past can also become a guideline for future expectations, and places or directions with space-time significance may herald that-which-is-to-come as well as that-which-has-been. Ancestral association may also provide a major focus for the association of horizontal spatial axes with vertical ones, i.e., for correlating horizontal distance or directions with "up" and "down" or with "high" and "low." Space-time associations, in other words, can show a range of nuances, all of which conjoin localities "outside" the home territory with events or conditions "outside" the present.

Cosmographies that correlate distant places directly with distant times offer settings in which contemporary activities, if they can be extended to include such domains, can acquire temporally related significance within the immediate world of time and space. Gossen's reception in Chamula reflects this situation in that his presence represented the arrival in Chamula of a living element directly derived from a place of an earlier epoch (see also

cannibalistic "savages," whereas forest groups spatially farther away, like the Campa, are regarded more favorably as wise and respected shamans or good and brave warriors. Similarly, mestizos, who at present compete with the Shipibo for the mainstream, are despised and deprecated, but ancestral Cocama Indians who formerly competed for the same niche in the temporal past and now live spatially farther away, are admired and regarded as shamans and culture heroes. Shipibo myths present the Incas, even more remote in time and more distant in space, as even more culture hero- and godlike. Clearly, groups close in space-time are held in negative regard while groups more distant in space-time are held in high regard, probably because those closer are more likely to be more immediately competitive in some way or another (Roe 1982:75, 82–83, 88–89).

Chapter 5). Certain aspects of the *ceque* system of the Incas also utilized the notion that association with distant space-time can affect immediate actions in the here and now. The administrative apparatus of the Inca empire included a sophisticated system for the organization, measurement, and ritual ordering of terrestrial (and political) space in which a network of forty-one sightlines (*ceques*) were directed out from the temple of the Sun in Cuzco toward and even beyond the horizon. At select points along the various sightlines were located places of worship (*huacas*) that could also serve as oracles. The Inca consulted these oracles, not only those directly visible but also those that were distant and out of sight, to ascertain "the past and the future, those times that the king by personal experience could not know. The spatial distance of existing huacas, which were invisible but which affected his own existence, allowed him to know things distant in time" (Zuidema 1982:432, 434).

In other situations, the significance of distant space-time is determined not so much by place or location per se (e.g., as a site hidden from immediate view), as by association with the concept of ancestors and/or the continuity of genealogical descent. The fact that the Barasana associate prestige with the east and downstream rather than with west and upstream relates to the former as the source of ancestral origins. In like manner (though with reversed symbolism), the inhabitants of the Quiché *municipio* of Momostenango in highland Guatemala associate the east (using a term meaning "rising sun") with the present or future, and the west (using a term meaning "sunset") with ancestors and the past. In addition, the northern and southern boundaries of the Momostenango universe are associated with marriage and patrilineages, that is, with descendants. Thus, the entire directional space-time package associates the past, present, and future with the partnered continuum of social life (Tedlock 1982:140, 142).[11]

As was the case with qualities of directionality, the values accorded ancestors or antecedents either as highly regarded teachers

[11] Similarly, for some Polynesians the significance of the west or northwest lies in its association with the land of the dead as an ancestral home frequently believed to be located in a westerly direction (or at least reached from such a direction) at, or beyond, the horizon (Williamson 1933b:306, 318).

or culture heroes or as asocial beings in an age prior to the origins of human socialization, can influence cultural attitudes toward distant locations and peoples. The Lugbara of East Africa believe that the original miraculous sibling pairs who existed before the beginning of socialized life lived in an incestuous manner outside present Lugbara territory in the Sudan, in territory that is currently (or still) associated with asocial, inverted beings who walk on their heads (Middleton 1960:233). In contrast, in West Africa the prestigeful tradition of literacy and education associated with elite Islamic teacher-scholars (*ulama*) among the Dyula and related groups (see Chapter 3) originated outside West Africa, in the north, and was linked to still earlier generations of Islamic scholars associated with the highly regarded intellectual centers of North Africa (Wilks 1968:167, 172–79). The significance of the high, swampy plains (*páramo*) of the Paez country of southern Colombia (Tierradentro) as supernatural frontiers where the human world ends and the realm of the supernatural begins, derives at least in part from the significance accorded páramo lakes as places both of origin and of death for past mythical culture heroes who one day will reappear (Rappaport 1983).

Since ancestors (or other types of spiritual beings) are currently "hidden" or "distant" or "out of sight," their spatial-temporal locations can also be freed from the spatial constraints affecting current mortals. Ancestors thus can be associated with the above and below as readily as with the horizon, river mouths, or swampy frontiers. Their location may thereby combine horizontal and vertical spatial elements, an expression of the common conjunction of horizontal geographical distance with the above and the below. The Barasana again offer a good case in point. Ancestral figures are said to be both in the *east* (downriver, river mouth) and in the *sky*, while cannibalistic forest spirits to the *west* (upriver) are closely associated with spirits of the *underworld*; thus, the horizontal east–west axis directly transforms with a vertical high-low or up–down axis (Hugh-Jones 1979:267–69). Furthermore, in the native scheme of things the horizontal axis of cultural relations originally derived from the vertical axis, particularly from that portion associated with the sky. Thus, the ancestral anacondas, who initiated the genealogical or "descent" era of orderly hu-

44

man existence on earth by their upstream east–west journey from the river mouth (paralleling the sun's daily journey), derive from an earlier "vertical" association with the sun in a "pre-descent" era. (In like fashion, a mythical tapir found in the west derives from the primordial underworld) (ibid., pp. 269–71).

Belief in the creational primacy of the vertical axis, which is transformed into a horizontal, terrestrial counterpoint in a later stage of cultural origins, is not limited to the Barasana. In epics told by the Kuna Indians of Panama, which basically describe journeys by heroes into an outside or unknown world, creational adventures during the time of the earliest, still uncivilized, people are located in spheres of the heavens and the underworld. At a later heroic stage (and reflecting European contact) the great culture hero-ancestors (*neles*) of the Kuna, who come from the heavens, may also conduct their adventures in geographically distant lands, perhaps in far away islands, in Peru, or in other earthly countries of which the Kuna now have knowledge (Kramer 1970:91, 97; Chapin 1970:58). A similar sequence occurs in Hawaiian mythical history. During the earliest, mythical era of cosmogonal existence gods and other supernatural beings and humans interacted freely, apparently moving easily between celestial, earthly, and subterranean realms. In a later heroic era the gods are replaced by great heroes, ancestors of the ruling lines of the islands, whose adventures involve travels not vertically up and down between earth and otherworlds, but horizontally and terrestrially between Hawaii and various distant lands, whence they bring new cultural goods and cults. In Hawaiian ethnography overseas lands, located invisibly over the horizon (where sky or heavens meet earth), still retain the connotation of "above" as well as of "distant" or "original" time (Sahlins 1981:15–16).[12]

[12] The Iraqw of Tanzania make a much sharper distinction between two-dimensional space, associated with absolute contrasts of good–bad, safe–dangerous, etc. and the third dimension of time. Time and the events of temporal contrast associated with it, such as generational differences, are symbolically associated not with the surface of the earth but with things that cut into the earth's surface and spring upward from it, like trees, or derive from its depths, like springs and rivers. It is interesting that the geographically distant wilderness zone is symbolized by the tree, which seems to imply an association again of geograph-

CHAPTER 2

Concepts of geographical distance as temporal distance associated with past ancestral heroes or progenitors and/or with the "above" and "below" can coalesce in activities in which contemporary actors travel to a "distant" realm, sometimes even assuming the guise of ancestors. Scoditti's (in Montague 1980) interpretation of kula activities within the context of Trobriand mythology and oral literature and Montague's (1980) interpretation of Trobriand cosmology suggest that the kula voyager, as he sails to a distant island, is enacting the adventures of a mythical culture hero; indeed, he becomes a direct expression or "double" of the hero. Williams (1977) reported a similar situation among the Elema of eastern Papua New Guinea when (under European pressure) traditional mask ceremonies were replaced by long-distance voyaging. The captain of such a voyage was in sole command of the secret by which the magic necessary for a safe trip could be made truly effective. He alone knew (and inaudibly breathed in a spell) the secret name of a mythical ancestral hero of the "long-ago people" who was associated with successful long-distance voyaging in ancient times and, therefore, could provide an example for contemporary trips. The use of the sacred name, Williams emphasizes, was *not* to appeal for protection but to contact and establish identity and "sympathy" with the hero so that the captain, in effect, might impersonate him (Williams 1977:15–17, 20, 64, 69).

Similar impersonations are affected by Warao canoe makers and bowmen of northeastern Venezuela, who supervise long-distance voyages from the Warao mainland north, over the horizon, to Trinidad. Such trips across the sea that encircles the disk-shaped earth and stands between it and the end of the universe are fraught with peril from sea monsters identified in origin myths dealing with the misdemeanors and long-distance travels of a culture hero (the inventor of canoes) who also went to the northernmost part of the earth, where he still dwells. Therefore, to safeguard the excursion the canoe bowman who heads north dresses in the guise of the hero on his ancestral crossing. Indeed, it is not

ical distance and the "above" and "below," for trees are links between the underworld, where its roots descend, and the sky (cf. Thornton 1980:76–77).

46

unlikely that the entire voyage constitutes a latter-day version of the "original" trip (Wilbert 1977; 1979).[13]

Long-distance "voyages" in the guise of ancestral journeys into time need not be limited to sea travels. A case in point are the extensive Tupi-Guarani migrations in search of God and the Land without Evil. According to Tupi-Guarani myth, human beings may survive the inevitable destruction of the present world if they rid themselves of evil and join God in his abode in the east, the Land without Evil, just as the culture heroes of the first creation, which was destroyed by flood, escaped destruction by joining God in his abode across the sea. Periodic historical migrations of Tupi-Guarani, which seem at least partly ideologically motivated, moved these seminomadic tribesmen from the Brazilian backlands to the coast (where the ocean halted their easterly trek) and then north along the coast (Ribeiro 1970:55–58). Huichol pilgrims of north-central Mexico also journey considerable distances to reach the high desert called Wirikuta, several hundred miles from their present homes, which was their original homeland (perhaps historically as well as mythically), and was inhabited by "First People," the quasideified ancestors. Wirikuta is representative of the paradisiacal condition that existed before the creation of the world and that will prevail again at the end of time when the First People will return. In order to re-enter Wirikuta, Huichol pilgrims must move out of present time and identity into a past–future time state; they must, in other words, not only assume the identity of, but actually "become," First People deities. To accomplish this transformation they practice a set of inverted behaviors during the pilgrimage to and from Wirikuta (Myerhoff 1978).

[13] In comparable fashion, headhunters in Southeast Asian hill tribes travel upriver or downriver to geographically and cosmically remote regions to the east or west to seek ritually important heads among "non-human" strangers considered to be comparable to the dangerous spirits that also inhabit such distant, strange, wild places. In addition, McKinley (1976) has illustrated that these journeys parallel mythical headhunting expeditions, and it is noteworthy that at least among some groups the formal war dress of a successful headhunter includes ornaments associated with the exploits of these legendary heroes. McKinley also points out that headhunting warriors' journeys are comparable in many ways to shamans' trance-induced soul journeys into far away spiritual realms; that in a sense a headhunter is a "shaman on the march" (p. 102).

47

Examples of comparable pilgrimages to distant locations associated with distant space-time events are numerous (Turner 1972). The Hindu pilgrimage shrines described above, particularly those at the highest, pan-Hindu level (e.g., Badrinath), contain a temporal dimension. The most famous shrines—those eulogized in the traditional Sanskrit literature—provide a perpetual link with the distant era of the epic period, just as they define the widest expanse of Hindu religious space. Pilgrimages to such shrines and the conduct of rituals there constantly reactivate this tie with the past, for celebration of a rite at a holy place not only commemorates the sacredness of the site but also re-enacts the event being celebrated; the celebrant feels that he can return to the specific time and be directly involved in the original event (Bhardwaj 1973:149, 169, 173). Expectations of the same experience drew medieval Western European pilgrims to the holy city of Jerusalem for centuries. These travelers sought not just to review but to relive with mystical experience the life of Christ by reciting the deeds of the Old Testament prophets and the events of Christ's life on the very spot of their original enactment. These ascetics and visionaries often referred to their own pilgrimages as an *imitatio Christi* since, by re-enacting in their own lives (and sometimes by their deaths on the dangerous pilgrimage route) the sufferings of Christ, they felt that they too were performing an act of personal redemption and were "tear[ing] down the barrier of remoteness that separated a man of the thirteenth century from the events of the first" (Sumption 1975:94; Turner and Turner 1978:1–39).

In virtually all these examples and in many others, places in the geographical landscape have been imbued with sacred, supernatural, or at least "otherworldly" significance by virtue of their association with temporally distant eras, events, or culture hero-ancestors. The illustrations presented also associate temporal distance and territorial sacredness with geographically distant localities that, through their identification with that which is "beyond" or "outside" the here and now, are charged with some manner or degree of mystical significance or potency. As we shall see in more detail in later chapters, those who presume to leave the safety of their homeland and venture to these power-filled lands are, accordingly, no longer ordinary people.

The Politics of Distance

The dimensions of space and time in terms of which territorial domains and especially geographically distant regions have been described above derive from paradigms of universal order contained in native cosmologies and in the creational schemata of native cosmogonies. In these paradigms and schemata, distant places and things carry various moral connotations that assist members of society, living in the here and now, to understand their place and significance within a wider cosmic setting. But "distant" beings and places are more than resources to assist the intellectual structuring of cognitive order out of otherwise undifferentiated cosmic (and personal or social) chaos. The position or significance accorded distant places in cosmic ideologies can also identify a type of resource useful within the very diverse and very dynamic systems of political activities and controls (broadly defined) by which members of society in the here and now give overt or tangible expression to their cosmological assumptions as part of the implementation of social and economic order and political superiority. In other words, concepts of geographical distance can signify more than the quaint expression of myth; places, peoples, creatures, and material items from the world "outside"—even the very concept of "distance"—can be used directly and concretely to regulate and operate the world "inside." Cosmic ideologies, including concepts of geographical distance, can be put to use, as we well know, to identify and activate political intents and ideologies.

Much of the remainder of this book will be concerned with arguing and illustrating selected aspects of this point, particularly as they have been expressed in long-distance travel and in the political utilization of knowledge of distant places/peoples/things. To bring the issue generally to mind and to better appreciate the range and the nuances possible in such perceptions, it will be useful to set the stage further by reviewing briefly a potpourri of political-ideological perceptions of geographical "distance" as factors in various types of political and ideological activities.

A common and familiar thread in many relevant ethnographic examples identifies foreigners and foreign lands both as persons and territories beyond the effective formal or official political-religious control of the home society and as places where personal lifestyles differ significantly from those of the heartland. The difference is often weighted in negative terms, as, for example, in the traditional Chinese conception of "barbarians" as cultural inferiors (particularly pastoral nomads of the northern and western steppes and aboriginal tribesmen of the mystical and dangerous tropical forests of the far south) who lacked the Confucian code of conduct, did not use written Chinese, and did not recognize the supreme position of the emperor as political and ritual representative of *all* mankind before heaven by performing the kotow and offering tribute (Fairbank and Têng 1941:137–39; Schafer 1967:12, 34). Recalcitrant "savages" in the hinterlands of the expanding European ecumene were interpreted in exactly the same way. Spanish friars considered the Ilongots of the Philippines to be living in a "deplorable state of nature, caught up in a web of evil-doing without access to knowledge of the laws for ordering their political and moral lives" (Rosaldo 1978:245). Similar opinions have been expressed many times elsewhere in the colonial world, as has been the corresponding and directly parallel association made by these friars and their colonial descendants between the deplorable social character of the Ilongots and the alleged wild, untended, and "uncontrolled" nature of their habitat prior to its being "reworked" and "civilized" by an orderly layout of roads and schools (ibid.).

To be sure, the morally (and politically) uncontrolled frontier need not be geographically very far away to be perceived as a "distant" place. Consider the venerable tradition in Western European thought of the wild man, ugly, libidinous, and solitary, except perhaps for an equally loathsome mate, who lived in caves or crevices or under great trees in the desolation of the forest, desert, mountain, or hills. Such areas, like the wild man himself, may have been geographically nearby but were still beyond the world of morally and politically ordered civilization (see Braudel

1984:42). In the case of the wild man, however, the question of what was "uncontrolled" contained multiple facets. In European literature and popular tradition, the wild man was placed beyond the pale in the geographical and moral senses, but his physical power and agility and his inherent intelligence were perceived to increase in direct ratio to the diminution of his conscience. "In most accounts of the Wild Man in the Middle Ages, he is as *strong* as Hercules, *fast* as the wind, *cunning* as the wolf, and *devious* as the fox. In some stories this cunning is transmuted into a kind of *natural wisdom* which makes him into a *magician* or at least a master of disguise" (White 1972:21, my emphasis).

This intriguing association between acquaintance or identification with lands (and powers) "outside" the bounds of formal society and the acquisition of unusual abilities as manifestations of natural (magical) power are considered further below. It may be noted here, however, that, as previous examples have already evidenced somewhat, the attributes accorded foreign ethnic groups or other types of beings that live outside society in space-time generally include assessment of mental capabilities or agility either as exceptionally above the norm (i.e., wise culture heroes or better shamans or especially powerful witches or deviously sly), or as exceptionally poor or "subnormal" (asocial or stupid and easily duped).

The political-ideological relationship between the home society and those who dwell in lands "outside" may not be merely a matter of negative contrast between those who obstinately stand beyond effective political-religious control from the heartland and the enlightened populace who accept such beneficial directives. It may well behoove political authorities to purposely elaborate and deepen such contrasts by *actively* denying access to special privileges and benefits associated with life in the civilized polity to peoples beyond the boundaries as an act of political and ideological superiority. Consider, for example, the stringent regulations surrounding the distribution and use of precious textiles (silks and purple and gold embroidered stuffs) in the Byzantine Empire of the early Middle Ages. Precious textiles were prime requirements for ecclesiastical ceremonies and formed the brilliant, iconical attire of the emperor and the aristocracy. They were,

CHAPTER 2

therefore, an indispensable symbol of political authority. The right to manufacture and/or wear precious textiles of varying qualities helped to differentiate among social and political statuses within the empire, but any subject, even slaves, could wear silken fabrics of at least second quality as a mark of identification with the state and as differentiation from the "skin-clad barbarians" living without. Control of the distribution of precious cloth into foreign lands was a powerful political advantage that the Byzantine emperors fully exploited through tightly regulated monopolistic manufacturing and export controls. The efforts of distant Western and Central European rulers to obtain such prestigious textiles marks an entire chapter of early European political history (Lopez 1945).

Outsiders who are to be "denied," avoided, or "distanced" may be considered foreigners or aliens not only because they are perceived as political inferiors or feared as potential competitors, but also because they are ideologically different and therefore ritually impure. Consider the curious situation that developed in early India when Indo–Aryan-speaking nomadic pastoralists, regarding themselves as the epitome of all that is noble and civilized, arrived in northern India and came into contact with the indigenous tribal remnants of the former urban civilizations of the Indus, whom they promptly excluded from proper society as demonic barbarians (*mleccha*) because they spoke a strange language and failed to perform correct rituals and to use correct Sanskrit (Thapar 1971). Exclusion extended not only to occupational and ritual status and avoidance of kinship ties, but to geographical locations as well, since for a long time particular frontier hill regions within India, as well as the Himalayan regions where *mleccha* languages were spoken, were designated as *mleccha desá* (country of the *mleccha*) and "cordoned off," at least in theory. On the other hand, people and lands that were ritually polluting nonetheless contained useful material goods, and although disapproval and dire punishments were prescribed in the traditional literature of the period for those who visited such regions, even high-caste Aryan traders did, removing the taint of pollution by the performance of expiatory rites (Thapar 1971:417, 425).

Acquisition of material goods from "pagan" territory while

52

under ritual protection and conduct of ritual purification upon re-entry into the heartland also appears in other contexts involving long-distance journeys (see also note 6), a reminder of the truism that there certainly is no perfect fit between political ideology and political economy and that the dynamics of such systems allow for necessary practical adjustments. The lack of perfect "fit," however, should not be taken to mean that the two cultural domains are unrelated. On the contrary, as we shall see, the value accorded to foreign material goods may in some (though not necessarily all) cases derive from the very fact of their derivation from spiritually (as well as physically) dangerous or powerfully charged locales. Association of material gain with lands that are regarded as dangerous or as ideologically lacking (or superior) may provide a statement of the political or moral worth or status accorded both to certain classes of material goods and to their purveyors or exhibitors in the home setting. Such associations may also serve as metaphors to identify social values, as in the book of Genesis, where (as Pocock has pointed out) the patriarchs seem to be more or less constantly on the move on a predominantly north–south axis, and where the north and things therefrom are associated with that which is socially and morally good (e.g., lineage ties, fruitful marriages), while the south (Egypt, Sodom and Gomorrah), though morally bankrupt and seemingly ritually impure (place of bad marriages and sterility), is a land of promise and of material increase and prosperity (Pocock 1975).

On the subject of exclusion, social and moral distance within a context of geographical separation may be accorded not only to persons who originally lived in lands of pollution, but also to those members of the home society who have become ritually impure through misdeeds and are permanently or temporarily socially "distanced," cast out, or exiled to roam the "outside" world bereft of the solace of an earthly hearth and home. Compulsory pilgrimage as assigned penance for serious social crimes in the Middle Ages is a case in point.[14] Irish churchmen in partic-

[14] Another fascinating example of exile as penance for social misdeeds is found among the Tanzanian Iraqw where temporary exile into surrounding "cursed" frontier lands also becomes a mechanism for territorial expansion. In addition, as Thornton points out, the power of community elders to decree and enforce such

ular favored the use of pilgrimage as penance for serious transgressions such as murder, incest, and sacrilege, and especially for the sins of monks and the higher clergy. On the mainland similar journeys were also ordained, again for public figures such as clerics or noblemen, whose misdeeds would be particularly public and scandalous. Yet many of these latter pilgrimages were short in duration and were oriented towards a particular shrine or city (Rome, Jerusalem), after which the penitent returned home to a normal life. The sentenced Irish pilgrim of the early Middle Ages, however, if judged guilty of a most heinous crime, underwent the most profound of penances, for he was often doomed to be a perpetual wanderer, "like Cain . . . a fugitive on the face of the earth, never to return to his native land." For the most serious offenses, such as kin-slaying, the offender was put into a hide boat with few provisions and only a single paddle (or even entirely without oars), pushed out to sea, and left to the mercy of wind and wave so that he might no longer pollute either the society or the soil of his native land. For lesser offenses pilgrimages of up to twenty years were deemed sufficient (Sumption 1975:98–102; Charles-Edwards 1976; Rees and Rees 1961:317; Turner and Turner 1978).

Political exiles, too, could be doomed to a miserable existence in a savage wilderness far from the civilized amenities and sensitivities, not to mention political advantages, of life at the center. In traditional China exiled metropolitan office-holders, disgraced politicians, and favorites of unpopular rulers banished by royal successors "cleaning house" often met such a fate, being assigned to minor posts amid the wild beasts, hot jungle, tree demons, and barbaric tribesmen of the far south, as far as possible from kinsmen, friends, and the comfort of venerable tradition. In an exquisite expression of letting the punishment fit the crime, disgraced politicians were banished to a distance proportional to the degree of their opprobrium such that the more heinous the crime, the farther south they were sent. Fortunately the reverse fate was possible, too, and the unlucky functionary could be gradually re-

---

sanctions "derives, in part, from their control over the danger inherent in the outside . . ." (Thornton 1980:27, 29, 80–81, 135).

habilitated and slowly moved back, post by post, to the north, to the capital, perhaps even once more to the court itself (Schafer 1967:38, 263).

Some wanderers in geographical distance, however, chose this fate themselves, purposely renouncing civilization and regarding rootless travel or a hermit's isolation as more virtuous than sedentary life or as an escape from the public confines of village life. In the early centuries A.D., ascetic monks of the Egyptian desert espoused perpetual travel, apparently as a means of literally signifying their advancement in spiritual life as well as combating the lethargy of a settled existence (Rousseau 1978:42–43). Bands of Syrian holy men in the late Roman era similarly sought the mysteries inherent in the demon-filled wilderness. Seeking to avoid the limitations of settled society, holy men "fled women and bishops" and preferred the life of the hermit (Brown 1971).

Voluntary pilgrimage in renunciation of urban civilization and as salvation through self-exile flourished in the Middle Ages, too (a direct descendant of the Egyptian and Syrian desert fathers). Once again, Irish pilgrims, voluntarily this time but still wandering freely without destination, set the standard for austerity and complete abnegation of this world. Early Christian wanderers either moved throughout the island (though outside their native territories) in the "lesser" grade of *peregrinatio* or crossed the sea to roam across Western Europe in the "superior" grade of pilgrimage. Anglo-Saxons did likewise, so that as Irish pilgrims moved to England, Anglo-Saxons exiled themselves to Ireland or to the continent. Not until Benedictine monasticism became a stabilizing force in the ninth century did itinerant clerics begin to settle down to a different expression of renunciation (Sumption 1975:94–97; Charles-Edwards 1976:43–46; Turner and Turner 1978:7–8).

On the other hand, the state of ritual grace that pilgrimage could provide sometimes permitted re-entry into society at a very high level. Irish ascetic pilgrims, "exiles of God" (*deorad Dé*) in legal terms, in fact were accorded considerable power and prestige in Irish society, and, like the bishop or chief poet, could hold a legal status equal to that of an Irish king, for the pilgrim was judged the representative on earth of God and the saints. Thus, "the *peregrinus* might have renounced the world, but the power which he held prevented the world from renouncing him" (Charles-Edwards 1976:53). Similarly, Egyptian desert fathers, with their gaunt, unkempt, "spectacularly holy" appearances and reputations for spiritual wisdom, were soon "discovered" as tourist attractions for pilgrim tourists, who traveled great distances to admire, seek advice, or even become disciples themselves, and the monks' lonely cells took on the appearances of well furnished consulting rooms (Rousseau 1978; Brown 1971:93; Casson 1974:310–13). Syrian hermits, too, though regarded with considerable suspicion and hostility by settled villagers, were valued as mediators in village life for the express reason that they *were* disassociated "strangers" from society. Some even provided sanction for high-level international arbitration (Brown 1971:91–93).

Of course, it is not necessary to permanently renounce life in normal society to achieve a state of ritual grace. The ethnographic literature fully attests that ritual grace and social respect can also be accorded those who venture into the wilderness temporarily to seek visionary experiences as part of life crisis rites or for personal spiritual renewal. Others may have such grace bestowed upon them by the simple fact that the "wilderness" is their homeland. Gardner (1982) has described how Paliyan hunter-gatherers of southern India, who have retreated into a most inhospitable peripheral hill region to avoid harrassment within Tamil Hindu society and who are forced by circumstance to live in a most austere manner, seem to be regarded by their Hindu neighbors as being ritually pure and as living in a state of ritual grace; consequently, they are invited to participate in Hindu religious rituals. The extreme simplicity and mobility of Paliyan lifestyle and their apparent freedom from sedentary social constraints appear similar, in Hindu perceptions, to the austerities assumed by religious recluses who also have withdrawn from Hindu life and live in the same forests as the Paliyan. Consequently, by dwelling in the wilderness as refugees from the wider society, the Paliyan, like Egyptian and Syrian hermits and medieval Irish pilgrims, find themselves reinstated at the very top of the social-religious system.

Before proceeding further, we should briefly review the truism (well evidenced in the previous pages) that in traditional societies geographical distance, like social, political, or ideological distance, generally is a relative quantity or even quality that is not likely to be measured with the standardization that we impose on topographical distances. Obviously, distance, like space, is culturally meaningful only in its relation to particular places, times, or people, and what is meant by "distance" in the sense of locale will depend entirely on context (see also Bowen 1964:52; Daniel 1984).[15] What is intended may be simply a contrastive geographical setting or sociopolitical situation "somewhere" beyond the boundaries of one's own society or its territorial expanse. Thus, for one group of Lugbara, the location of the superhuman beings who walk on their heads may be ten miles away (by our neutral scale of topographical measurement), while for another group these beings may live twenty or fifty miles away (Middleton 1960:237). Syrian hermits lived at a "distance" by dwelling without social amenities in the desert, even though sufficiently close to settled villages to serve as arbiters. As we have seen, a concept of degrees of geographical distance corresponding with degrees of social and political distance also underlay Chinese theories of political exile. Differentiation between a "lesser" grade of pilgrimage for the Irish wanderers who chose to remain in Ireland and a "superior" grade for those who traveled overseas reflects corresponding concepts correlating degrees of geographic distance with degrees of sacred distance (Charles-Edwards 1976). Similarly, Gossen reports that when a Chamula man drew the location of places in his world view on a map, he located distant Chamula hamlets closer to home than they "actually" were (by standardized measurement) and pushed places occupied by non-Chamulas farther outward towards the margins of the universe to the degree that they were thought to be dissimilar from Chamula (1974:19).

[15] Identification of what constitutes that which is near and that which is distant can also be individually or personally related or defined rather than group or socially related or defined, as Daniel describes for the Tamil. In other words, individual ("person-centric") conceptualizations of near and far may differ from more

What constitutes geographical "distance" can also be a factor of means of communication or transportation. To the Tapirapé, for example, distances are expressed by time and the effort of human exertion. Distance to a garden or between villages is expressed as "walking until the sun is there" (pointing to sky), or as "walking and sleeping three times" (Wagley 1977:370). Australian aborigines of the Western Desert have similar concepts. Here, too, time spent in walking, with variations depending on exhaustion, sore feet, availability of water, or burden carrying, decides whether localities are "close by," "a normal day's walk," "a long way," or "a tiresomely long distance" (Tindale 1978:158). In another sense, the type of available transportation relative to other forms can define "distance," too, as is known by every field worker who has flown into his field site by air in twenty minutes to avoid a two-day river trip by dugout and pole.

Clearly distance can also be extremely variable depending on external conditions such as weather. Braudel provides an excellent example of this relativity. Speaking of the sixteenth-century Mediterranean world, he points out that, instead of a sense of a shrinking world as we express it today, "in the sixteenth century there was too much and it could be both an advantage and an obstacle" (1972:355). The uncertainties of mail delivery (postal complaints have an honorable antiquity) became the preoccupation of statesmen and ambassadors. Chance and luck determined time spent in travel as much as did the vigilance of the traveler; on a sea trip, favorable wind and a spell of good weather could make the difference between requiring six months for a voyage or completing it in a few weeks (ibid., p. 357). On land, war, flooded roads, and snowed-in mountain passes all made distances anything but invariable. Modern transportation, Braudel points out, has not only increased the speed of travel but has eliminated much of the real uncertainty caused by bad weather.

In terms of the sacred or symbolic significance of geographical distance, the uncertainty or variability associated with distance, that is, the sense of "distance" as constituting some kind or degree

formal, standard, fixed, or "universalized" social or political concepts (Daniel 1984:67-70).

of obstacle, may be as significant as the association of distance with concepts of the unknown or the "known about." In terms of the political use of geographical distance, conceiving of distance as an obstacle allows for the active expression and utilization of distance as a means of evidencing exceptional personal qualities; i.e., if distance is an obstacle, he who overcomes, "controls," or "conquers" distance may evidence superior ability, power, wisdom, and worth.

Origin and migration myths often express the significance accorded the conquest or control of distance in the general format of ancestors beginning a journey at a place (and time) of origin distant from the present and proceeding to move closer geographically (and temporally) to the eventual heartland, in the process overcoming difficulties and temptations and surviving an often hostile environment. Heroic epics of the travails and victories of great heroes who, like Ulysses, overcome great odds, survive great dangers, and conquer great perils of land and sea before they come home as wiser and better men, are also relevant (cf. Campbell 1949). Indeed, for heroes (and as if to make the point), the obstacles to be conquered are usually more awesome and the rewards gained generally greater than those of ordinary men, at least in part because the powerful incantations, magical spears, and other exceptional means frequently utilized to meet these challenges are also not available to mere mortals except as imitative belief in the efficacy of protective rituals for the traveler and his conveyance.

At home obstacles can be used directly to express the political-religious "hiddenness" or restrictiveness of power, knowledge, and authority at the center. Physical obstacles used purposely to obscure can be found in the man-made interruptions—the "seemingly interminable succession" of gates and towers and walls, staircases and sunken courts—in the processual avenues that defined the major directional axes of ancient imperial capitals such as Peking or Teotihuacan (Wheatley 1971:425). Such obstructions limited visible space and made progress difficult as the official visitor made his slow progression deeper and deeper into the heart of the political-religious center. Conceivably this design symbolized the hidden, restricted, esoteric nature of high government and religion. Eliade's comments on inaccessible mythical cosmic trees guarded by monsters and sought by heroes is appropriate in this more earthly context: "[That] which symbolizes absolute reality, sacred power and immortality, is hard of access. Symbols of this sort . . . are always closely guarded and to get to them is equivalent to an 'initiation,' a 'heroic' or 'mystical' conquest . . ." (Eliade 1958:380–81).

Eliade's comments are directed toward central places that are difficult to access so as to protect that which is within from physical and spiritual dangers without. But, as Turner has emphasized (1972:211–13; Turner and Turner 1978:1–39), it is quite possible also to view such "centers" from a distance and see them as places or states of being "out there" to be attained after lengthy and arduous effort, the difficulty of which directly correlates with the good to be derived from reaching the final destination. Conditions of pilgrimage are obvious cases in point (ibid.). In the Middle Ages the reduction of purgatorial time pilgrims could "earn" with indulgences varied according to distance traveled. "At the end of the twelfth century, visitors to St. Peter's on Maundy Thursday won an indulgence of two years if they were Italians, three if they came from further afield" (Sumption 1975:230). In like fashion, Alexander III used to inform Swedish pilgrims that those who made a good confession would receive an indulgence of one, two, or three years, depending on the distance they had traveled; presumably Scandinavians could expect to win a full three years (ibid., pp. 230, 231).

Similarly, latter-day pilgrims may feel that shrines at a greater distance, requiring greater efforts to reach, may allow for greater benefits. Thus, the villagers of the Upper Nansa Valley of Spain make more important promises to more distant shrines, the principle involved again being that the effort expended to reach the shrine must be commensurate with the favor requested. Alternatively, if time is not available for a long trip to a more distant shrine, closer shrines may be approached for more important promises provided obstacles are added to the trip, e.g., promising to go barefoot, or without speaking, or without drinking, or adding other penances such as the purchase of masses or exvotos or saying novenas (Christian 1972:122).

The same correlation of sacred distance and effort expended relative to reward for those who reach the goal can be found in Hindu India, particularly with respect to sacred places in the Himalayas (like Badrinath) which are remote and inaccessible for much of the year. As Bhardwaj has pointed out, "Their very remoteness may have been of special value. Being remote and isolated, they were, so to speak, away from the profane world and hence suitable places for the abode of gods. The greater the effort required to reach these places, the greater would have to be the conviction of the pilgrim and hence perhaps his expectation of religious reward. This attitude follows directly from the stress on austerity in Hinduism" (Bhardwaj 1973:32–33).

Conquest of "distance as obstacle" with exceptional effort in order to gain religious grace is perhaps most literally demonstrated in situations where travelers choose their route directly, "as the crow flies." For Swat Pathans, "religious merit acquired is proportional to the degree of effort expended on the visit; it is greater if one takes the direct route over rough country than if one follows the road" (Barth 1965:58). The same procedure is described for Incaic Peru, apparently as part of the *ceque* (sightline) system described earlier. In an important imperial ritual, any social group or local chief could send an immaculate child to Cuzco or another ritual center to be sacrificed or, after participating in various rituals, to be returned to the home locale for sacrifice. From a description of the children's travel home, it appears that the retinue accompanying them went not by the royal road but "straight, without turning off to any place, crossing the gorges and mountains that they had in front of them, until each came to the place where they were waited for to receive the sacrifices . . ." (Zuidema 1982:430–31; Urton 1981:201–2 also notes priestly pilgrimages in a straight line).[16]

The ability to surmount and "conquer" distance can be expressed not only in terms of great endurance and great effort in moving across the terrain, but also in the belief in a more "literal"

---

[16] The Incaic myth of the creation of the god Viracocha also describes his travel in a straight line from his point of origin at Tiahuanaco to Ecuador. Similarly, contemporary pilgrims try to travel in as direct a manner as possible to this shrine (see Zuidema 1982:439–45).

means of "rising above" the landscape or of capacity for exceptional speed. Many shamans are believed to have the ability to travel through the air to distant places, including the sky, but do so in an altered state of being in which the spirit or soul may soar but the body remains motionless at home. Some curers and ritual leaders, however, are believed to physically move at a far faster pace than ordinary persons and even to become airborne in the process. Consider Elkin's report regarding the capacity of southeastern Australian aboriginal "men of high degree" for fast travel. While long-distance walking is commonplace among aborigines, the shaman-curer's abilities are said to be even more exceptional. Not only can "medicine men" fly to distant places in sleep or in visions, but they "can also run at a surprising pace for any distance, faster than anyone can run, and without getting tired or out of breath. They apparently run less than a meter above the ground. . . . it has been said that the air has been made soft and solid, and that it moves along, carrying them with it" (Elkin 1977:55). Elkin notes a similar circumstance in Tibet where, according to some observers, certain lamas, as a result of physical and psychical training, are able to walk without stopping at a rapid pace for long periods (ibid., p. 60). These runners apparently travel in leaps and bounds in a state of half-conscious trance in which "one does not feel the weight of one's body. A kind of anaesthesia deadens the sensations that would be produced by knocking against the stones or other obstacles on the way, and one walks for hours at an unaccustomed speed, enjoying that kind of light agreeable dizziness well known to motorists at high speed" (David-Neel, quoted in Elkin 1977:61). It is further claimed by some that, after traveling over a certain distance, the feet of the "runner" seemingly no longer touch the ground and to all appearances he "glides on the air with an extreme celerity" (ibid.; David-Neel 1953).

Alleged ability to travel spatially through the air or to travel at a fast speed is found in other settings, too. Part of the exceptional nature attributed to the wild man of medieval European belief was his capacity to travel or move "fast as the wind" (White 1972:21, see above). Some of the supranatural character of Europeans when the Lugbara first encountered them was their purported capacity not only to walk on their heads when they weren't being seen (as did other distant "inverted" peoples known to the Lugbara), but to cover vast distances by this means. Europeans were also believed to walk across country at fantastic speeds, so that just when people thought the district commissioner was far away and began to plan warfare he would suddenly appear among them (Middleton 1960:234–35).[17]

On the other side of the world, in the epic Mesoamerican myths associated with the political-religious hegemony of Tollan and the Toltecs and their hero-god Quetzalcoatl, the superiority of the Toltecs and their culture hero is also expressed in terms of their exceptional ability to conquer geographical distance. "[For Quetzalcoatl's] vassals, the Toltecs, nothing with which they dealt was too distant. Very quickly they could arrive whither they went. And because they were fleet, they were named Tlanquacemilihume (those who walked the whole day without tiring). And there was a hill [where] . . . a crier stationed himself . . . in order to announce [necessary things]. He was heard clearly in distant places. Everywhere was heard what was said, the laws that were made" (Sahagún, quoted in Carrasco 1982:89).

Evidencing control with the metaphor of speed and evidencing superiority with exceptional speed are part of the symbolism of the kula exchange, too. The concept is expressed mythologically in the famous myth of the flying canoe in which a kula trader, setting off on an expedition, has a canoe of such superior power that it need not be launched at the beach but takes off directly into the air to travel. Eventually the canoe owner is killed by kinsmen jealous of his superiority and ostentatious display (Uberoi 1971:77–78). In more immediate terms, Tambiah discusses how kula men correlate their fast-sailing canoes with flying pandanus streamers that speed on the sea with their perception of the kula trip as a very unanchored, loose, fluid state of existence away from lineage

[17] In addition, Europeans could disappear underground, if attacked, and come up some distance away, a means to defeat distance that seems to be the inverse of the more common mode of rising into the air to travel. But, as we have seen, for the Lugbara, inversion was the basic characteristic of asocial and amoral distant peoples, and the first Europeans known to them were put into this category (Middleton 1960:234–38).

restraints in search of an equally volatile state of personal fame (Tambiah 1983:175–76). Munn also notes how the speed of canoe travel is an important aspect of canoe symbolism, and that motion—"the swift traversal of space"—expresses control, particularly in the sense of a kula actor's ability to encourage his exchange competitor to decide quickly to give him a shell. Conversely, the capacity to show control by *slowing down* movement is equally important, as when ego deals with a competitor who wants to obtain his shells. Senior kula men are able to incorporate both speed and slowness in their rituals and other transactions and thus achieve maximal control over motion and distance (Munn 1983:281–82, 286, 293).

IN THE preceding pages an ethnographic peregrination among cultural concepts relating to geographical space and distance has been presented, not with any intention of providing a full overview of such concepts, but rather to focus attention on the general subject of the cultural interpretation of geographical distance, to review some basic concepts related to this topic, to appreciate the variety of approaches to the cultural interpretation of geographical space and distance recorded in the ethnographic literature, and thereby to serve as introduction to following chapters that explore particular aspects of this subject in more detail. Recognition has been given particularly to the fact that symbolic differentiation may be accorded geographical space as a means of expressing basic ideological and cosmological contrasts between the known, visible, familiar, socially controlled, and morally ordered heartland, and the strange, invisible, uncontrolled, disordered, and morally extreme (very good or very bad) lands "beyond," where geographical distance and its cultural contrasts may merge with temporal distance and its cultural contrasts or where horizontal distance may flow into vertical distance as the sky meets the earth at the horizon. Examples have also been presented to introduce the idea that the symbolic significance accorded to geographical space and distance can acquire more dynamic dimensions as the characteristics or attributes of geographical distance are given overt expression in the affairs and activities of various political-religious practitioners. As the following chapters illustrate more fully, acquaintance with geographical distance and manipulation of its significance and its attributes may be particularly important for those political-religious specialists for whom acquaintance with esoteric knowledge, access to strange material goods, and/or control of cosmological powers are crucial aspects of political-religious status.

3

The Investigation of Cultural Distance

It seems either irony or ill-fated prescient wisdom that, even as the European Age of Discovery initiated an unprecedented era in European thought and experience, the "ideal state" was conceived by European philosophers as one where foreign contact was regarded with considerable skepticism. Sir Thomas More's *Utopia* (written in 1515–16), for example, evidences a very cautious view toward travel and contact with strangers, seeing them as conducive to social and political discontent. Those who wish to travel can do so only under strict passport controls that describe the limits of the trip. To ramble about without such a document would be to court punishment as a fugitive or even to be condemned to slavery (Becker 1933:148–49). A century later, Francis Bacon's *New Atlantis* (1627) allows only slight, though significant, modification, for even as the good King Salomana fears the negative consequences of contact with strangers and foreign ways and forbids to all citizens navigation to any place outside his rule, he nonetheless authorizes two ships to be sent forth every twelve years, each with a staff of three "research fellows" whose mission it is to acquire knowledge of the sciences, arts, manufactures, and inventions of the world, and thus to "maintain a trade, not for gold, silver, or jewels . . . nor any other commodity of matter; but only for God's first creation, which was light . . ." (ibid., p. 150).

Motives for Travel

The king is not alone, either in his ambivalence or in his goal. Ethnography and history are both replete with examples of the truism that the consequence of foreign contact can be a two-edged sword. Ethnography and history also give much evidence of the importance accorded to the search for (or sometimes the

66

display of) knowledge as a major motive for travel. Knowledge (personal learning or experience) is one of a number of reasons, all containing a high degree of individualism—including adventure, curiosity, self-realization, fame and prestige, and freedom from social constraints—that are frequently cited in the ethnographic literature as providing motivation for travel beyond the home territory. These highly individualistic themes are often in tandem with motives that may be more relevant to immediate political or social needs, such as pilgrimage to holy places to seek personal or family help, curing, exile or penance, acquisition of ritual or other highly-valued goods, and official government business. Even a cursory overview of travel motives as they are expressed in ethnographic accounts suggest that (1) reasons for travel outside the home society are diverse, even for single cases; (2) the majority of motives expressed contain a high degree of self-realization or personal benefit; (3) many, perhaps most, expressed reasons for travel are of a *political, ideological*, or *intellectual* nature; and (4) economic benefit, when cited in the literature, frequently though not inevitably, is part of a more diverse set of motives or goals.[1]

Obviously, individual reasons for travel vary greatly depending on a great range of circumstances that reflect the social, ecological and political environments of diverse societies. Consequently, *a priori* assumptions as to reasons for long-distance

[1] Economics inevitably comes into the picture, too, in terms of financing travel in general, regardless of the motive. In Europe, the development of monarchical state capitalism out of commercial capitalism allowed extensive and expensive long-distance travel (generally seeking remunerative wealth) to be subsidized from royal coffers (cf. Chaunu 1979:269–70). In less complex traditional societies other means must be utilized, undoubtedly on a smaller scale, to defray expenses. Many types of solutions to this problem can be identified, although the topic falls outside the scope of this study. Suffice to note by way of suggestion and example that itinerant barter with whatever can be carried and disposed of may accomplish this on a small scale for individual travelers, such as missionaries or pilgrims (cf. Lewis 1966:21; Sundström 1974:16). Presumably the sale of magical amulets by itinerant scholar-priests would serve this function, too. The Dyula, famous trader-scholars of West Africa, wove textiles to help finance their outside activities (Launay 1982:41–44). In traditional states, royal ambassadors and agents were supported at least in part by their patrons, as the Aztec emperor supplied the pochteca with large white pieces of cotton cloth (*quachtli*) to exchange for long-distance trade goods in the market place (Sahagún 1959:7–8).

contacts can be hazardous either because they are too simplistic or because they assume motivational primacy (e.g., "trade") when such is not always the case. Even when trade, for example, *is* cited as a reason to journey the entire context of the trip should be kept in mind. In his description of traveling traders of northern Thailand in the late nineteenth and early twentieth centuries, Moerman notes that while traders were delighted with the large profits they sometimes made, "a more dominant memory is of the fun they had, of the sights along the way, of opportunity for song and riddle" and of the many contacts and good hospitality enjoyed. "Adventure, fellowship, popularity, and prominence—as well as profit—rewarded the trader" (1975:158–59). It may be argued by some that, in terms of the "really significant" operations of cultural systems, the movement and sale of rice (in this case) is the most important factor here. Nonetheless, the non-tangible motives and rewards of the journey should not be automatically dismissed. As Moerman makes clear, pleasure and especially prestige as well as profit can, indeed should, be considered as part of the cultural matrix. In the succinct words of a reminiscing trader, "we went in part just to travel, in part to visit age-mates, in part to trade" (ibid., p. 166).[2]

Adventure and a different type of "goods" underlay the extensive travels of Akawaio men in the Guiana Highlands of South America. According to Colson, young men, who are the most inveterate travelers, may "take a walk" to visit other groups, partly to seek jobs for cash, but also simply out of curiosity about other peoples and places. The goods acquired may be of an intangible nature. "Personal contacts of this kind usually result in the visitor bringing back songs, stories, and perhaps ritual knowledge [that will] gradually diffuse within his home group"; Akawaio songs are probably "exported" in a similar way to neighboring tribes. "The basis for such exchange is the novelty of items

[2] A comparable mix of motives is recorded by Hill for Navajo trading parties. Although trade produced ceremonial goods, status items and horses, it "was also significant because it offered a means for enhancing personal prestige and satisfying a desire for adventure" (Hill 1948:393).

of foreign culture, interest in the variations and, in some instances of ritual, a belief in superior efficacy" (Colson 1973:7, 52).[3]

The Akawaio are not unique in their interest in the songs and rituals of other peoples. Curiosity about ritual knowledge or other customs in general as a reason for travel is frequently encountered in the ethnographic literature, often in contexts in which male initiates or a shaman or shaman neophyte do the traveling perhaps to take training among peoples other than their own. Among the Murngin of Australia, "a recognized way of gaining ritual knowledge is to travel widely and see ceremonial performances organized by distant groups. Such journeys are built into the structure of male initiation" (Morphy 1978:209). Similar reports are found from southeastern Australia where aborigines "often travel great distances" to learn a new song. "Sometimes picked men may be sent to a distant tribe just for the sake of learning [a corroboree]" (McCarthy 1939:409, 83. A similar quest by shamans-in-training may account for part of the Akawaio travel and exchange of knowledge and songs mentioned above; see Gullick 1981:10).

Similarly, Harner has described the information chain recently developed among Canelos, Jívaro, and Achuara shamans of the eastern Ecuador Upper Amazon region whereby shamans seek essential magical darts needed to effect their curing and bewitching powers from as far away as possible. The most powerful, and, therefore, most valuable, darts are believed to belong to Canelos shamans who themselves have exceptional power because they are in closest contact with Europeans. Jívaro and Achuara shamans closest to Canelos visit Canelos shamans directly to obtain power, while Jívaro and Achuara shamans farther away (who fear to travel far because of feuds) go as far as they think safe to get power from a shaman who obtains his darts directly from the Ca-

---

[3] Other Akawaio, we may note, are afraid of strangers as potential sorcerers, and, if they must travel, do so in a state of perpetual apprehension. In response to this state of affairs, Colson notes that trade with tribes that are not neighboring ones or which involves journeys through the territory of intermediate peoples does not seem today to provide a motive for distant travel. It should be noted, though, that the Akawaio are involved in extensive indirect trade as middlemen (Colson 1973:9, 64–66).

nelos, or to get darts from a shaman who got them from a shaman who got them from the Canelos. "Thus, among the Jívaro
and the Achuara, there is a regular traffic of shamans making pilgrimages . . . from their neighborhoods to secure strong supernatural power" (Harner 1973:119–21).

In like fashion, Taussig reports that a network of long-distance
contacts links local curers of southwestern Colombia with reputedly more powerful shamanic healers and herbalists of the eastern
highland Andes. These shamans travel about the countryside,
sometimes alone and sometimes with friends or family, selling
plant medicines, dispensing advice, and serving as healers particularly for local folk doctors who are impressed by the high-
landers' knowledge of hallucinogens and require the services of
these more powerful outsiders as protection against the occupational hazard of local sorcery. The highland curers (Inganos), in
turn, obtain their healing power and their hallucinogenic brews
from great shamans of the Amazon lowlands, whose source of
spiritual insight is the hallucinogenic experience that derives from
taking *yagé*. Amazonian shamans, however, repute greater power
to highland curers who, in addition to (lowland-derived) knowledge of hallucinogens, have access to non-Indian black magic, including that obtainable by literate persons who can buy books
(see below regarding the power of literacy and books) (Taussig
1980b:235–40).

Of course, the complement to shamans' seeking training from
afar is found in the also widespread preference of their clientele
for specialists from afar. Thus, the Brazilian Kayapó make long
journeys to consult especially powerful shamans (Posey NDa:4–
5), and the Mehinaku are convinced that shamans from other
tribes are better than their own and, especially if a patient is extremely ill, summon a curer from outside (Gregor 1977:351; cf.
Seeger 1981:59; Villas Boas 1970:262). Ecuadorian and Peruvian
highland Quichua-speakers avidly seek the services of lowland
forest shamans (Salomon 1981:194; cf. Urton 1981:177), and for
centuries native Andeans "anywhere between Bogotá and Bue-
nos Aires," as well as whites and mestizos, have utilized the skills
of traveling Callahuaya (Qollahuaya) ritualists and curers from
the border region of the altiplano and eastern valleys of Bolivia.

FIGURE 3 1

A Callahuaya "traveling doctor" of the Andes. The woven bag and large silver cross are said to be distinctive. From G. Wrigley, The travelling doctors of the Andes: The Callahuayas of Bolivia. *Geographical Review* 4 (1917): 187, figure 2. Copyright by and reprinted with the permission of the American Geographical Society.

In the course of extensive tours, they exchange their news, ritual knowledge, and aromatic gums, barks and curing herbs derived from the lowland jungles of the Upper Amazon for a wide range of highland merchandise, money, and mules (Wrigley 1917; Taussig 1980b:229–31).

The traveling Andean Inganos of Colombia mentioned above also wander over great distances, carrying in their medicine bags "rare herbs and plant medicines from all over Colombia, from the Amazon lowlands, from the high plateaus of the Andes, from the temperate slopes, and from the jungles of the Pacific coast. In addition, they sell charms, along with iron filings, blocks of sulfur, beaks and feathers of jungle birds, and desiccated paws of the jaguar and the bear" (Taussig 1981b:236–37). In the course of these travels, Taussig notes, the Andean healers learn to modify their practices in accord with the particular beliefs and problems of different locales and themselves learn of different drugs, disease categories, and other types of healing and magical powers (including those associated with European and black beliefs) (ibid., pp. 237–38).

Traveling in order to acquire the esoteric knowledge necessary to develop ideological powers and expertise is certainly not limited to Australian Aborigines or to native peoples of South America. There is, for example, an extensive literature regarding the education of Islamic scholars in West Africa where the pattern of learning required considerable peripatetic traveling about from teacher to teacher to acquire greater knowledge and more esteemed credentials. Libraries at centers such as Kano and Timbuktu "drew men to travel from country to country in order to sit at the feet of more learned scholars and so increase their wisdom through the study of books." This peripatetic system could be combined with pilgrimage to Mecca, for as a teacher traveled the country on his way to and from the East, his students went with him (Goody 1968:208, 218, 225). Indeed, not only for West African scholars but for many others, the pilgrimage was not only a religious duty but "a unique vacation, an initiation into the great world of Islam, and for scholars, the exact equivalent of our journeys for study abroad" (Sarton, quoted in Kimble 1938:50).

FIGURE 3.2

Greek cart and mules, sixth century B.C. From L. Casson, *Travel in the Ancient World*, p. 33, figure 1. Allen and Unwin, publisher. Copyright by and reprinted with the permission of Allen and Unwin.

A similar scholarly bent drew learned patrons to early Mediterranean centers, such as the Ptolemaic museum and library at Alexandria, and lured pilgrims to the Christian *axis mundi*, Jerusalem. Here "Christian travelers were chiefly interested in its remarkable library which made it, by the end of the second century, a meeting place for the foremost scholars of the first age of Christian philosophy" (Sumption 1975:89). Indeed, most of the cities of the Roman Mediterranean provided a field for learned clerics and churchly intelligentsia, "a small but highly important group, [who] restlessly moved from center to center in their search for education" (Casson 1974:302).

The eastern journeys undertaken by aristocratic Tibetan youths sent by their fathers to China for reliable interpretations of the Chinese classics appear comparable in general motive (Schafer 1963:11), as do the western journeys of innumerable

73

Chinese Buddhist pilgrim-monks through the desert sands, burning winds, and demon-created mirages of the wilderness to India (during the T'ang era, seventh to ninth centuries A.D.) to study Sanskrit texts and commentaries at great intellectual monastic centers (e.g., Nālandā in Magadha) and to acquire sacred texts and relics to bring back to China (Mirsky 1964:29–114).

Conversely, those who cannot or will not travel to acquire esoteric knowledge or foreign curiosities must obtain these benefits by the travels of others. A case in point is Chinghiz Khan's request to the famed Taoist master, the aged Ch'ang-ch'un, who was reputed to know the secrets of long life. Summoned by the Khan, Ch'ang-ch'un, at about the age of seventy, left the cities of China in 1219 to endure a slow, difficult, and painful trip thousands of *li* long across the vastness of Central Asia to the Khan's camp in what is today Afghanistan. Three years later, after innumerable delays, the long-awaited meeting began. Chinghiz ordered a pavilion set up, two trusted lieutenants were detailed to guard the entrance, and, except for an interpreter and two of the master's close associates, everyone else, including the Khan's women and all the officers of his retinue, was sent away. In comfortable privacy (secrecy), Chinghiz and the venerable Taoist settled into a discussion of various mysteries, including the secret of longevity and astute political advice (Mirsky 1964:119–71).

In similar style, a few centuries earlier the T'ang Chinese Empress Wu had sent envoys to Khotan to obtain a particular original Sanskrit text that she desired. Her emissaries not only found the book, but brought back a competent Khotanese translator. "The holy pages, pressed between boards, and the learned scholar were both installed in the palace in the Eastern Capital, and the latter set to work making a Chinese translation, with the lady sovereign sitting nearby—a presence which could not have made his philological work easier. He will serve, however, as a specimen of the hundreds of foreign scholar-priests who were summoned to the splendid court of T'ang, clutching their precious books to their bosoms" (Schafer 1963:274; Wheatley 1961:108). It was in the same spirit that Kublai Khan some centuries later graciously requested the brothers Nicolo and Maffeo Polo to ask the pope to send him a hundred men of learning and oil from the sacred lamp of the sepulchre at Jerusalem.[4]

Similar motives of curiosity and desire for foreign rarities and beneficent wonders (such as strange animals) from the ends of the earth underlay to some extent the series of great maritime explorations undertaken by the Chinese Admiral Cheng-Ho in the early decades of the fifteenth century (and earlier explorations as well), which reached as far as the Persian Gulf and East Africa. While these voyages also may be seen as an unsuccessful effort to incorporate the sources of Chinese maritime trade into the imperial tribute structure (Fairbanks and Têng 1941:204), it is noteworthy that upon the return of the first expedition a school was founded to promote the study of the languages of the barbarians encountered in such distant parts (Chaunu 1979:216–17; Mirsky 1964:237–59; Wheatley 1975; 1961:88–89).

The remote frontiers may also be more surreptitiously observed for pragmatic political reasons, again utilizing long-distance travelers as knowledge-seekers for official purposes. As is well known, information gathering was part of the assignment of the "disguised merchants" of the Aztec pochteca who, when they returned home, recounted their observations directly to the emperor (Sahagún 1959:22). A comparable tactic of combining at least the appearance of trade with official information gathering was apparently used by the Inca in regions of the Oriente, east of the Andes (Oberem 1974:347; Bittman and Sullivan 1978:214). (In western and northern regions priests of oracles established in lands beyond the imperial frontiers provided necessary information; see Patterson 1983:6.)[5] A more straightforward means of acquainting potential men of influence with necessary knowledge of distant peoples is described in de Laguna's excellent account of the Yakutat Tlingit. Long-distance contacts for these natives in-

[4] The Khan eventually received the holy oil, but of the hundred men of learning only two started the long journey to the east, only to desert the expedition in a panic. In their place, the Khan received the services of young Marco Polo (Power 1926:132–33).

[5] The *Mindalaes* or "merchant Indians" of Ecuador, also long-distance specialists, may have acquired similar information for the lords of Ecuadorian highland chiefdoms from the remote lowland and maritime zones they visited (Salomon 1970:238; 1986:102–6, 214–15).

cluded trading expeditions to acquire foreign "luxury" goods to distribute as a sign of wealth and rank, but, in addition, "one motive for trading expeditions was to visit foreign lands, to see one's distant relatives, and to exchange news. I [de Laguna] suspect that many trips were made primarily for these reasons, and that trade was a relatively secondary consideration. Certainly, the return home of travelers was a time for gossiping, recounting of adventures, and storytelling. . . ."

Furthermore, "for the youth, traveling to strange places and meeting strange peoples was not only an exciting adventure, but was considered a valuable part of his education, especially if he were the nephew of a sib chief and might later act as interpreter or adviser to his uncle when foreign guests came to visit" (de Laguna 1972:356–57). Such young people, especially if they showed promise, were sent away to travel "all over" to learn the songs and stories of other groups. Each youngster, at about the age of ten, went to a different foreign tribe to live with the local chief until he reached manhood, and to learn the language, history, songs, and traditions of his hosts. On their return home, these young men acted as interpreters for foreign visitors and instructed the incumbent chief in what they had learned. This education in foreign customs, songs, and stories was essential for a future chief and for any person of rank, for whom display of esoteric languages and superior learning were an essential requirement (ibid., pp. 465–66).

Travel and direct experience with foreign peoples and places is also a means by which an individual may gain some degree of self-realization, escape for awhile from the limitations of village society, acquire fame, and perhaps even obtain some assurance of personal immortality. Travel to be free of social confines was noted earlier as a context for pilgrimage and hermitic life in early and medieval Europe, where "a surprisingly large number of pilgrims seem to have left their homes solely in order to deny their parish priest his monopoly over their spiritual welfare" (Sumption 1975:13). A fifteenth-century writer reflected that the excessive devotion to pilgrimage included not only curiosity to see new places and to experience new things, but also "impatience of the servant with his master, of children with their parents, or wives with their husbands" (quoted in Sumption, p. 13). Bhard-waj, in the context of Hindu pilgrimage in India, seems to agree, particularly with regard to the significance of pilgrimage for the scheduled castes. In contrast to the village or home locale where the status of the scheduled castes is low and well defined, various sacred places provide a religious and social setting in which caste distinctions can melt away, at least for a time, in the crush of pil-grims and the hectic pace of activities. Briefly at least, a person of a scheduled caste can escape the limitations of his position and en-joy the freedom of a semblance of equality (Bhardwaj 1973:151–52).

On the opposite side of the world, the Mehinaku of Brazil sometimes feel some of the same sense of social claustrophobia and the need for relaxation of social constraints. "The man who wants to avoid his comrades simply packs his bags and leaves the tribe. His destination is either another tribe, the Indian post, a dry season village, or just the forest, where he can wander about" (Gregor 1977:213, 317). But perhaps the most elaborate expres-sion of this need to affirm individuality against the wider social whole, and to do so by traveling, is found in the ideology and pol-itics of the kula exchange in which the search by kula men for self-realization and expression of individual ability, prestige, fame, even immortality, as well as for some degree of esoteric knowl-edge, has been institutionalized in the formalities of long-distance voyaging and exchange. In the words of Scoditti, regarding the Trobriand Islanders, "Men say their true personality can only be expressed in kula, all other social contexts being more con-strained and distantiated [sic]. Their behavior is observably more extroverted on the kula, especially on overseas expeditions. Kula is said to make men more sophisticated, to allow them to use their intelligence more openly than any other occasion, and to make them physically stronger. . . . Kula men see their ceremonial ex-change activity as their best potential avenue for immortality. Or-dinary men . . . carry their names with them to the spiritual un-derworld after death. Famous kula men, however, leave their names behind linked to prominent shells" (Scoditti 1983:272; Uberoi 1971:142–44; Weiner 1976:234). "When men embark on overseas *kula* expeditions, they leave behind the symbols of their

FIGURE 3.3

Twelfth-century pilgrim with the scallop shell of St. James, signifying a visit to Compostela. From A. Kendall, *Medieval Pilgrims*, 1970, p. 85. G. P. Putnam's Sons, publisher.

power: their yam houses, wives, sisters, and children. The only objectifications of power men take are themselves, their canoes, their beauty, their decorations, and their magic" (Weiner 1976:217). The rewards of this travel, Scoditti also notes, are not only a measure of personal freedom and fame and the challenge of self-responsibility but also fuller knowledge of the cosmos (represented symbolically in kula ideology by the closed circular shape of armshells, as well as other circle motifs), for such knowledge can be realized at least in part by exploration not only of birds and stars, caves and mountains, but also by "knowing the world through travel" (Scoditti 1983:271; see also Chapter 4).

Travel is fun; travel is exciting, often dangerous; travel provides tactical or esoteric knowledge, valuable experience, and a variety of material goods. Travel also can give a measure of indi-

FIGURE 3.4

Pilgrim from Erasmus's *In Praise of Folly*. From A. Kendall, *Medieval Pilgrims*, 1970, p. 18. G. P. Putnam's Sons, publisher.

vidual freedom and of personal renown. In addition, the experiences of travel can place the traveler in a peculiar position or endow him with a different aura or status not only while he is adventuring but also when he returns home. Knowing more of a wider world than those at home, the traveler has been corrupted, becomes an outsider, an odd one, extraordinary. He may no longer easily remain entirely within the confines of the old, nor, as Burridge has noted with respect to millenarian prophets, can he really adequately express this wider, greater outside experience with the language of narrower, smaller everyday concerns, "to explain an experience in an idiom which does not contain it" (1969:158). To a greater or lesser extent, depending on the circumstances and the consequences, the traveler, like other specialists in esoteric matters, is likely to be "different." Regardless of

79

his motives, to the majority who choose to stay at home, he who travels will be distinctive simply by virtue of the act of travel itself.[6]

The Ritual of Travel

The preceding pages have briefly reviewed several basic points: that geographical distance is accorded symbolic (cosmological or cosmogonic) significance in traditional society; that geographical distance or distant locations can be an active element in political-religious affairs; that motives for travel can be diverse and can include the search for intangible esoterica, including political or ritual knowledge, as well as for tangible goods. In the following discussion this background should be held in mind as a framework within which to consider additional salient characteristics of a selected sample of geographical long-distance specialists that are reasonably well described in the ethnographic literature or are intriguing in spite of fragmentary data. The political-religious contexts frequently involved in long-distance activities are again emphasized. This approach is not intended to deny or denigrate recognition of long-distance travel or of long-distance traders as mechanisms through which material goods can be acquired or exchanged, but does emphasize the noneconomic environment in which long-distance travelers may pursue a diverse range of goals and activities, including trade.[7]

In general, it is argued that geographical long-distance travelers or specialists may be associated with categories of political-religious specialists already recognized in anthropology, including shamans and other political-religious elites, who are also expected to be especially familiar with esoteric strategic resources, whether tangible or intangible, and who are also familiar with

[6] The Navajo trader, for example, was marked "as a person apart from the ordinary" in light of the adventure, danger, and experience involved in his journeys (Hill 1948:393).

[7] An excellent general introduction to long-distance trade and long-distance traders by Curtin (1984) is highly recommended. Curtin's emphasis is basically on political and economic facts of long-distance exchange and the organization of "trade diasporas," and includes many of the cultural groups dealt with in this essay.

particular forms of distance. Distance per se constitutes an esoteric resource because it is nonlocal and is therefore likely to be
physically and/or spiritually dangerous, and because it requires
special effort and expertise to reach or traverse. It was noted
above that geographical distance (not unlike vertical supernatural
distance) may be considered as an "obstacle" to be "conquered"
for political-religious purposes. By now regarding this form of
distance as an extraordinary strategic resource by virtue of its
physical/spiritual dangers or powers, geographical distance can
again be seen to offer political-ideological challenges not unlike
those posed by other dimensions of dangerous and powerful
supernatural distance. Consequently, experts in the control and
exploitation of geographical distance may be equated with experts who control and exploit other forms of distance as political-
religious elites.

The directionality of a trip in geographical space involves a
starting point or beginning, and a destination or end, joined by a
journey through space and over a period of time. The journey
through space-time becomes a "middle passage" experience
through a domain that may have its own distinctive liminal quality in addition to (or as expression of) whatever "uncontrolled"
physical or cosmological dangers may exist, just as the "traveling" portion of a trance shaman's trip may have its own distinctive quality and can be particularly hazardous (e.g., if his soul
should be lost en route) (see Turner and Turner 1978:1–39). Consequently, the act of travel for voyagers in geographical space as
much as for trance-induced travelers in psychological space may
require appropriate protection and expression in ritual. Members
of such an expedition may be enjoined to participate in periodic
ceremony and observe appropriate behaviors, while the leader of
a travel party or caravan may be expected to provide protection
not only against physical depredations by bandits or thieves or social disorganization if the travel party or caravan is not well dis-
ciplined, but also against spiritual perils encountered in the "wilderness."

It may be expected, too, that those who brave the hazards of
geographical sacred space and reach geographically distant locations are given recognition at home and/or abroad comparable to

81

that accorded other "distance" specialists. In fact, in many (but certainly not all) cases, those who are interested in geographical distance are often in some way also involved with other types of "distant" or "restricted" affairs, perhaps as religious experts, scholars or diviners, or agents or advisers to political elites, or as political elites themselves. In other cases, long-distance travelers may simply assume political-religious distinctiveness for the duration of the trip. In either event, in the home society travelers may be both reverenced and feared for the power and aura their distant experiences and activities provide and represent. Away from home, as travelers or residents in a foreign setting, long-distance specialists again may be both reverenced and feared, either because they have come from a distance and display exotic, probably "supernaturally" powerful talents, abilities, and valuable goods that surpass in kind or in quality what is locally known or because, coming from a distance, they are simply by definition not the same as local homebodies and, therefore, must be "exceptional," for better or for worse, in some way. Consequently, long-distance experts and traveler-strangers (not unlike shamans and ruling elites) may expect either high honor or possible attempts at destruction. They certainly will not be ignored.

In view of the above, it is to be expected that one of the most consistent elements characterizing long-distance travelers and their activities in traditional society is the frequent involvement in the enterprise of some aspect of ritual or some concept of the sacred. Whatever the motive or goal for travel or contact, whatever the particular occupation or role of the long-distance specialist, ideology is likely to be involved. Some of this association is pragmatic. Not infrequently, in traditional societies lacking effective secular controls over distant territory that can guarantee safety to travelers, to journey under some guise of religion is the only safeguard. Thus travelers may seek somehow to be "sacralized" as a practical means of protection (Netting 1972). To understand the role of religion in long-distance activities as strictly protectional, however, may not always be sufficient. Such an interpretation implies that, except perhaps for pilgrimages, the real significance of travel lies in some other more "secular" intent that lures individuals to face the peril of distance; perhaps the desire for profit or wealth through trade, or the need to deliver an urgent ambassadorial message, or pursuit of scholarly studies, or the urge to visit distant relatives. Such may well be the case to some extent. Yet the full significance of long-distance travel and contact and of the roles of long-distance travelers may also lie in the fact that even such seemingly "worldly" activities do not just fall under the protective aegis of religion, but may be heavily imbued with symbolic significance by the very fact that geographical distance in traditional settings is itself imbued with symbolic significance and that travelers or visitors from a distance are likely to be similarly invested.

By way of example, let us consider in some detail the elaborate ritual context in which Navajo traders traveled and operated when they left their territory to visit Pueblo and Ute festivals. After forming an aggregate group of perhaps twenty-five to thirty persons, a designated leader was chosen on the basis of knowledge of trading ritual, songs, prayers, and prescribed behavior. Such knowledge could be considerable. "While nearly all Navajo were equipped to practice some esoteric ceremonialism pertaining to trade, certain individuals commanded immense bodies of religious knowledge devoted to this activity. Such a man would be selected to conduct the group" (Hill 1948:382–85).[8] Such a man could, in fact, be a recognized chanter, one of whom was a member of any trading expedition of any magnitude, for much time en route was consumed by ritual. Songs were sung and prayers were said the evening before the group left, but "the trip actually began, i.e., *became a religious matter*, 'when you reached the edge of your own country' " (ibid., my emphasis). At this point songs and prayer were given and prescribed rules of

---

[8] Descriptions of caravan organization elsewhere (Africa, for example) also note the special care with which a leader may be selected, perhaps giving preference to sons of former leaders who may be credited with special powers or explicitly requiring ritual leadership along with other organizational and protective abilities (Curtin 1984:55; Edwards 1962:9) The use of fetishes and medicines by caravan traders to ensure a successful trip is also widely reported (Sundström 1974:33–34) For example, the caravans of the Mbundu often carried the skull of a defunct caravan leader as magical protection and to serve as an oracle to be consulted about suitable routes, while the "secretary" of the caravan performed necessary magical rites (ibid.; see also Yao travel rituals described later).

conduct commenced. Actions were to be circumspect; no frivolity or nonsense was allowed and conversation was limited to subjects related to the success of the venture, including stories of other successful trips. Songs, initiated by the leader, were sung at intervals; songs pertinent to the desired goods, to ensure successful bargaining, friendly treatment, and safe return. Whenever stops were made for food or rest short rituals were performed which incorporated the "secret" names for the Ute and the Pueblos.

According to Hill, the use of secret names was the most essential part of these rituals, for no success was possible unless they were known. Employment of secret names is very widely encountered in the ethnographic literature as part of the ritual formulas used by shamans and ritual leaders in a wide range of circumstances involving control over spirits of nature or forces of the unknown (see also the Elema boat captain's long-distance travel preparations involving the invocation of ancestors' names described in Chapter 2). To utter such a name is a powerful magical action, for the use of a secret name in a ritual or supernatural context indicates to the "force" or spirit involved that the knower knows the essential nature or meaning of the spirit, knows the name that originally brought the spirit or force into cultural existence, the name that in and of itself contains the power of the spirit. He who knows such a name can control the designated spirit or being for his own use. Recitation of Ute and Pueblo secret names by the Navajo chanter seems to imply that a similar context is involved here, one in which, by involving secret names in ceremony, the knowledgeable Navajo ritualist will be able to successfully "control" the portending contact with foreign entities (viewed as comparable to forces of nature or of the unknown?), and thereby help assure successful trade.

When a Navajo trade party halted for the night further ceremony and prescribed behavior was required, including construction of the camp so that openings faced in propitious directions, the sprinkling of pollen to the sun, and many songs. Similar practices were repeated each morning and evening until the travelers arrived at the place of trade. After exchanges were completed the travelers left for home as soon as possible, and the trip was accomplished as speedily as distance and ceremonial observances would allow, curbing any tendency along the way to express exuberance over trade success. Upon arrival home ceremony was again performed to sanctify the goods and to remove such malignant influences in them as would result from contact with dangerous outsiders.[9]

According to Hill, trade was important to the Navajo not only for "economic" acquisitions (many of which were ceremonial and prestige goods) but also because trading was a religious activity. Those who participated in trading journeys had undergone a unique experience not known to every Navajo and, therefore, enjoyed a distinctive status reflected in the buffalo robes, turquoise earrings, or ceremonial equipment they wore and displayed. As was noted above, some of these distinctive trader-travelers were already distinguished as religious chanters and leaders and, as Hill makes clear, regardless of the goods acquired, their journeys into dangerous outside territory were themselves of an extraordinary nature.[10]

The ritual and symbolic contexts of Navajo journeys are certainly not unique, and are evidenced elsewhere in the ethnographic literature, though not always in such satisfying detail. For example, travels undertaken by Australian aborigine elders contained much of a sacred nature. In aborigine cosmology distant places were generally regarded with much circumspection, and the landscape was rife with ritually dangerous locales. Travel was directly correlated with physical and ritual danger and was restricted to all but properly initiated elders with full ritual knowledge and protection, whose persons were regarded as sacred even to enemies, and who were able to safely enter strange or unknown places. Such messengers, sometimes traveling in pairs, could cover great distances generally to announce and assemble

[9] Trading trip ritual "remarkably paralleled ritual performed for hunting trips and journeys to get salt" (Hill 1948:393). Both game and salt may well have carried significant symbolic connotations and involved travel "outside" the protected sacredness of Navajo territory.

[10] The careful behavioral prescriptions and constant attention to ritual also suggest that these religious observances encouraged or facilitated a sense of personal discipline and determination while the trade expedition was in "dangerous" territory.

intertribal gatherings for a variety of reasons. Since they came as visitors and news bearers carrying sacred paraphernalia, and since they were properly painted or decorated, they were accorded hospitality and prestige. The ability to speak several dialects facilitated such visits, and linguistic ability, general intelligence, and skill as orators were requisite for messengers. On a lesser scale, boys approaching puberty periodically undertook trips in company with teachers to territories associated with their grandparents as part of their ritual training and preparation for initiation. (It is noteworthy that in some groups, if the message sent or the circumstances involved implied treachery, dispute, or other danger, women rather than elders were sent as messengers. The use of women, small boys, or socially irrelevant persons as long-distance contacts in potentially dangerous situations is not infrequently encountered in the ethnographic literature) (Wheeler 1910:109–15; Mulvaney 1976:78, 84, 86; Biernoff 1978).

The Yao of east Central Africa, enthusiastic long-distance travelers, also took care to assure the success and safety of their caravan journeys by ritual means. Before setting off on safari it was necessary to obtain the blessing of the ancestors of the village headman or the chief. Confession of any crimes was also strongly encouraged, and those who had need to do so were given protective charms and medicines. En route special charms were carried for protection. A man on his first long-distance trip sprinkled himself with water from each stream he crossed to ensure safe return. While husbands and wives were separated both observed taboos on bathing and on wearing any but plain cloth, and men were not to use salt. On return from the trip men were greeted by women who sprinkled them with ashes and flour, offerings were made to ancestors, and the taboos were ended at a feast by placing a charm in the banquet dishes (Alpers 1969:410, 416–17). (See Frazer 1922:101–16 for a wide range of examples of purifying ceremonies performed when travelers returned home or when strangers appeared "to disarm [them] of their magical powers," which were generally considered potentially harmful; see also van Gennep 1960:28–38.)

Considering the various symbolic contexts noted above relevant to Melanesian cosmological concepts of distant land, sea, and sky, the liminality associated with the sea, and the particular association of travel with separation from ordinary social existence that kula trips hold for kula men, it is not surprising that considerable ritual is associated with kula travel, too. Referring to a composite of Uberoi's analysis of the ritual of the kula ring and Munn's discussion of kula symbolism, we find that the journey begins with rituals performed privately by the canoe owner, followed by a preliminary ritual halt in which members of the travel party spend a day sitting on the beach to clear their minds of everyday distractions, develop a sense of solemnity, and separate themselves "from dogs, women, and children" and from bad luck. Meanwhile, the prow of the canoe in which they will travel has been elaborately carved, painted, and bespelled to express the symbolic mobility and speed associated with this trip outward into space. The pandanus streamers that flow from the prow-boards and the arm streamers with which the men decorate themselves have been similarly ritually treated. After the major portion of the sailing trip has been completed the most important rites are performed at an isolated spot not far from the final destination. Every man, now privately, individually, and ritually separated from association even with his local lineage group, performs magical incantations and attends to the personal washing, face painting, and body annointing that, hopefully, will overwhelm and therefore "control" his trading partner and assure a fruitful, "speedy" outcome in the final ritual of trade competition on which his "name" and his fame depend (Uberoi 1971:141–47; Munn 1983, 1977).[11]

[11] Turning in quite a different direction, the Ibo of eastern Nigeria affected an ideological context for long-distance trade, travel, and other activities both through the recognition of supernatural protections and through the operation of a highly regarded network of oracles (Ottenberg 1958). Although distant travel for the average Ibo was not a common occurrence, traders and religious specialists, including diviners, medical men, and priests, who also sometimes conducted trading activities, did travel considerable distances over selected routes, safely protected by their supernatural associations as much as by their value as traders. In addition, oracle agents traveled and traded widely under the protection of various oracles, the most influential of which was that of the village of Aro Chuku. Feared and respected as agents of the oracle (which was reported to have great powers either to kill or to help people), and also with the aid of mercenary warriors, the Aro Ibo established settlements and dominated trade routes over a con-

As a final example of the religious and ritual context of long-distance travel let us consider in some detail the *pochteca* of pre-Columbian Mesoamerica. Although these long-distance specialists are generally viewed as merchants and state spies ("vanguard merchants" and "disguised merchants") in frontier regions at or beyond the edges of the Mexica (Aztec) empire, who clearly played an important role in long-distance exchange (cf. Berdan 1982b:31, 40), the ethnohistoric descriptions of travel activities also reveal pochteca travels to have been religiously militant adventures outside the realm of civilized Aztec society in chaotic and dangerously disorganized "wastelands" on the edge of the Aztec universe.

In the discussion of pochteca activities by Sahagún, emphasis is placed on the hardships endured and glory won. Returned travelers, representatives of a particular category of pochteca known as "vanguard merchants, who knew distant lands" were scornful of those who stayed at home by the ashes of the fire, and boasted of their wealth, their valor, their achievements, and especially of the places they had been. High-ranking pochteca elders, relating the rewards of their calling to novices about to depart for the first time on such a journey, also spoke of the honor, wisdom, and authority to be won by their profession. These benefits were to be obtained by a singularly difficult experience; by departing, disappearing from view, abandoning and forsaking kinsmen, home and homeland, by suffering misery, hunger, thirst, and fatigue, by facing menacing rivers, scorching heat, and dust-laden winds. If honor were to be gained by these afflictions and privations, the

siderable area. The Aro also encouraged persons with problems or engaged in legal disputes to go to the oracle to seek advice or settle the matter. Oracle agents, for a fee, would then escort their clients over long distances to the shrine, relying on the belief in the oracle's power to make ill those who harmed its agents, as well as on armed mercenaries, for safety during the trip. Other less influential Ibo oracles did not utilize mercenary forces and did not dominate as extensive an area, but their general mode of operation was the same. Thus, the Agbala oracle at Awka was associated with famed blacksmiths who safely traveled long distances throughout Ibo country as agents of their oracle and as traders, diviners, circumcizers, and doctors (Ottenberg 1958:308) Not surprisingly, since members of the oracle groups were engaged in activities of considerable prestige, they were differentiated from other Ibo in the communities where they lived, and were considered "superior" (Ottenberg 1958; Netting 1972:230–32).

FIGURE 3.5

Mexican merchants on the road. From B. de Sahagún, *General History of the Things of New Spain*. Book 9: *The Merchants*, figure 13. Published by the School of American Research and the University of Utah Press. Reprinted by permission of the University of Utah Press. Drawing by Paso y Troncoso from the Florentine Codex.

novice had to enter into the experience totally and completely, "devoted and dedicated to suffering," as were their elders before them, so as to become prudent, mature, and to gain understanding. "For not without reason did the merchants take and find leadership and the wisdom of old age, become leaders, and receive their authority in exchange" (Sahagún 1957:60–64; 1959:14). Against these perils, the elders continued, one had to take care to perform rituals and seek godly protection. "Go praying to our lord for mercy. Be not negligent. Think only of and be dedicated to penances. Be diligent in providing water for the washing of face and hands, and in sweeping and gathering up rubbish" (1957:63–64).

The travelers and novices, according to Sahagún "animate[d] and encourage[d]" by the preceding advice, sought an auspicious day sign on which to set out. The day before departure, rituals began. "Once and for all [they] washed their heads with soap and cut their hair here in Mexico. And all the time that they went traveling in Anauac, nevermore did they wash their heads with soap [or] cut their hair. They only bathed up to their necks, not submerging in water; all the time they traveled abstaining." After bathing, the travelers prepared staffs painted and wrapped with paper to represent various gods. Stout traveling canes were prepared the same way, and were carried throughout the trip (Sahagún 1959:9). Finally, the highest ranked merchants admonished those about to depart regarding proper reverence and respectful behavior and all the details associated with performance of penances and vigils while en route (see note 10). And so they left, without looking back or to one side, without returning to claim a forgotten item, for turning back was an omen of evil and of danger (1959:13–16).

While the travelers were far away, their families performed rituals too, letting themselves also become dirty. "No longer did they wash their heads with soap, though they could bathe their bodies. Nevertheless, no more did they submerge in water. But every eighty days they arranged the washing of heads with soap. Thus, they showed and made it known that they did penance for the sake of their children, their young men, who were still absent. All the time they thus went about doing, however long he was gone" (1957:69). Upon the successful return of the traveler ritual was again observed. Eventually, on the appropriate annual festival, an elaborate feast was held involving, among other delicacies, ingestion of hallucinogenic mushrooms (Sahagún 1959:27–31; Berdan 1982b:33).

These excerpts not only clearly indicate that the journeys of pochteca "merchants" were undertaken in an ideological context of ritual and penance (see Turner and Turner 1978:1–39), but also suggest conditions that are generally recognized as underlying ritual initiation of boys into manhood in many societies.[12] Poch-

---

[12] References in conquest literature to Yucatán "pilgrims" probably also refer to merchants who visited shrines to offer prayers and to burn incense while traveling (de Landa 1978:47; Thompson 1970:130–31). De Landa notes, too, that Yucatecan travelers carried incense and censors with them and conducted rituals each night of their journey to pray for safe return home (de Landa 1978:46). Merchants

teca novices seem to have been preparing to enter an initiatory journey in the real world; one that, as Sahagún notes, could entail years of difficult travel, toil, and ritual penance, but which would eventually gain for the novice the prudence, maturity, and experience that would mark him as an exceptional man for the rest of his life. These difficult years of travel, in fact, can also be seen as analogous to the long years of training, penance, and toil endured by Aztec priests. Townsend has suggested a similar interpretation based on the pochteca annual sacrifice of slaves to sanctify the future leaders of the professional group. "The rites," Townsend says, "were initiated by young traders wishing to consecrate themselves in their profession, as if they were postulants or neophytes in a religious order" (1979:31, 32). The ingestion of hallucinogenic mushrooms at pochteca feasts provides a further parallel with priestly rites and obligations, and suggests some sense of association with the cosmological order not unlike that falling under priestly responsibility. Such parallels would not be surprising at all if pochteca experiences in distant lands were charged with symbolic significance.[13]

Pochteca activities also reflected aspects of the life of the warrior, whose role in Aztec society was heavily ritualized, too. (Yet in this role they again resembled priests, who frequently engaged in warfare and were distinguished for their military services; Berdan 1982b:132). As we know, pochteca traveled dressed for battle and often had to fight. As warriors, Sahagún says, pochteca "exalted the city and the Mexican state; because indeed everywhere they were surrounded by [foreign] lands" (1959:19, 17). Given the hazards of this life, as the elders pointed out in their admonishment to novices, the long-distance traveler might never re-

---

of the lowland Gulf coast were also known to the Aztecs as great sorcerers, meaning, probably, herbal curers (Roys 1972:109–10; de Landa 1978.37).

[13] León-Portilla (1963.12) notes a distinction in Nahuatl thought between two types of wisdom: that passively handed down by teaching of tradition and that acquired by action. The knowledge of learned priests seems to exemplify the first category in that they mastered the secrets of the universe through reading and interpreting sacred books and by passive scholarly training, while the pochteca, although also highly educated, acquired additional knowledge of the nature of the universe through action "in the field," "learning of war, performing the life of the road."

turn. "Perhaps somewhere in a gorge, at the mouth of a canyon, on some high place, at the base of a rock, at the foot of a tree shalt thou sleep. Perchance somewhere thou shalt be destroyed . . . our lord will end thy existence." If such occurred, the traveler's remains were disposed of with honor, as those of a sacrificial warrior. His body was adorned, then bound to a carrying frame and carried to the top of a mountain. "There they stood him up; they leaned the carrying frame against [a post]. There, his body was consumed. And they said that indeed he had not died, for he had gone to heaven; he followed the sun, and just so was it said of those who had died in war" (Sahagún 1959:25). Pochteca travelers, in short, combined aspects both of the priesthood and of warriors with a profession that appears to have been construed as a major form of "wilderness experience" both for novices and for experienced travelers, and as an exaltation of the Aztec state in distant realms. Small wonder that Aztec emperors raised up the merchants, along with priests and warriors, considered them even as noblemen, and rendered them honor (Sahagún 1959:23; cf. Durán 1971:137–39; Sahagún 1959:6–7, 19).

What of the nature of the distant lands that contained such dangers, required such ritual protection, and served as pochteca battlefields? In his analysis of commemorative sculptural monuments of Tenochtitlán, the Aztec capital, Townsend suggests that "the inhabitants of Tenochtitlán automatically perceived their city as the center of the world, beyond whose sphere of influence lay chaos and the unconsecrated territory of foreign nations" (Townsend 1979:37). "Social space was automatically translated as sacred space, to be separated and purified against the inchoate, threatening forces and phenomena of regions barely known, of foreign territories beyond the zone of Mexican habitation and control" (ibid., p. 48). Similarly, Sahagún's commentary describes inhospitable places of torment, of deserts, forests, gorges and mountains, of strange and dangerous cities, of places and roads to be traveled with caution, for "desolate, ferocious, cruel, and peopled by evil men spreadeth the wasteland" (1957:65–66). Sahagún also defines these lands as those of "Anauac" (Anáhuatl), which is to say (according to Seler's definition of Anauac), pochteca traveled and fought as representatives of civilization in

FIGURE 3.6

Ekchuah, Yucatecan god of merchants and travelers. From the Madrid Codex, printed in Friar D. de Landa, *Yucatan Before and After the Conquest*, 1978, p. 46. Published by and reprinted with permission of Dover Publications, Inc.

distant and dangerous areas "at the edge of the water" (that is, the ocean), the "divine water" or "celestial water" that surrounded the earth and merged with the heavens at the horizon; lands (actually Pacific and Gulf coastal areas) virtually at the edge of the Aztec world (Seler, in León-Portilla 1963:48).

Viewing pochteca travels as ritually suffused, religiously militant adventures outside the realm of civilized Aztec society in lands conceived of as dangerous and chaotic wastelands on the edge of the Mexican universe, certainly suggests that the pochteca themselves were regarded with a respect and symbolic significance that went beyond their services as searchers for material wealth. Not only were they as honored as noblemen and priests, not only did their activities include both pragmatic and ideological aspects of the priesthood and the military, but by serving also as advisers to Aztec rulers they provided information on dangerous and "uncultured" distant realms that paralleled the counsel, prognostications, and reports made to the emperor by exalted senior priests who also studied and advised on the nature of distant portions of the cosmos, though with insight gained through

93

penitential and educational means other than physical travel (Durán 1971:137–38).

Men of Learning from Afar

The combination of travel experience with trade, religiosity, esoteric knowledge, and advisory services to eminent rulers evidenced by the pochteca, is also characteristic of other specialists in geographical distance, particularly those involved, like the pochteca, with centralized polities where a distinct ruling elite must seek the services of a variety of political-religious specialists (including priests and military generals). In more egalitarian societies and simpler forms of ranked society it is more likely that single individuals—shamans, lineage or household heads, or initiated elders—will combine these roles and experiences into overall leadership capacities directed toward general understanding of the exceptional forces and expressions of the universe regardless of location (i.e., both in horizontal and vertical space and distance) and will themselves act as religious authorities and as long-distance travelers and traders, as well as providing some of their own advice, perhaps with the aid of hallucinatory trance. In archaic states and possibly more complex chiefdoms, however, specialized long-distance experts (where long-distance refers to geographical distance) were more likely to be separate from, though closely involved with, members of the ruling elite per se. As such, they put their ideological eminence and esoteric knowledge and experiences at the services of those who ruled, and gained in return prestige, honors, and protection both in trade and against others who were less sanguine about such royal favoritism.

These characteristics are particularly evidenced in situations where long-distance specialists were ethnically foreign to the polity in which they lived and served, and where their political-ideological role and influence was also viewed as competitive by local courtiers and advisers. Such conditions prevailed to some extent in Aztec society, for it is evident that the pochteca, who were a closed, hereditary group and who may also have had ethnic origins separate from the Mexica, went to considerable pains in daily life to avoid conspicuous display of their wealth and of the riches awarded to them by the emperor. This humility may have been intended to avoid the jealousy of noblemen whose rank rested on birth and lineage more than on material wealth (Sahagún 1959:31–32; cf. Berdan 1982b:31–32, 57, 66). Possibly, too, the jealousy of those of noble birth derived from the fact that the pochteca, as highly regarded purveyors to the supreme ruler of esoteric knowledge and goods regarding geographically distant places and people of the universe—knowledge and wealth gained by arduous religious-militant toil—constituted a competitive threat to the "establishment" religious and military orders who guarded and transmitted esoteric knowledge of other portions of the universe. In other words, the apparently delicate relationship between principal pochteca and other religious-military advisers may have reflected not only relative positions of wealth but also an atmosphere of competitive knowledge, learning, and esoteric understanding among men of wisdom, as is frequently mentioned in the ethnographic literature from many lands.[14]

The spread of Islamic influence in West Africa by networks of Muslim trader-scholars and by particular ethnic groups such as the Hausa and the Dyula, who adopted Islamic learning in combination with warfare and long-distance trade, provides another case in point for the general association of long-distance trade

[14] The contrasts in dress and behavior between pochteca and noblemen seem to make a visible, tangible statement of the "distance" of pochteca from "normal" life at home. For example, where aristocrats wore rich garments indicative of their status, pochteca dressed humbly; where aristocrats worked by day, pochteca, in a sense, worked at night—at least they took care to enter the city at night on their return from journeying; and where land-owning aristocrats represented the social hierarchy and economic base of traditional society, the pochteca were associated with goods derived from outside society and, as highly honored but commoners, held a rather anomalous social position (Sahagún 1959:31–32). In sum, pochteca lifestyle appears almost as the antithesis of aristocracy, not in the sense of low versus high birth and status, but in the sense of association with that which is esoteric and "hidden" versus that which is known and understood. Pochteca in this sense again seem closer to the priesthood who also adopted unusual dress and unkempt appearance, knew the things of the night, understood forces existing outside society, and held special liminal status. An interesting parallel to pochteca–aristocracy rivalries is also suggested in rivalries between hereditary chiefs and *nouveaux riches* commoner-traders on the northwest coast of North America (Hickerson 1973:35).

with intellectual and religious roles that serve both to facilitate long-distance contacts among specialists themselves and to enlighten elite employers. With respect to the former, as Cohen has pointed out, the association of Islam with long-distance trade in West Africa has provided a foundation for the establishment of networks of communities in which the interethnic, "universal" nature of Islam serves "*not* as an epiphenomenon, but as the *blueprint* of a politico-economic organization which has overcome the many basic technical problems of the trade. Indigenous traders become Moslems in order to partake in the moral community of other traders." The "ideal man" in this far-flung moral community is likely to be "the successful trader who is also learned in Islam and to whom the crowning goal of success in life is pilgrimage to Mecca to acquire the title *Hajji*" (Cohen 1971:277–78, my emphasis).

The antecedents of contemporary groups of long-distance specialists such as the Manding-speaking Dyula and closely related Diakhanké, can be traced to the Mali empire of the thirteenth to sixteenth centuries and even to the ninth century and the early days of the Soninke empire of Ghana. They include a number of earlier West African itinerant trading groups (particularly the Wangara) whose influence underlay the emergence of still other Islamized long-distance trader organizations such as the Hausa. Like the Hausa, the Dyula provide a good example of families of long-distance trader-scholars who have tended to live as unassimilated immigrant minorities in other communities where they have served as intermediaries between the chiefs of local populations, who have not necessarily been Muslim, and other regions where Mandıng-speaking Islamized traders have also operated (Launay 1982:1–3). The Dyula have specialized in warfare, Islamic scholarship, and trade, especially highly prestigious long-distance trade; "of the three activities, trade was the most important; *it provided the wherewithal to support the other two*" (ibid., p. 20, my emphasis). Since the dangers of long-distance travel could necessitate protection by armed guards (usually armed slaves), Dyula youths could also choose a military career. Scholarship and warfare, however, have been antithetical. Thus, scholars generally did not pursue a military life. But a trader could also be expert in the study of sacred texts, and scholars could participate in at least local trade, although the time-consuming nature of their extensive education made trade problematical in many cases, particularly for those who left the region to study under teachers outside. Yet a rich trader could also become a scholar in his later years, turning over his business to young sons and pursuing learned studies as he got older.

In order for adherence to Islamic law and ritual to continue and to maintain important jural and moral ties with other Islamic traders in West Africa, it always has been necessary for at least some Dyula men to be literate in Arabic, particularly in communities with the most active long-distance contacts. Hence, Islamic scholarship has been important to the Dyula themselves and to members of other Islamic trade communities in West Africa. But Dyula scholars, like Islamic scholars in similar situations elsewhere in West and North Africa, also serve as diviners and advisers for the non-Muslim local population, particularly because of their literacy and ability to consult written books (Launay 1982:25–48; Curtin 1971; Goody 1968; Cohen 1971). Education in Islamic tradition has been useful in a comparable manner to the Hausa, whose scholars (*malams*) have traditionally served as administrative advisers, consultants, diviners, prayer makers, curers, and especially sellers of the reputedly most potent Muslim charms and amulets to royalty and commoners alike. Hausa migratory traders, like those of the Dyula, have also been responsible for the establishment of a wide network of Muslim influence resting essentially on the brisk sale of written amulets and other commodities.

In fact, since Hausa scholars (particularly itinerant malams who moved about with a few pupils seeking positions as Muslim clerics) could also act as traders (trading through their pupils and local clients) and traders could serve as scholars, no rigid line is drawn between itinerant Hausa traders and malams; great malams may have even greater fame as traders, while great traders have been famous for their powerful charms. Hausa young people, whether in their home communities or in foreign lands, might spend half their time learning to read and write in Arabic through the Qur'ān, and the rest of the time in the market acting as trading agents for parents and teachers. Reaching adulthood, those who were academically inclined would specialize in Islamic studies, but would maintain contact with business, mainly through agents (Adamu 1978:9–10, 73–75, 82–84).

Hausa trader-scholars have been particularly invaluable as advisers and sources of support to local rulers, both Muslim and non-Muslim. The reputed power of the superior charms sold by a malam-cum-trader often made him popular with, even essential to, local chiefs, who would then invite the malam to become an adviser and pray for royal prosperity (ibid., pp. 36, 75, 83). Sometimes Hausa malams even converted a king, as the following excerpt regarding the education (acquired, it should be noted, by traveling to foreign lands) of a pagan ruler of Dagomba (Volta Basin) describes:

> It was the custom among the princes of Dagomba in those days to leave home and go to other places to learn the arts of warfare and government and then return home to face the struggle for the throne. It was during such a journey that Wumbei went to Hausaland and became Al-Kashnawi's pupil, and on being converted by his teacher, took his name as Muhammed Zangina. They came back to Dagomba together, and their association continued even after Zangina became king (Adamu 1978:69).

In this case, the malam Al-Kashnawi is also credited, culture hero-like, with bringing a "whole civilization" to the kingdom of Dagomba, having introduced, among other things, the use of cotton clothing to replace animal skins (ibid., p. 72).

The roles of Hausa trader-scholars in the Asante (Ashanti) kingdom in the late eighteenth and early nineteenth centuries exemplify many of their services to royal patrons. In the community of Kumasi, Muslim traders were employed as administrative department secretaries, the leader of the local Muslim community was an influential adviser to the Asantehene (Asante king) on matters of foreign affairs, and the current king, Osei Kwame, was so affected by Muslim religion and Islamic influence that his chiefs conspired and arrested him to forestall his eventual Islamization (ibid., p. 79).[15] It is interesting to note, too, that traveling and settled Hausa immigrants also provided drummers, musicians, and praise singers for royal entertainment and, not surprisingly, sometimes served as scouts and spies for chiefs in outlying areas (Adamu 1978:41, 94, 100). Sometimes, too, as in Dahomey, the king, though not a Muslim, would take leading malams with him on military campaigns so they could pray for the success of the mission and advise the king through their arts of divination (ibid., pp. 115, 131).

Since Islamic trader-scholars were welcomed for their knowledge of the book as much as for their trade goods, and since literacy has relevance, too, for long-distance associations, the significance of the written word requires further explication. Goody has explained most succinctly the potency believed to exist in the power of literacy. Referring to northern Ghana, he notes that the efficacy of written charms inscribed in Arabic characters on fragments of paper lay in their magic. To the illiterate farmer, for example, who cherishes these charms, these writings are associated with the power of God, specifically the Allah of the Muslims more or less combined with the Jehovah of the Christians. Even if the farmer were not a follower of the prophet, "he saw in the Muslim's capacity to write a more effective means of supernatural communication as well as of human intercourse: the very fact that writing enables man to communicate *over space and time* makes it more effective as a way of getting in touch with *distant deities*" (Goody 1968:201, my emphasis).

Similar uses of the written word, particularly verses from holy scriptures, are found throughout the written world of the Middle East and parts of Asia in association with literate "believers," as well as with illiterate "pagans" or partially Islamized groups, and among both chiefs and commoners, all of whom feel that the magic inherent in words and formulas is all the more potent when words are given material, graphic form in writing. The belief that through prayers Muslim holy men can actually converse with the

[15] Court influence and positions were also useful ways for Muslim trader-malams to augment their incomes with money, gold, and slaves given them by the king, which helped to recompense for limitations sometimes placed on the energetic Hausa traders to protect Ashanti traders (Adamu 1978:81–82).

deity is encouraged by the fact that Muslims can control a superior form of human "conversation" through the technology of writing (ibid., pp. 202, 203, 205, 227). Conversely, the magic of the written word is also enhanced by association of writing with the Muslim priesthood, whose members reveal their power by using books that "talk" (as it were) and reveal significant truths and from the high prestige of the Islamic cultures of which literacy is part.

In addition, contact with Islam, as Goody points out (1968: 215–16), has meant that some of the most highly valued members of the receiving culture are absorbing ideological ideas and acquiring skills that derive from quite a different time and that link the local region with the Islamic world of North Africa and the Middle East, i.e., with higher cultures that are also distant in space. "The links in this system of intellectual communication are the books in which information is stored and the men who have been trained to interpret them" (Goody 1968:216, 239; Bloch 1968:296). As we have seen, many of these learned scholars obtained at least some of their education while away from home, studying with already prestigious clerics. Others were purposely brought from the "ideological heartland" of the Middle East by rulers desirous of their advice and magical protection, as when Mansa Musa, king of Mali in the fourteenth century, brought learned men back with him on his return from pilgrimage (cf. Wumbei, king of Dagomba, discussed above) (Goody 1968:219). These scholars were valuable both because they came from a distant place and because they understood and represented the esoteric quality of written words and the knowledge they encapsulated; words and knowledge that were "*secret* formulae for the revelation of *hidden* truths, possessed and interpreted by a *few* book-owning scribes, and deriving power from their position in an international network of cultural communication. *It was often the fact that book or practitioner filled the role of stranger that gave them authority in dealings with the esoteric*" (ibid., p. 228, my emphasis). In other words, these strangers, and all learned Muslims, members of a potent and prestigious community of scholar-traders, were possessed of a far wider appreciation of geographical distance and space-time through trade, pilgrimage to ancient sacred centers, and learned books than were ordinary persons. It was this wider experience, conjoined with their mystical divinatory talents and literate-magical abilities, that made them valued associates, particularly of ruling elites.[16]

The same combination of wider experience, esoteric knowledge, and foreign origins, combined with strategic trade positions and excellent organizational structure, supported the Order of the Sanusiya of Cyrenaica (Libya) among oasis dwellers and Bedouin tribes of Cyrenaica, the Western Desert of Egypt, and the former French Sahara. As Evans-Pritchard has recounted (1949), the Sanusiya was a fraternity of orthodox Muslims of the same general Islamic tradition as that of West Africa established by an extremely learned Muslim scholar and his followers in the early nineteenth century in the isolated stretches of the Cyrenaica plateau and regions to the south. The Order was conceived as a missionary movement aimed at countries of the Sahara, the Sudan, and equatorial Africa. It was particularly effective among semi-nomadic Bedouin who controlled major caravan routes leading from these interior regions to the Mediterranean. Consequently, scholarly communities (lodges) of Sanusi were strategically situated at oases on these major pilgrimage and trade routes, and their participation in caravan trade, both directly and by collection of customs duties, provided a profitable means of logistic support.

The missionaries trained at these oasis centers, particularly the early disciples of the founding Grand Sanusi, were foreigners to the Bedouin area (many came from Algeria and other countries of the Maghrib) and to the Bedouin tribal structure. This separation from local lineage and political systems was a major factor

---

[16] Certain nobles of the Taimoro of southeastern Madagascar were the only Malagasy group to possess knowledge of the manufacturing of paper and of writing—in this case using Arabic script to render Malagasy words—and consequently served as itinerant specialists in ritual and esoteric knowledge in the courts of a number of other Malagasy rulers for at least two hundred years. Their services included work as diviners, magicians, doctors, scribes, and scholars. They traveled widely selling charms and inscriptions, recording genealogies and serving as advisers to chiefs and kings. They were eventually replaced by London missionaries, another group of learned men from afar (Kottak 1972:118, 123; Kent 1969:45–47; 1970:88–115, 244–46)

in facilitating the successful role of the Sanusi as local holy men, mediators, and advisers. The success of the Order in Cyrenaica was also due to the ancient devotion of the Bedouin to holy men, saints (Marabtin) or "Marabouts," for the Grand Sanusi and later his followers were considered as members of a long line of saints with baraka (spiritual grace) to impart to ordinary folk. Although the exceptional success of the Sanusiya Order rested ultimately on its unusual internal organization, for our purposes it is the traditional role of the Marabtin or saints which the Sanusi filled that is of most interest.

In earlier centuries Marabtin in Cyrenaica came from regions to the west; many settled in Cyrenaica on their return from pilgrimage to Mecca. "Their fanaticism, asceticism, ability to read and write, and thaumaturgic power, impressed the simple Bedouin, who accepted them as holy men and magicians and used them to write charms, to perform religious rites, and to act as mediators in inter-tribal disputes" (Evans-Pritchard 1949:66). The tombs of these holy men became cult centers or defined neutral border locations for intertribal gatherings, fittingly enough, as Evans-Pritchard notes, since the Marabouts themselves were "regarded as standing outside the tribal system, to which indeed, being foreigners from the west, they did not belong . . ." (ibid., p. 67). Thus, long before the Sanusiya Order developed the Bedouin were used to the sight of the learned man, "for anyone who can read and write is a learned man to the Bedouin—coming from the west to heal their children and beasts, break droughts, write talismans, and teach them the beliefs and laws of Islam," as well as to arbitrate (ibid., p. 68).

Marabouts of this sort were still coming to Cyrenaica when the Grand Sanusi arrived with his disciples, also from the west (Algeria). After organizing a few lodges (zawiyas) in trading oases the system spread as local tribal leaders vied with each other in requesting a shaikh from the Order to establish a zawiya near them and to teach, tend to religious needs, and arbitrate both among local tribes and between tribes and the outside Turkish administration. The shaikh and his assistants also directed trade and subsistence activities at his lodge, which served as a hospitality center, caravan stop, commercial center, and general point of settled social, religious, educational, administrative, and economic stability in the nomadic pattern of the surrounding population (ibid., pp. 77–80, 88).

As Evans-Pritchard emphasizes, the shaikhs of the Sanusiya lodges enjoyed a reputation for sanctity among the Bedouin because of their esoteric wisdom, that is, their knowledge of the Qur'ān and of reading and writing, and their strict performance of religious duties, and doubtless also because of their foreign origin, "for the Bedouin of Cyrenaica were accustomed to look to the west for piety" (ibid., pp. 82–83). To the Bedouin, the learned and pious Marabout, with his baraka, is both respected and regarded as a "different kind of person" who is not intimately part of Bedouin life and with whose families Bedouin do not intermarry.

The universalistic nature of Islam allows for the development of far-flung networks or "diasporas" (Cohen 1971) of "foreign" scholar-traders whose point of commonality rests on literacy, a common sacred text and moral community, and a holy center (Mecca), and whose political-religious aura and trading capacities are enhanced locally because they are "outsiders" by birth and by learned tradition. The same phenomenon has been characteristic of other Old World interethnic political-religious traditions at various times. The extensive missionary and trade network of Nestorian Christians that stretched from "China to the Tigris and from Lake Baikal to Cape Comorin" during approximately the fourth through the tenth centuries A.D. also seems to be of this order.[17] Itinerant Nestorians of the Eastern or Assyrian Church,

[17] The far-flung Jewish communities of the early Middle Ages should also be mentioned in this context. In Europe, mainly because of their international connections, Jews enjoyed a protected legal status as wards of the nobility in return for services as kings' confidants, agents, and commercial intermediaries in the Carolingian centuries when, after the spread of Islam, Christians could not trade in Muslim countries nor Muslims in Christian countries. In the Orient, as the spread of the Caliphate empire opened the way for better communication, Jewish communities were established in India, Ceylon, even northern and southern China. Consequently, Jewish communities in France or Germany, in India and China shared a travel and communications network that stretched from the land of the Franks on the Western Sea to the Far East. A small, unique, and little-known group of long-distance specialists, the Radanites, then emerged, who traveled freely along this extensive network, supported along the way by the com-

centered in the Tigris–Euphrates valley and then in Baghdad, apparently were particularly effective among the elite of the equally nomadic ranked societies of the Turks and Tartars of Central Asia. Here they served their chiefly potentates not only as proselytizers but also as learned men, i.e. doctors, scholar-priests, scribes, interpreters, secretaries, and tutors to their children, in large part because of their ability to read and write, which skill they also introduced and taught to their followers among the Turks, Uigurs, and Mongols. A number of high-born women and wives of native khans were also converted to Christianity, as apparently were some rulers and many commoners. However, even those Mongol khans who did not convert to the faith "used to take off their headgear and genuflect before [the Nestorian] Patriarch" (Mingana 1925:342).

Many of these Nestorian missionary-scholars apparently also engaged in trade; mention is made, perhaps apocryphally, in several chronicles of the time, of "Christian merchants" who discussed and instructed upon matters of faith with a ruler of the Keraits after he was purportedly miraculously saved by a saintly vision when lost in a blizzard in the mountains.[18] More generally, Rowbotham also notes that Syrian Christians, as nomadic merchants, were "the pilgrim of the highland, the disseminator of news and even the banker of western and central Asia," and that Nestorians were often merchants rather than missionaries, but

mon linguistic ties and cultural kinship that underlay Jewish solidarity regardless of locale (Bronitsky 1982, Roscher 1944). Unfortunately, the nature of their activities, other than general association with long-distance trade, apparently is unknown. In the later Middle Ages, even though the extensive east–west communications network was broken, Jews in Europe and the Middle East enjoyed high, even if unpopular, positions as royal advisers and intelligencers, providing both wealth and knowledge from their wide network of contacts maintained through the travels of itinerant Jewish merchants, craftsmen, and scholarly rabbis. Jewish scholars also became royal physicians, and it was their skill as doctors that gave Jewish rabbi-statesmen their positions at many of the courts of Europe and the Middle East. The family backgrounds, education, and careers of these royal favorites—at once men of business, scholarship, and statecraft—reveal a familiar combination of long-distance trade, medicine, learned scholarship, and royal counseling emerging from general training in literary, scientific, and philosophical instruction (Abrahams 1911; Noveck 1959)

[18] This incident may be somewhat confused with the legend of "Prester John" if "John" is originally associated with a Kerait ruler, as some have suggested.

spread their religious influence (and, we can add, their skills as learned men) nonetheless "literally into the remote confines of ancient Asia" (1942:5). Other Nestorians, living in China during the seventh and eighth centuries A.D. under the tolerant T'ang dynasty, became rich, held sundry offices under the emperor, and enjoyed great privileges (Power 1926:138; Mingana 1925; Rowbotham 1942:4–14, 30–31).

The Nestorian impact in Central Asia and the Far East was gradually assimilated into more indigenous religious systems and disappeared, but the impact of learned religious scholars from the far west was strongly felt again when Jesuit missionaries were recognized by the Chinese court during the late sixteenth and seventeenth centuries. The story of the Jesuit fathers in China is remarkable in many respects. For us, it is another supreme example of a group of foreigners of undoubted learning coming from a distant land who were imbued with an aura of the exotic by virtue of their foreignness and were accorded highest honors at a royal court as men of great wisdom and knowledge and as masters of specialized arts and crafts (see Rowbotham 1942:218, Fülöp-Miller 1930:210–20, 230–34 regarding similar experiences of Jesuits in Japan). In addition, the Jesuit fathers are of interest because they clearly understood the basis for their elevated (though sometimes politically rather shaky) positions, and worked hard to develop, elaborate, and exploit their reputations as foreign curiosities and intelligentsia and masters of hidden understandings.

Indeed, the success of Jesuit missionary efforts, and probably their lives, lay in their ability to play this role, for they understood that conversion had to begin at the top of the social pyramid and that learned Chinese scholars would respond only to those who were also men of letters and astute politicians (Spence 1984:152–53; Rowbotham 1942:212–37; Fülöp-Miller 1930:238–41). But in addition the Jesuits seem genuinely to have enjoyed the challenge of their undertaking, and actively engaged the Chinese literati, as fellow specialists in esoterica, in competitive rivalries as men of wisdom. Their status was further enhanced on the occasions when they won such competitions, provided, of course, that the emperor approved, as a number of them did, particularly since Jesuit displays of exotic learning were frequently mounted at their

Le Père Matthieu Ricci.   Le Père Adam Schaal.   Le Père Ferdinand Verbiest.

FIGURE 3.7

Three Jesuit leaders in China: Ricci, Schall, and Verbiest. From A. Rowbotham, *Missionary and Mandarin*, 1942, p. 101. Published by University of California Press. Reprinted by permission of the press.

request or in their service. For the Jesuit fathers in general, and select individuals (such as Fathers Ricci, Schall, and Verbiest) in particular, became interpreters, close diplomatic, military, and "scientific" advisers, foreign ambassadors, doctors, personal friends, and private tutors to the imperial throne. Some were honored with high titles (and the accompanying pomp and circumstance) making them mandarins of the first class, and were able to enjoy direct access to the emperor, particularly those rulers who became personally interested in the science and philosophy of the West (Rowbotham 1942:81, 94–95; Fülöp-Miller 1930:241–45, 252–57; Spence 1984).

In pursuing their vocation as foreign sages, the Jesuits utilized two major areas of knowledge: an understanding of physics and mechanics and expertise in mathematics, astronomy, and cosmography, as well as an appreciation of books, both as inherently beautiful objects when carefully printed and artistically bound and as repositories for wisdom (Rowbotham 1942:218; Spence 1984:142–49, 154–55). Chinese officials, themselves reflective of an ancient scholarly and magico-literary tradition, appreciated

106

books for largely the same reasons.[19] They were intrigued by the principles of mechanics, which were new to them, and recognized astronomy and cosmography, particularly as evidenced in the astrological value of the imperial calendar, as the cosmically ordained foundation for the continued strength and well-being of the emperor and of the state. Perhaps the greatest triumph of the Jesuits as learned men of wisdom was achieved when, by imperial decree, they were given important duties as assistant director and technical advisers in the Bureau of Mathematics or Astronomy and, therefore, were involved with preparation of the imperial calendar, the arbiter of the destiny of everyone and everything in China (Rowbotham 1942:67–72; Fülöp-Miller 1930:250–51). This highest honor derived from the precision of the Jesuits' astronomical calculations, which allowed them to forecast major cosmological events, such as the exact time of eclipses, with greater accuracy than their Chinese counterparts, and thus evidenced their more closely tuned connection with cosmic workings. (It is noteworthy that in the earlier T'ang era, when the Chinese court was highly tolerant of foreign goods and peoples and Buddhism was popular, official calendrical calculations were virtually monopolized by three families of Indian astronomers whose success also lay, at least in part, in more exact methods of predicting solar and lunar eclipses. Obviously, the celestial wisdom of learned foreigners was appreciated and applied to one of the highest expressions of political ideology on more than one occasion; see Schafer 1963:279; Eberhard 1965:126–28).

Yet to many Chinese scholars the mastery of astronomy was no greater achievement than mastery of the intricate details of clockworks and other mechanical devices,[20] or ingenious solutions to technical problems of bridge-building, or manufacture of

[19] Indeed, in traditional China books were more than aesthetic objects holding wisdom. As Weber noted, written sacred books were considered magical objects, and the men conversant with them were viewed as holders of a magical charisma. The prestige of the literati lay in their knowledge of writing and of literature as a form of magical power (1946:417).

[20] "A volume might be written concerning the influence of the clock on the infiltration of Western ideas in China, so great was the importance of this popular form of gift" (Rowbotham 1942:219; Fülöp-Miller 1930:241–48).

hydraulic machinery to operate fountains for the royal gardens. Of the monarchs themselves, those who were most accepting of the Jesuits were frequently most interested in acquiring information not only of Western sciences but also of the customs, histories, and court etiquette of the distant Western countries (Rowbotham 1942:224). The Emperor Ch'ien Lung even requested that, as part of a miniature city complete with personnel that he had built for his edification and amusement within the palace grounds (since the Son of Heaven was not at liberty to venture forth into the real streets of the capital proper), a whole street be built according to Western architecture "which in his imagination he must have peopled with such crowds as daily passed the Porte Saint-Martin or crowded the Pont Neuf in that capital of France about which he had heard so much from his Jesuit servants" (Rowbotham 1942:226).

Yet there was a viper in the emperor's garden. Foreign wise men, because they are sagacious, can also pose a threat to local men of knowledge, for being foreigners they are, quite simply, intrusive elements into the local cultural system.[21] If, in addition to being foreign, they also hold highly effective command of prestige-conferring knowledge and seemingly magical powers and are highly influential as advisers to the crown, it is not surprising that local literati and royal counselors find their patience strained even as their intellectual and political acumen is challenged. Thus the Jesuit presence at the Chinese court met with opposition from traditional mandarins on various occasions. This opposition can also be understood as comparable in its own, short-lived way to the ancient and long-standing rivalry between traditional mandarin literati and the powerful eunuchs employed in the Chinese court. Unlike the mandarins, eunuchs had unimpeded access to all parts of the royal household and frequently monopolized communication channels to the emperor (Stover

[21] The ethnographic literature readily indicates that many long-distance or foreign specialist groups live in separate towns or in special wards or quarters of the local community. This separatism, often combined with separate courts of law and/or a distinctive language, gives physical as well as political expression to their distinctiveness vis-à-vis the local setting (see Curtin 1984:38–41, 86).

1974:25, 196; Fitzgerald 1961:250–55, 305, 468; Weber 1946:416–44). Like the Jesuits, the eunuchs also represented access to potential political-ideological power bases other than the landed wealth, high birth, and restricted access to traditional literacy that underwrote mandarin status. For a thousand years eunuchs had been entrusted with overseas expeditions designed to display the greatness of imperial prestige, encourage tribute (see Chapter 4), and bring back exotic and precious products from distant lands. During the T'ang dynasty eunuchs of the imperial palace were appointed to the crucial post of "Commissioner of Commercial Argosies," a sort of customs office, at the port of Canton where much foreign merchandise was received and where ambitious imperial officials could become very rich (Schafer 1963:16; Mirsky 1964:237–51).

Eunuchs and Jesuits, then, shared not only access to the royal ear but an interest in, knowledge of, and access to foreign barbarian wealth and curiosities, while mandarin officials were committed to wealth in taxes and to traditional Confucian truths that had no use for such inferior heresies.[22] Consequently, just as mandarin officials destroyed the official records of the eunuch admiral Cheng Ho's expedition to Africa in the fifteenth century to discourage later attempts at maritime ventures (Wheatley 1961:88–89; Fitzgerald 1961:474; Mirsky 1964:247–52), so a century or so later Jesuits and mandarins enjoyed at best an uneasy truce.[23]

It has been my contention that whatever motives impel them to travel, long-distance specialists are also frequently regarded as

[22] Eunuchs of the Chinese court obviously suggest comparisons with the pochteca for, like pochteca, they supplied the emperor with information regarding the state of "outside" things (including controlling the flow of information to the monarch from "outside" his palace), while Chinese literati, like Aztec aristocrats, controlled the internal esoteric knowledge of society.

[23] As is well known, Jesuits also became unpopular in some European ecclesiastical and court circles for a complex set of reasons including their enviable roles as royal advisers and diplomatic agents during troubled times. In addition, they were challenged because of their willingness to accommodate foreign customs and to condone foreign practices in the mission fields, particularly China (the so-called rites controversy). In both China and Europe, then, Jesuit familiarity with foreign matters was a factor in the mix of circumstances making them suspect (Fülöp-Miller 1930: Duignan 1958).

learned men, and often rightly so. In the traditional societies we are considering, knowledge and wisdom of "distant" affairs is, by definition, knowledge and wisdom of the nature of the cosmos and, therefore, a matter for political-religious elites in whose company, one way or another, long-distance travelers are properly included. Appreciating this, we can better recognize the potential significance of several otherwise rather enigmatic, and seemingly passing, commentaries in the literature; for example, reference to the likelihood that the Callahuayas, the traveling curers of the Andes, once served as litter-bearers of the Incas (Wassén 1972:16), or that the pre-Columbian merchants of highland Guatemala, who shared the hospitality and leisure activities of the lords of the towns where they traded, could also "read and write the painted codices," presumably the same type of codices that contained the ritual calendar and divination charts and were under the general charge of the priests (Carmack 1976:8, 16).

We can begin to appreciate, too, why organizations of ostensibly long-distance merchants such as the itinerant Coromandel traders of the eleventh to thirteenth centuries in southern India, should be described in a contemporary temple inscription as enjoying unrivaled fame and brilliant glory for things that seem to have little directly to do with trade: "like the elephant, they attack and kill; wise as Brhaspati [the teacher of the gods]; fertile in expedients as Narayana [Vishnu, the great deity]; perfect in disputes as Nareda Rsi [a divine sage] . . . clay they set fire to; of sand they make ropes; the thunderbolts they catch and exhibit; the sun and moon they draw down to earth . . . they are not ones to fall" (quoted in Stein 1965:51). Undoubtedly the largesse conferred upon the temple (which the inscription also records) helped encourage such glorification, but the tone of the tribute draws a picture of bravery, renown, wisdom, skill in mediation, and a degree of seemingly magical expertise in understanding and controlling portions of the universe denied ordinary mortals which, though proclaimed rather exuberantly here, can, as we have seen, be paralleled elsewhere by calmer ethnographic statements of the exceptional expertise of long-distance specialists.

The Strange and the Precious

The Greek god Hermes was represented by a variety of guises that, for all their apparent disparateness, were not unrelated. He was the god of the thief, the shepherd, the craftsman, the herald, the musician, the athlete, and the merchant. He was associated with mental cunning and with trickery ("thievery") as manifestations of magical powers expressed, for example, in charms and spells. His magical abilities, in turn, were closely associated with his role as craftsman, a role with a number of implications appropriate to long-distance concerns that are also neatly encapsulated in Hermes' various appearances.

"Primitive magic is a technology of a sort; its aim is the manipulation of the external world. The primitive craftsman supplements his technique with magical practices, and success at his craft is taken to indicate possession of magical powers" (Brown 1947:21). As craftsman, Hermes' magic also represented mental ability and the god, thereby, emerges as a culture hero; in the *Homeric Hymn* he is credited with inventing music (the lyre, the pipe) and with discovery of the art of making fire (ibid., pp. 21, 22, 24). He is also recognized more generally as the "giver of good things." As a wise craftsman, Hermes is further associated with the royal herald or ambassador who served kings in many skilled capacities, including that of the wise and knowing personal servant and adviser, as functionary in ceremonies of sacrifice and divination, and as sacred and inviolate messenger and sacrosanct agent of international ("foreign") negotiations (ibid., pp. 26–27).

In dealing with foreigners Hermes was associated with people and things that stood outside the boundaries of society, that existed in the uninhabited "wastelands" where shepherds tended flocks, where precious metals and other natural goods were found and worked by the sacred magic known to craftsmen, where foreigners were met as merchants come to trade. Indeed, as Brown has pointed out, the name "Hermes" probably derives from the Greek word for "stone heap," and signified "he of the stone heap." The stone heaps in question were boundary stones that marked points of communication between strangers, e.g., at a house entrance, at crossroads, in the wild wastelands of a forest or on some hilltop. Such points of habitual contact with strangers were hallowed ground in that dealings with strange foreigners in ancient Greece were surrounded with magical protections. Consequently, magical rites associated with strangers encountered at boundary points were readily associated with the god of the boundary stone, and Hermes became the god of roads and of doors, the guide who watches over comings and goings, and "the 'ambassador' who protects men in their dealings with strangers" (ibid., pp. 34, 45); dealings which involved, in effect, the skilled and essentially magical "craft" of dealing with "forces" of the outside which must be controlled.

The boundary not only provided contact with strangers but also access to their products. The boundary was crossed "by enterprising men bent on procuring raw materials from the wasteland that lay between the neighboring communities or engaged on a 'merchant adventure' into alien territory" to acquire good things. Thereby Hermes, the god of craftsmanship and the culture hero who provides "good things," also becomes the god of merchants; merchants being, in Homeric terms, "professional boundary-crossers" and procurers of desired goods (ibid., pp. 38, 45).[24] Craftsmen themselves ventured into the "wastelands" searching for raw materials; "the legendary discoverers of the art of iron-smelting, the Idaean Dactyls, lived and worked in the mountains. The god of the wasteland became a patron of such enterprises: the silver-producing Mount Pangaean was known as the haunt of Hermes, and the silver from Mount Laurium was called the gift of Hermes" (ibid., p. 46).

Dealings with strangers, merchant adventurers, good things from afar, the "riches of the earth" sought by craftsmen; all are now combined under the patronage of Hermes, the god also of crafts, of magic and intellect, of royal ambassadors, advisers, and diviners. In short, Hermes is the god of "distant" things and experiences in general (as represented in time by divination and in space by access to the wealth of the wasteland and to strangers'

---

[24] Exchange at the boundary in ancient Greece refers to practices that were followed before the establishment of exchange at the agora or city center (Brown 1947:39, 40).

goods), and the god of the exceptional magical-intellectual skills needed to contact distance (by divination, by foreign travel, or boundary trade) and to acquire foreign "goods" or manufacture them from foreign raw materials.[25]

Hermes' multiple attributes are reflected in the ethnographic examples noted in previous pages in which travel beyond the border into uncivilized "wastelands" is portrayed as a ritualized "sacred" experience; where priestly scholar-traders from afar control the magical "craft" of literacy and serve as royal advisers, astronomers, and diviners; where "craftsmen of wisdom," such as shamans or youthful initiates, travel in search of additional esoteric knowledge and seek good things from distant places (whether potent herbs, magical darts, or knowledge of foreigners' customs, songs, and rituals) to enhance their skills still further. We have seen, too, the suggestion in the Coromandel inscription that "magical" skills in working with the resources of the universe was one of the attributes of Coromandel traders. In these areas of skilled and extraordinary expertise and in others not mentioned here (e.g., as skilled musicians and entertainers; cf. Hermes as musician) we find long-distance specialists involved.[26]

"Hermetic wisdom" or insight regarding the functioning of the universe includes knowing the "purposes" for which the elements of the universe were originally created. This knowledge and the ability to control cosmic forces and to put them to use for human beings, either for good or for evil, can be an important part of the sacred wisdom and associated magic of religious practitioners in many traditional societies. In addition, although in traditional world views cosmic powers or forces are believed to be inherently intangible, they often are thought to be expressed in tangible forms. Many "curious" things of the earth, the sea, and the heavens, many "riches of the wasteland" are thought of as

[25] Hermes also was patron of wandering or itinerant unskilled laborers (vagabonds), who were also travelers who made things

[26] The Guatemalan merchants who could read the painted codices could also play the musical instruments of the lords (Carmack 1976:8); Hausa musicians were royal drummers and praise singers in some host communities (Adamu 1978:41, 100); the Siassi Islanders, trader-voyagers of the Vitiaz Straits, were also famous dancers and participants in religious ceremonies and festivals in host communities (Harding 1967:142–44).

curious or as representing natural riches because they are believed to contain or express cosmic powers. "Everything unusual, unique, new, perfect or monstrous at once becomes imbued with magic-religious powers and an object of veneration or fear according to the circumstances . . ." (Eliade 1958:13).[27]

The curious or unfamiliar objects that are most marked by cosmic power are frequently those that are not immediately at hand, but must be obtained by some exceptional effort. The difficulty of acquisition and/or the need for exceptional skills to acquire or craft exotic goods become, in turn, part of the measure of their potency. It is no accident that material goods that come from a distance—like those that are extracted from the earth or sea—are likely to be considered as unique and powerful, as containing exceptional potency and magical strengths and abilities. If the things that come from a distance are also acquired from a mystically charged source—and I have argued that geographically distant locations are likely, virtually by definition, to be charged with some sort of supernatural, sacred, or mystical connotations—then potency is virtually assured.

Similarly, long-distance "merchants" and local and traveling craftsmen (such as the itinerant Ibo smiths mentioned in note 11), who are intimately involved in the acquisition or preparation of such goods are ipso facto agents in an ideologically powerful process of acquiring cosmically charged "wealth" from the uncontrolled, chaotic outside world and making it available and useful (by transporting or crafting) for society's consumption. So it is that Hermes can be the god of merchants and of magic and of craftsmen, and can be associated with the "wealth of the wasteland" extracted and manufactured by craftsmen's magical skill. Those who, like ironworkers or goldsmiths, take minerals and other products from the body of the earth and fashion them into valued objects are "controlling" the power of the universe. Those

[27] "But power is an invisible mystery. It erupts out of nature in storms, volcanoes, meteors, in springtime and newborn babies; . . . The only way we know it is there is to see it in action. And so the idea of *mana*, or special power erupting from the realm of the invisible and the supernatural, can only be spotted in the unusual, the surpassing, the excellent, that which transcends what is necessary or expected" (Becker 1975:46).

who, like shaman-curers, tame unruly spirits by ritual and with curative herbs or, like royal adviser-diviners, acquire knowledge of distant time and ascertain the future, are performing comparable tasks. Those who, like long-distance travelers, acquire symbolically potent material goods or knowledge from a geographically distant, supernaturally charged realm and make them available for the good of the polity, are also involved in comparable tasks of "harnessing" the power contained in things from afar.

In the following, emphasis will be placed on the symbolic significance of material items derived from symbolically charged geographical distance, either as already manufactured goods or as valuable raw materials (i.e., as products in their "natural state") derived unformed and unshaped (uncrafted) from the earth, air, or sea and which are thereby redolent with the power of the universe. Yet a brief digression may be useful concerning the importance of the act of crafting such products into cultural objects of some sort. (Some products, of course, such as strange animals or exotic natives brought from far away places for display at royal courts, may not lend themselves to crafting, though efforts to domesticate and to civilize can amount to the same thing).[28]

The abilities recognized as crafting skills are frequently accorded special significance not only because they are acquired or exhibited by relatively few persons or because they may identify a given individual's particular area of expertise and perhaps personal identity, but also because crafting skill indicates a special gift or a special power. "The artisan is a connoisseur of secrets, a magician; thus all crafts include some kind of initiation and are

[28] Like Schneider (1977), I prefer to consider material items in terms of whether or not they derive from a distance rather than whether they are "luxury" or "utilitarian," given the difficulty that can arise when the political usefulness of luxury goods is considered (see also Polanyi 1975:135). Where Schneider is interested in exchange of long-distance goods as relevant to the capture of energy, however, I prefer to emphasize political-ideological facets associated with such materials. Again, my approach is intended to complement, not oppose, concerns of political economy. I also feel a distinction between natural products and crafted goods, although not pursued here, may be a particularly useful distinction in terms of the political-ideological significance of such goods, especially for centralized polities where certain crafted goods, such as fine textiles, may be produced and exchanged for outside natural products, such as precious metals (cf. Schneider, ibid.).

handed down by an occult tradition" (Eliade 1962:102). It is instructive in this context again to remember the range of activities (such as Hermes' varied attributes) with which artisan skills may be associated in a single though multifocal symbolic expression. For example, the Mesoamerican culture hero-god Quetzalcoatl associated with celestial creativity, sacrificial nourishment and agricultural fertility was also symbolically associated with kings, merchants, priests, elite wisdom (education), and also artists (e.g., jade–metal–featherwork; Carrasco 1982:4; Roys 1972:76; Berdan 1982b:129–30). In a similar manner, Werner notes the various areas of expertise among the Mekranoti (Brazil) where individuals may exercise influence or achieve prestige: curing, shamanism, oration, hunting, body painting, warfare, cross-cultural mediation, knowledge of ceremonies, ancestors, and foreigners, and crafting (1981:365–66).

Each of these areas of proficiency reflects a particular expertise in manipulating some element or manifestation of universal energy. Crafting skills in particular may represent human intelligence and understanding which, in traditional societies like the Mekranoti, ultimately refers to understanding of the meaning and operation of the cosmos and its dynamic and animating powers. "When the Mekranoti want to express how intelligent a man is they often refer to the things he knows how to make" (or, alternatively, can't make, if they wish to indicate his stupidity; Werner 1981:366).

Association of crafting skills with extraordinary power can be found either directly stated or implied in ethnographies worldwide. Thus, McCarthy, speaking of crafting and trade in Australian aborigine society, notes that "articles are often sought after from a craftsman renowned for his skill . . . to personal skill, however is sometimes added a belief by others that a man is able to impart a personal magical potency to whatever he makes." Goods "are better because another man made them" (1939:172). Likewise, the Shona of Zimbabwe attribute any special skills or personal gifts—e.g., hunting, curing, divining—to secret "stranger-spirits," unsettled spirits of foreigners including whites (see Chapter 5) who died away from home or of young unmarried persons, who roam around seeking an expressive medium

(Bucher 1980:91, 96, 195). Similarly, the Shilluk interpret the special personal gifts and talents of certain people as the expression of the "stronger flow" of universal power or *juok* in such individuals (Lienhardt 1954:156). Concerning the Warao of the Orinoco delta, Wilbert, noting correspondences between skilled Warao craftsmen (such as canoe makers and basket weavers) and shamans, rainmakers, herbalists, and musicians as experts (*uási*) in their respective professions or arts, suggests that "in a way, all true Warao uási are religious practitioners who mediate the powers of their natural and supernatural environments" (1979:144–45).

The special power associated with crafting skills is also evidenced ethnographically by the attributes associated with particular physical materials. For example, to work with iron, exceptionally fine textiles, salt, or precious metals may require certain ritual precautions or abstensions. Thus in Incaic Peru select "chosen women" were periodically designated as chaste "virgins of the sun" and set to weaving ceremonial textiles for temple and priestly use (Mason 1957:181). Similarly, in many parts of Africa, Scandinavia, Central Asia, and elsewhere in the Old World, smiths were widely respected, feared, and sometimes socially distanced, for their highly ritualized work with iron and their seemingly extraordinary power to create tools involved them closely with powers of the earth, from which they dug ore, and of the trees killed for charcoal (Sundström 1974:188; Alpers 1969:3–61, 406; Eliade 1962:81–99, 57, 29). Certain purificatory rituals were associated with gold mining in parts of pre-Columbian Central and South America (cf. Lovén 1935:532; Sauer 1969:134; Feldman 1978:69), and sanctity was accorded brine springs and pools, just as elaborate rituals and special status have been associated with salt manufacture in many parts of the world (e.g., Meek 1969:428–31).[29] In Australia, localities where various

[29] Navajo journeys for salt, hunting trips, and trading excursions were all characterized by similar ceremony and ritual (Hill 1948:393), another reminder that hunting may be viewed not only as subsistence activity but as a special skill. Hunting magic may be enjoyed to some extent by all men, but it may also be the particular gift of a few. In centralized agricultural polities, hunting (at least of certain types of game) may be a specialty of the elite; a means of evidencing their control over nature's powers (creatures) as much as for recreation, and the value of animal

objects are made are those where spirit ancestors introduced them or their method of manufacture. Objects used by living natives must be made of the wood of that locality and have any necessary art designs applied.

It has also been argued that the mode and style of crafting may express political-ideological concepts associated with particular forms of social organization and government and that the display of these crafted products by those holding the appropriate status then becomes a succinct symbolic statement of the proper, "true," or legitimate form of social and political organization (e.g., Helms 1981, 1986a; Rabineau 1975; Fraser and Cole 1972). Adding this context to the others briefly summarized it becomes apparent that crafted goods may attest not only to the skills and powers of select craftsmen, or the supernatural characteristics of the material itself, but also to the extraordinary power, prestige, and ideological legitimacy of a given polity, its leaders, and its vested representatives, which now can include artisans as well as councillors and kings.

Let us now consider a few examples evidencing the significance of geographical distance in establishing the value of raw materials and crafted goods. In considering what makes foreign-derived goods, whether crafted or natural, desirable from the point of view of those receiving them, factors such as rarity of materials, strangeness of the object, cunning of the craftsman or value as a craftable raw material are cited in the literature (e.g., Elliott 1976:21; Berdan 1982a:18), while from the point of view of those manufacturing or transporting them portability and durability are mentioned (e.g., Mulvaney 1976:80; Harding 1967:72–73). All are summed in the general concept that in traditional societies goods derived from a distance or transported a long way will probably be high in value and low in bulk. There can be little quarrel with any of these points as generalities, particularly if we recognize that one of the most frequently exchanged types of long-distance goods is esoteric knowledge which is, by definition, rare, strange, in a sense cunning, can be very durable espe-

skins (and jaguar thrones) may lie in the skill and symbolism associated with their acquisition (cf. Wilson 1979:57; Feldman 1971:174).

cially in oral societies, and represents the highest degree of portability and lowest possible bulk of any transported good. Its high value, which has been well attested to in ethnographic examples given above, is succinctly expressed in comments such as that by Braudel regarding sixteenth-century Mediterranean societies where "news, a luxury commodity, was worth more than its weight in gold" (1972:365–68). In addition, only rich bankers, merchants, or governments could afford the exorbitant prices charged by couriers, especially for top-speed service, and only those elites had reasonable access to the scarce resource of letters.

Yet, leaving aside esoteric knowledge and focusing only on material goods, we can see from the ethnographic literature that sheer distance and the magical or symbolic potency associated with distance or with distant places and polities can be important factors in the value assigned to some resources. For example, in Australia, "the quest for magical power from afar lies behind the barter of many material media used in magic and ceremonies" (McCarthy 1939:173–74). A shield from far away, or steel axes from whites, pass unused from tribe to tribe, moving over great areas of the country "as though of sacred import." Certain ceremonial objects—pearl shells, bullroarers, songs—that had to be made at appropriate sacred locales associated with culture heroes, were bartered widely, treasured as magic in locales distant from their source, and "frequently travel longer distances than articles used for everyday purposes" (ibid., pp. 173–74, 437–38). Similarly, boomerangs received in trade may be considered objects of powerful magic. In short, "magical power is an important factor in the promotion of barter and exchange," and goods were prized for good or evil magic as well as for utility and increased in antiquity and in value as they traveled farther and farther (ibid., pp. 174, 438).

Salisbury has characterized inter-band exchange and the long-distance movement of goods among Narragansett, Pequot, and other native peoples of sixteenth-century southern New England, half a world away, in comparable terms of gaining access to new sources of spiritual power as much as discovering new foods or tools, and as necessary as interaction with spiritual nonhumans for keeping the world in proper sacred balance (1982:49). In like fashion, the ceremonial and special status goods sought by the Navajo in foreign trade included turquoise beads which, being particularly dangerous because of foreign association, were ritually treated to remove malignant influences and to purify and sanctify the beads under new ownership, as well as to "fix the color" so that they could be handled safely (Hill 1948:391; Ford 1972:44; see also Forge 1967:75 regarding potent ceremonial paint from afar).

De Laguna also notes that men of importance among the Yakutat Tlingit sought prestige by lavish distribution of "exotic foods" and "important objects," and sought a wide range of foreign goods, including guns and ammunition, cloth and Hudson's Bay blankets, Tsimshian wood carvings, Haida canoes, and Salish slaves, generally for this purpose, though it is not clear whether their value as goods from outside lay in their foreign associations per se or in the prestige accorded to influential men because of this evidence of their foreign associations, or both (1972:356–57). Wilbert is of the opinion that a major impetus for Warao overseas voyages to the mythically symbolic north (i.e., to Trinidad) was the need for ritual tobacco for shamanic exercises, though a number of other items were acquired there, too (1977:39–40). Colson attributes the Akawaio interest in foreign goods to the simple belief that foreign is finer, and that exotic goods carry prestige and aesthetic value because of their manufacture by distant craftsmen (1973:59). Taussig, however, makes it clear that the foreign, lowland ornaments worn by highland Andean curers in Colombia represent and in a sense also contain the esoteric knowledge and shamanic power derived from the Amazon lowlands: "The highland healers adorn themselves with the symbols of the jungle and the jungle shamans. High above the jungle and close to the arid and near freezing paramo . . . of the Andes, they put on the crown and train of jungle birds' feathers; 'these are from the birds of the jungles, they make the visions come.' Around their necks they wear the pods of the cascabel which tinkle as they move. 'These are the sounds of the jungle, they bring the sounds when you take yagé.' They wear the necklace of jaguar's teeth, for the jaguar is the owner of yagé" (1980b:238–39).

120

The exceptional significance associated with items from distant places is particularly evidenced in highly centralized polities, both because exotic or nonlocal goods are given considerable visibility in association with the high status and political legitimacy of the elite, and because many types of exchange goods are again accorded inherent magical and religious significance because of their source or physical characteristics. The basic premise underlying this valuation again rests on the identification by elites of natural or crafted "gifts" or "trade goods" from afar as power-associated or power-charged treasures acquired from extraordinary realms outside their own heartland.[30]

In pre-Columbian central Mexico, according to a manuscript published in part by Feldman (1971:77), ". . . it was said that the rare thing was the privilege of the rulers [in pre-Hispanic times]. Whatever came *from the lands of the coast*, the precious thing was theirs alone. The precious feathers, the rare bird . . . all were the privilege of the rulers. Likewise the jade, the fine turquoise . . . the rare vase . . . the rare wood *from far places* . . . the gold from which was made their jewels . . . likewise silver . . . and in truth, *all, every world rarity*, its different rarities are all the privilege of the rulers . . ." (my emphasis). That distant rarities were desirable for more than curiosity's sake (and remembering Eliade's injunction that that which is exceptional is sacred) is indicated by a comment from Durán, ". . . [the Aztecs] decided to send messengers to Cempoala in the province of Cuetlaxtla, asking the rulers there to send them some conch shells, live turtles and scallops and other curious sea products, since these people lived right next to the ocean. The Aztecs had heard about these objects and wished them for the cult of their god" (quoted in Berdan 1982a:8–9). Archaeology adds further verification to the likelihood that goods from a distance were not only curious but also powerful. Speaking of recent discoveries at the Temple Mayor excavations in Tenochtitlán (Mexico City), Carrasco notes that over 80 percent of more than ninety exotic offerings that have been uncov-

[30] If we accept that elites are concerned with publically related honorific (essentially sacred) motives more than with more domestic "profit" motives, elite-related long-distance goods, whether crafted or natural, must also be primarily honorific in concept or in qualities (Goldman 1970:478–82; Polanyi 1975:137).

ered at strategic points around the base of the pyramid came from distant and frontier provinces under Aztec domination, suggesting that "the offerings of [such things as sea shells, crocodiles, swordfish from distant seas] demonstrate the Aztec desire to incorporate the powers from the edges of their world into the sacred shrine" (Carrasco 1982:182–83).[31]

It is probable, too, that the exotic tropical materials—jade, turquoise, tortoise shell cups, wild animal skins, and multicolored precious feathers (including the long green plumes of the quetzel bird of the mountain cloud forests)—acquired from elites in distant lands of Anáhuatl by pochteca travelers in exchange for embroidered and embellished textiles and other high-status Mexica regalia, were also "world rarities" replete with sacred symbolism. It is interesting in this respect to read that the foreign goods brought back by the pochteca are described by Sahagún as being the "riches, the wealth of the protector of all," as "the reward of the gorges, the mountains, the deserts," and as "the property or goods of the master, or lord, Uitzilopochtli" (Sahagún 1959:52, 53). When considered as "hidden riches" of the earth and as property of the gods, pochteca wealth appears less as merchandise and more as revealed earthly "secrets," richly charged with the potency of their ideological exoticism. As I have also argued, such rarities were retrieved from their natural or cosmic setting in po-

---

[31] In Mesoamerica, as in so many places, the sky, sea, and landscape are all replete with symbolism. In Mesoamerican legend, the surface of the earth itself was believed to be derived from the destruction of a monstrous goddess who floated in a giant primordial sea. From parts of her body hills and valleys, trees and plants were created. Her eyes became springs and caves, her mouth rivers and large caverns. "It is easy to see that, with a mythological tradition such as this, all geographic phenomena were seen as both animate and sacred" (Heyden 1981:6). Hunt (1977) has noted some of the sacred qualities and associations given to such phenomena. To take only a few examples, many culturally important minerals were associated with celestial images of the gods (salt, an important exchange item, was associated with water–moon deities; it is now associated with the Virgin of the Rosary), while precious metals, such as gold, the reddish-yellow metal of ornamentation, were associated with the reddish-yellow of the planet Mars and the god Xipe and with the vegetation that ornamented the earth. Images of the gods were fashioned with turquoise and other precious minerals (jadeite, obsidian, rock crystal, etc.), turquoise representing, among other things, the light of the sky and water. "Hence the precious jewels of the sky, the stars and planets with their sacred colors, become solidified into the precious jewels of the earth, the metals and gems" (Hunt 1977:156).

litically and ideologically uncontrolled wastelands far from the civilized Aztec heartland through the heroic efforts of ritually protected and knowledgeable long-distance adventurers. We can also conclude that the earthly rulers and elites of the Aztec universe who received these valuables received them not only as material wealth but as evidence of their command of the earth's powerfully sacred riches and of their esoteric knowledge of distant geographical-cum-cosmological realms (see Chapter 4).

The centralized polities of the Andes provide further evidence that exotic trade goods carried symbolic associations derived at least in part from their sources. Using contemporary ethnographic analogies, Reichel-Dolmatoff (1981) has suggested that the principal trade items in ancient Colombia included gold, semi-precious stones, necklaces, raw cotton and textiles, salt, sea shells, and narcotic snuff, all with "marked symbolic value which refers to concepts of fertility and fecundity."[32] These valued goods derived from various highland, lowland, and oceanic sources and were widely exchanged. For example, emeralds from highland Chibcha territory carried fertility symbolism and were considered as sacred stones in offerings to the gods. Many were traded as far as the Caribbean coast and it is likely that their sources and their symbolism provided a considerable part of their desirability as trade goods. In like fashion, salt from the mountains and salt from the sea, both of which carry connotations of sexuality among many contemporary native peoples of Colombia today, were extensively traded in pre-Columbian times (see also Salomon 1986:95).

In Andean highland and coastal kingdoms farther south the considerable traffic in *Strombus* and *Spondylus* shells, obtained from coastal Ecuador probably by long-distance sea voyagers from coastal Peru, provides another case in point. *Spondylus* and *Strombus*, which are limited to tropical waters and not found nat-

[32] Among Tukanoan tribes today, copper ear pendants, necklaces of silver triangles, and hexagonal rock crystals contain colors, shapes, and odors closely related to concepts of solar energy, cosmic order, and fertility. Similar concepts are accorded to gold by Kogi Indians of the Sierra Nevada de Santa Marta (Colombia), while rare and beautiful minerals of the Sierra Nevada and beyond, crafted into necklace beads, are valued for ritual use and as curatives or disease preventatives.

urally south of the Gulf of Guayaquil, were used in the coastal and central highland polities of Peru in rituals associated with assuring adequate water for crops and as offerings to springs. As products deriving from the ocean at Ecuador these shells would also be associated with the complex of ideas associated with the sea (water, rain, purification, earth) as opposed to the mountains and with the area (near Manta) where the Inca culture hero and creator, Viracocha, disappeared over the ocean after his travels from Lake Titicaca to Ecuador (Netherly 1980; La Lone 1977:4–6; Diez Canseco 1977:174–76; Davidson 1979; Zuidema 1964:168–69, 1982:432–34).

Foreign exotic goods in Old World empires could be charged with symbolic significance associated with the qualities of distant places, too. Schafer (1963) states the case for T'ang China very succinctly, noting "the old belief that foreign travel was full of physical hazards and spiritual perils, and that monstrous adventures were to be anticipated everywhere outside the confines of China. It was readily believed that spirits and monsters waited at every turn in the mountain trail and lurked beneath every tropical wave. People and things from abroad naturally partook of this dangerous enchantment . . ." (p. 34). The imperial courts of T'ang China received many such things from abroad. Some enchantments were human, people sent as tribute who, being "men from remote lands, given luster by distance and rarity, were sufficient curiosities in themselves." Exotic musicians and entertainers were popular, too, but the "best gifts of all were wise men from far countries, whose uncanny insights were the more believable because of their exotic source" (ibid., p. 50).

Other types of living creatures from distant lands were also acquired. Foreign horses of various types were eagerly desired, at least in part for their affinities with legendary and supernatural creatures of the venerated past. Thus from the far west came great "horses of heaven," handsome steeds associated with legendary dragon-horses that may have been kept more for ritual purposes than for battle, while even farther away were the lands of the Arabs whose mounts were believed to understand human speech (ibid., pp. 59–62, 70). Other creatures received from the far west included tigers and lions, whose awful majesty, described in verse, "must have been accentuated by distance and rarity, so that its [the tiger's] spiritual potency was exaggerated in Chinese eyes beyond that of the traditional tiger." Lions evoked images of India and Buddhism; lions' tails (like other animal tails) were powerful talismans; lions' dung was believed a potent drug with power over all crawling things, and was burned to drive away demoniac beings (ibid., pp. 85, 86–87, 109–10).

Inanimate objects contained comparable powers. Sandalwood, probably from India and Southeast Asia, was used for widespread religious as well as luxury applications and had medical value in that it was able (like lions' dung) to quell demoniac vapors and kill crawling creatures (Schafer 1963:136). A wide range of exotic spices ranked high among useful drugs, particularly because of their aromas, and served a wide range of magical needs as charms and panaceas. Precious gems and minerals were among the riches of the earth for T'ang China, too. Jades from distant Khotan came "rich in royal and divine associations and [were] . . . reserved mainly for ceremonial and magical objects" (ibid., pp. 139, 224), while from Rakshasa, "a country of black men with vermilion hair, the fangs of wild beasts, and the talons of hawks," came crystalline "fire orbs" that could set things on fire by focusing the energy of the sun, "which itself concentrated the invigorating and holy light of Heaven," and were revered as divine objects, "condensers of mana" (ibid., p. 237). The most wonderful and powerful pearls, which were able to control calamities of water, derived either directly from coastal waters or from the mystical lands of the south (ibid., pp. 242–44). Not to be overlooked, either, are the many holy and venerable sacred objects—scriptural texts and relics, images and statues—that moved from India and other Buddhist nations to T'ang, reminders of the "collecting zeal of Chinese visitors to the holy places of India" (ibid., pp. 265–68).[33]

Referring to Ming Chinese contact with and descriptions of East Africa, Wheatley (1975a) explains further why certain foreign products were so potent. He notes the particular interest ac-

[33] See also Schafer (1967) and Wheatley (1971) for the products associated with the frightful, magical, and exotic southern frontier of Nam-Viet.

corded to large animals within the "cosmo-magical scheme of universal relationships which underpinned the Chinese theory of government. . . . Strange or monstrous animals were conceived as beneficent cosmic creations born of the superabundant goodness generated by a harmonious reign" (p. 93). Consequently, elephants, rhinoceroses, ostriches, zebras, lions, leopards, and, above all, giraffes were of interest. Indeed, a giraffe (an animal of "supremely propitious portent") solicited from distant Malindi was met at the gate of the capital by the emperor himself, and, "set[ting] the seal of beneficence and felicity on the reign of the Yung-Lo Emperor, indeed on the Ming dynasty itself, was immortalized in paint and verse as 'an endless bliss to the state for a myriad myriad years' " (p. 94). In addition to animals, several other African products were in demand, including, among others, ambergris (popularly believed in China to be solidified dragon spittle and used in perfumes and in scenting lamp oil), rhinoceros horn (invaluable in the Chinese pharmacopoeia), frankincense, and myrrh (ibid., pp. 104–7).

Mention of frankincense and myrrh brings to mind the associations these spices and similar exotic products carried in the ancient Mediterranean world. As Miller has reminded us, "the word 'spice' derives from the Latin *species*, meaning a commodity of especial distinction or value as compared with the ordinary articles of commerce" (1969:1). The appeal and the potency of spices lay both in their symbolically anomalous identification as plants mediating between the celestial realm of the divine and the earthly home of mortals (Detienne 1977:xxii–xxiii), and in their sharp "fiery" scent or taste. These attributes made them invaluable in temple rituals and public ceremonials and as a seasoning for food and wine.

As magical means to invoke good spirits and to expel evil ones, spices were also fundamental ingredients in a wide range of remedies, antidotes against poison, love philters and charms, as well as for perfumes and fragrant incense compounded both for personal use and to recognize and attend the glories of the gods and of imperial triumphs. Yet spice plants were limited in supply and grew only in particular distant places, notably Arabia, India, the Far East, and East Africa. The rarity of these plants made them a form of royal treasure. "As an article of luxury, comparable with gems and silk, they were purchasable only with gold, and that itself was rare" (Miller 1969:vii, 1–2, 5–7). Nonetheless, the search to find the sources of the products and their transport across deserts, mountains, and seas was an important aspect of early Mediterranean exploration and trade.

A sense of the symbolism and exotic aura associated with these divinely associated products is readily captured by brief consideration of some of the uses and beliefs attributed to a few of the more famous ancient spices. For example, myrrh, together with frankincense, a constituent of perfumes, incense, and ointments in the Greco-Roman world, was also an ingredient in the sacred annointing oil of Hebrew priests and was one of a number of components used in Egyptian medicines, embalming materials, and incense (holy smoke or *Kuphi*). Myrrh and many other fragrant woods and rare exotics were sought by numerous expeditions to East Africa (the "Land of Punt" or Somalia) and to Arabia (God's Land or Yemen) (Schoff 1974:112–13; Miller 1969:102–5; see note 28).

Frankincense, also from the "incense-land" to the south and from Arabia, was also regarded as holy, and was used in sacred priestly oils and incense. The conditions under which frankincense was said to be found and the means of obtaining it are particularly interesting, as they are appropriate for a sacred treasure from the wilderness and quite in keeping with the special ritual restrictions that frequently surround the acquisition of potent earthly riches (e.g., salt, gold). According to Pliny's (slightly myth-like) account, the region in Arabia where trees yielding the aromatic resin grew was cliffed, rocky, and inaccessible except for a single, narrow road. Men of a single community held the privilege, by hereditary right, of working with frankincense trees, and "for this reason these persons are called sacred, and are not allowed, while pruning the trees or gathering the harvest, to receive any pollution, either by intercourse with women or coming in contact with the dead; by these religious observances it is that the price of the commodity is so enhanced" (quoted in Schoff 1974:125). Ritual restrictions and personal purity were required because the tapping of the trees was attended by special dangers arising from the supposed divinity of the trees themselves, for the virtue of the aromatic resin lay in the belief that it was the "blood" or essence of an animate and holy plant. The spirits of the trees (souls of the dead) were made manifest, too, in the plethora of small winged serpents that were believed to surround and guard the trees and that had to be appeased by burning particular other types of incense (Schoff 1974:130–32, 144–45, 120–26; cf. Miller 1969:103–4; Detienne 1977:6–10).

Pepper, which was greatly valued in the Roman Empire primarily as a medicine but also as a spicy fragrance and food condiment, was a principal import from India and, like frankincense, cost a small fortune. Pepper was a product of a distant "land of wonders" not far from the very rising of the sun (and the gold and silver-laden islands of Chryse and Argyre), virtually beyond the confines of the known world (at least from the Roman perspective). This land was known for its "strange beasts and birds, the basilisk and the phoenix, or [for its] wise men of strange powers and saintliness, the Gymnosophists" (Mattingly 1957:102). Being a product of such a place, pepper was also believed to be guarded by serpents that could be controlled only by burning aromatic substances (Schoff 1974:49, 213–16; Wheatley 1961:132; Wheeler 1955:134, 177; Miller 1969:80–83, 110). Diamonds, because of their hardness, invincibility, and protection against evil regarded as the most precious of all precious stones in the Mediterranean world, were guarded in the same manner. They, too, were known only from India, where they were said to exist at the bottom of great and deep mountain valleys surrounded by serpents, whence they could be obtained only by most exceptional means (Schoff 1974:224–26).

The virtue of these and other exotic goods (balms, ebony, gems, pearls, sandalwood; see Schoff 1974; Detienne 1977; Wheatley 1961:127–50) lay at least in part in their derivation from reputedly almost inaccessible and spirit-filled locations in strange and distant lands. In the words of Schoff, "there was no reason per se for the Egyptian faith in myrrh as a purifying and cleansing agent beyond the gums of their own trees, or for the trust of the Babylonians and Greeks in frankincense, or of the Romans in cinnamon, beyond their own pine-resin . . . ; *it was the result of the eclectic spirit which accepted that which was told them by strangers"* (p. 236, my emphasis). [34]

It has been the intent of this rather eclectic and clearly selective discussion to re-emphasize the point that for traditional societies valued goods may well be valued at least in part because of their associations with the sacred powers of a very dynamically perceived universe. As a corollary, it is suggested that while the dynamic powers of the cosmos may imbue all things and locales, near and far, the greater mystery of that which is unfamiliar, farther away, inaccessible (or believed to be) by virtue of geographical and spiritual distance and hazards, may contribute to the enhanced potency of goods acquired therefrom. (Again, it is useful to remember that, in contrast to our own encompassing global perspective where virtually no portion of the earth remains a mystery, traditional societies were well aware of the existence of unknown and therefore mysterious realms beyond the geographical borders of their worlds).

Such an approach, of course, may not be fruitful in understanding every case of long-distance exchange. Nor should it be expected to be. Clearly motives for exchange are diverse; types of long-distance travelers and specialists are diverse; the cultural (social, political, economic, ideological) results of long-distance contact are diverse, too (see Leach and Leach 1983; Polanyi 1975). The structural results of distant contacts can also vary. Sahlins (1981) has noted the contrast between trade as commercial exchange, which defines a "between" relationship, an ongoing *sep-*

[34] The Roman imperial culture was further supplied by a range of precious commodities in addition to frankincense from southern Arabia and pepper from southern India, including silk from China, ivory from tropical Africa, and amber from northern Europe (cf. Wheeler 1955:177). All of these products may be expected to carry very distinctive characteristics derivable, at least in part, from their association with geographically distant locales. Note, for example, that most Baltic amber is a coastal product. Baltic amber-bearing beds are often underwater and amber is frequently washed ashore, especially after storms, and collected as flotsam from the sea. This oceanic context, the likelihood that flotsam and jetsam fell by right to the rulership as strange and curious and potent goods (see Chapter 4), and the general distribution of amber in the earlier European bronze age, are suggestive of a mystically symbolic context for this fossil resin (cf. Shennan 1982). In addition, the significance of crafted products from afar, such as silk textiles, may well also lie in political-ideological associations contained in the concept of crafting.

CHAPTER 3

arateness, differentiation, opposition between the parties involved even though they may have complementary interests, and exchanges that are more on the order of communion, that signify a sense of *inclusion* as, for example, when men give gifts (sacrifices) to the ancestors or the gods or to foreigners whom they may regard in a comparable light (p. 38; see also Chapter 5). I would suggest that, in relation to the contexts discussed above, even in situations where the mechanics of acquiring various types of goods from beyond the borders of the heartland may entail conditions of separateness, of seemingly "commercial trade," motives inspiring the exchange and/or anticipated results (acquisition of sacred or potent materials) may be more appropriate to exchanges of inclusion. In other words, while the acquisition of shields or shells or stones or holy incense may require careful hard-headed trade and commerce between distinctly separate trading agents and polities, the ultimate goal of those seeking such goods may well be directed toward obtaining (maintaining) access to material manifestations of the power and potency that imbues their cosmos, thereby continuing their close association and inclusion with the dynamics of the universe of which they are an integral part.[35]

[35] Obviously access to valued distant products may be effected by many means, including commercial or "economic" transactions of the kind engaged in, for example, by the author (perhaps a merchant or an agent of imperial Rome) of the *Periplus of the Erythraean Sea*, the first written record (perhaps ca. A.D 76–100) of organized trade of western (Mediterranean) peoples with nations of the East (cf. Schoff 1974:153–55; Mathew 1975; Miller 1969). Alternatively, they may be acquired by expeditions of a more openly political-ideological nature, such as that described in an inscription which recounts how the great king, Amon-Re, like earlier pharoahs, bypassed commercial sources and organized great royal expeditions to the legendary Incense Land of Punt to bring back great store of valuable and curious treasures for his kingdoms (Schoff 1974:121–22).

4

The Authority of Distant Knowledge

Kingship and the Power Outside

Wishing to satisfy his ambition, the Chinese Emperor Mu (1001–945 B.C.), fifth ruler of the Chou dynasty, decided to tour the world and to "mark the countries under the sky with the wheels of his chariot and the hoofs of his horses" (Hsün Hsü, quoted in Mirsky 1964:4). After being entertained by a barbarous tribe who lived to the north, the emperor marched west to the kingdom of Pëng-jen, whose people were descendants of the god of the Yellow River, and offered sacrifice at the mountains where, in ancient days, the god had established his family. The emperor then ascended the sacred K'un-lun mountain to visit the burial place of the Yellow Emperor, who had ruled a peaceful realm a thousand years before. Next he visited the rich Ch'un mountain, a store of precious stone and valuable jades where tall trees and the most flourishing crops grew, and gathered some species of plants so that he might cultivate them at home. Proceeding still farther, the emperor arrived at the distant court of the legendary Royal Mother of the West and offered his compliments, which were graciously accepted (excerpted and summarized from Mirsky 1964:3–10).

Disregarding the rather moot question of historical accuracy, the tale of the travels of the Emperor Mu very nicely combines the imperial ruler's rightful association with gods and other royal rulers with his equally rightful interest in the distant frontiers and lands beyond his realm and the richly sacred places and products found there. Both dimensions attest to his involvement with exceptional things and events, subjects that are the proper domain of political and ideological specialists of any polity, large or small, centralized or segmented. "Exceptional" in this context can refer to a considerable range of phenomena, including things and events that are "outside" or "beyond" the ken of ordinary folk and the mundane experience of everyday life; that are unusual (i.e., rare, curious, esoteric, exceptionally dangerous); that are situated at a distance, either vertically above or below or horizontally removed from the hiero-geographical center (or are held and comprehended in the separate confines of the mind); or that are acquired by contacting outside realms by shamanic trance, oracular pronouncements, chiefly rituals in the privacy of sacred enclosures, or physical travel in foreign domains or offering protection and hospitality to foreign visitors. Phenomena associated with all these circumstances may be regarded as "exceptional," and, in addition, may well be imbued to greater or lesser extent with some aspect or degree of sacredness and hold symbolic significance within the dynamic, animate universe that political-religious elites are expected to understand and control.

To be discharged successfully, the elite's responsibility to understand and control the forces of the universe must be openly evidenced and activated, and in this process political-religious specialists themselves will be separated or "distanced" from society proper. As a corollary, association with distant phenomena may be expected of or attributed to elites as validation of their status. It is the intent here to illustrate that such distancing and distance-related attributes apply not only to specialists' concerns with nongeographical distance, but also to their concerns with geographical distance.

Let us begin by considering various circumstances in which political-religious specialists or hopeful specialists either are derived from sources outside the polity in question, or (attempt to) validate their position through associations with foreign contacts. Such involvements may well be sought for the secular, "pragmatic" assistance that might be rendered, but they may also be desirable because foreigners may be associated with greater powers of a more mystical sort. For example, in discussing the "minimal" politics of the Hadza, nomadic hunters and gatherers of northern Tanzania, Woodburn (1979) relates how so-called Hadza "chiefs" were men with long experience with powerful and "potentially dangerous" outsiders, especially with Europeans or chiefs of a neighboring agricultural tribe. The neighboring chief whose recognition was particularly sought, expressed power as a rainmaker, while Europeans (like other outsiders in Hadza eyes) were considered generally powerful in the same way that storms and earthquakes, arrow poison, and sorcery are powerful, i.e., by being unpredictable, uncontrollable, and potentially dangerous. According to Woodburn, successful alliance with such potentially dangerous and powerful outsiders would be the only way in Hadza society that one man might in practice be able to acquire certain types of controls over Hadza followers (pp. 224–66, 349, 363).

Among the Hadza such attempts to bolster internal influence with external contacts were not notably successful, but many other societies have accorded recognition to leaders with foreign associations. The Iraqw, for example, believe that persons of other ethnic backgrounds whose origins lie in zones of dangerous wilderness outside the Iraqw homeland (see Chapter 2) have special powers by virtue of their identification with such wildness, which is itself a source of power. Consequently, in the last century the Iraqw paramount ritual office was successively granted to representatives of three foreign ethnic groups whose medicine was considered superior by virtue of its derivation from the outside. During the colonial period, when in the course of their official duties headmen and chiefs were required to travel widely outside Iraqw lands, such leaders were also accorded special status and respect as men who had "walked in the wilderness" (Thornton 1980:27, 74, 210, 215).

Among Nilotic groups (Dinka, Nuer, Mandari) of the southern Sudan, where intrusive foreign spirits or "powers" are widely believed to invade given societies from neighboring groups or are derived from aliens, the "doctors" best equipped to deal with such outside influences may be those trained outside the group (Buxton 1973:69, 110; Leinhardt 1961:163–65). Similarly, "wizards" who have traveled beyond their society's borders may acquire powerful foreign fetishes which may be used to increase their positions as men of importance at home (Evans-Pritchard 1956:99, 101–4).[1]

---

[1] Among the Dinka, "powers" may be derived from experience with Arabs of

In like fashion, foreign diviners are regarded as more reliable by the Lovedu, who have borrowed the institution of the *mugome* ("smelling-out diviner") from the Shangana-Tonga as a means of settling difficult disputes. After private consultations and accusations, a journey is made to a Shangana-Tonga "smeller-out" who lives far away to the east, under the theory that the more distant the diviner the more reliable will be his verdict (distance also protects the diviner from vengeful neighbors; see Krige and Krige 1943:204–5, 208, 224, 259).[2] Similarly, doctors with foreign experience have more status among the Azande, who think the "medicines used by foreign witch-doctors are more powerful than any they possess today, so that a witch-doctor who has visited foreign countries and learnt new medicines and major techniques from alien leeches and diviners is regarded by colleagues and laymen alike as a more than ordinary witch-doctor" (Evans-Pritchard 1937:200–1).

The belief illustrated by these few examples, that superior magical power can be derived from lands and peoples outside society, can also be used to legitimize the origins of ruling houses. Myths and traditions of peoples of the Nyasa–Tanganyika corridor describe a number of situations (perhaps also reflecting a degree of historical reality) in which ruling chiefs are derived from external sources sometimes as lineage founders, sometimes as knowledgeable and skilled culture heroes, sometimes by marriage to local princesses. The first chief of Namwanga was said to be the brother of a chief from the country of the Bisa who, culture hero-like, brought the art of iron smelting and the seeds of various crops and taught the hunting and gathering Namwanga how to make hoes and to cultivate. He then became their chief "because he knew much that they did not" (Wilson 1958:21). The ancestors of the Fipa royal line, in contrast, were a mother and two daughters who came from a far country north of Lake Tan-

---

the northern Sudan and from outsiders to the south. Among the Mandari, the doctors best equipped to deal with Dinka-derived powers are Dinka-trained. Certain foreign fetishes owned by Nuer "wizards" had been purchased on journeys to the west of the Nile.

[2] Following the same logic, litigants from other tribes seek consultations with Lovedu diviners.

ganyika and succeeded in supplanting the local Fipa chief by sitting on his stool. The two daughters married local hunters and found favor by cooking the game their husbands caught with salt which (culture heroine-like) they had brought with them (ibid. p. 22). The founders of the royal lineages of the Hehe and Bene were brothers from the east, hunters said to be the sons of a white man who married the daughters of local rulers. Although the brothers returned to their own country, the sons of their wives eventually became rulers of the royal houses (ibid. pp. 32–33).

A very similar tradition is related for the Sangu, whereby a tall, fair foreigner with many medicines and famous as a war doctor had a son by the daughter of the local chief, who, in turn, became chief (Wilson 1958:34). The Nyakyusa-Ngonde chiefs and priests also came as culture heroes from afar (the mountains to the east) bringing fire, cattle, and iron, as well as the institution of chiefship, and were welcomed as sources of wealth, as advisers to settle disputes, and as sources of mystical power to increase rain and fertility (Wilson 1977:8). These and several other similar traditions all associate the arrival of strangers with chiefship and the introduction of new goods and techniques and (in some cases, but not all) the growth of foreign trade which not only introduced material goods (e.g., textiles, rings) for chiefly benefit, but also gave access to powerful foreign medicines (Wilson 1958:49, 54–55; Wilson 1939:10, 38, 44–48).[3]

Powerful foreigners who established chiefly lineages are attested to in a number of other African traditions, too, often because, as among the peoples of the Nyasa corridor, they have exceptional ritual powers or introduce new civilizational characteristics. In Madagascar several sets of Betsileo mythical-historical traditions associate noble descent groups with external origins, in one case identifying them as descendants of a princess descended from Arabs who settled on the coast. The princess and her entourage migrated from the coast to the interior highlands, where her seven children became apical ancestors of noble descent groups. Similar traditions derive noble lines from other, less

[3] "Among the Nyakyusa-Ngonde, as elsewhere [in the corridor area] the most powerful medicines were traded from afar, and certain outstanding families of doctors were known to be of foreign descent" (Wilson 1977:167, 168).

glamorous, outside areas. Regardless of details, the significant point is that those groups that claim to be nonlocal in origin also assert seniority or greater sanctity over others (Kottak 1980:64–65). In the eastern Sudan, the introduction of Islam as the court religion was indisputably facilitated in matrilineal societies when Muslim newcomers married chiefs' daughters and secured dynastic rights to the throne by right of succession (Lewis 1966:36; Hasan 1966:150, 154). The Tegali kingdom of the Nuba Mountains offers a particularly good example. According to Tegali tradition an Islamic holy man, a "wise stranger" who came from the north, so impressed the Tegali chief by his piety and conduct that he was allowed to settle and teach, married the chief's daughter, and founded the royal lineage of Tegali kings. Once established, Tegali kings encouraged further immigration of "holymen, merchants and adventurers of every sort," who preached and traded and accordingly enhanced the power of the kings (Stevenson 1966:214–15).

Southall's well known discussion of the expansion of Alur chiefs among neighboring non-Alur polities in search of more focused leadership is another case in point. Alur rulership is sought by non-Alur peoples on the periphery of Alurland because Alur chiefs have always been just and fair advisers (because of their nonlocal ties) and are famed rainmakers. Rainmaking is the most closely guarded chiefly secret and the most esoteric ritual complex, the efficacy of which is inherent in chiefly power and in chiefly lineages and is evidence of very strong control over the supernatural. In turn, some Alur chiefs also look outside for legitimacy and recognize Bunyoro as the origin of their sacred power, acknowledging their ritual tie by going to Bunyoro for confirmation of their title after accession to chiefship (Southall 1953:13, 94–95, 147, 218–19). The continual outward emigration of Alur chiefs to non-Alur peoples also creates a spatial zone of political authority on the order of center to periphery, in which the oldest and most completely Alurized groups form something of a chiefly Alur center bordered by semi-Alurized lineages, with relatively newly dominated groups lying beyond, and still independent peoples at the fringes of Alur influence (ibid., pp. 146–48, 181–82). Conversely, from the perspective of those on the periphery, the introduction of supernaturally potent foreign (Alur) rulers provides alliance with the ideological potency of the concept of government (rainmaking) as expressed at the distant center.[4]

In comparable though reverse fashion, there are cases where local rulers are themselves drawn into more distant contact with a civilizational center, the allure including a hope that the ideological legitimacy of the center will become a distant *axis mundi* for local elites. The association of native West African rulers with Islamic legal, scholarly, and ideological traditions deriving from the north and focusing ultimately on Mecca is illustrative, particularly when Islam is used to enhance the power of local chiefs through associations with Islamic advisers and diviners, or to legitimize chiefship in rites of investiture in settings where a significant proportion of the population remains pagan. The act of pilgrimage to Mecca could also enhance a ruler's prestige. Although the journey was formidable and costly, many rulers of Sudanese states made the trip, partly for religious motives but also as a way for newly converted chiefs to affirm their adherence to a world faith, to enhance their standing in the new religion, and, hopefully, to reinforce their authority and acquire power by virtue of pilgrimage to a sacred center (Trimingham 1959:85, 87, 139; Levtzion 1973:208–14).

That such political bolstering might be necessary is understandable when it is realized that, at least in Sudanic states, the chief was chief not only by virtue of his office but also by virtue of less tangible qualities acquired through the ceremony of investiture, which sanctified him and set him apart from profane life. Dynastic stability also required a delicate balance of power between the separate ruling lines of king and heir apparent or electoral power, as well as between factions following native pagan

---

[4] The arrival of a wise and powerful outsider as culture hero and ruler also is found in Yucatecan tradition in the myth-history of the great Kulculcán or Quetzalcoatl, a name given perhaps to several lords, one of whom came to Yucatán with his followers from foreign parts to the west (Mexico) to establish a capital at what later came to be called Chichen Itza. Later, another foreign company, whose leader claimed the same title, founded the city and ruling lineage of Mayapan and re-established a golden age of orderly government before returning to Mexico (cf. Roys 1972:76; de Landa 1978:10–11; Thompson 1970: chapter 1).

FIGURE 4. I
A trading caravan and pilgrimage from Cairo to Mecca. From *The Book of History*,
Vol. V: *The Near East*, 1915, p. 1939. Published by The Grolier Society.

religion and those of royal elites who had adopted Islam. The
troubled political history of the Songhay Empire is a case in point
(see Hunwick 1966). Songhay rulers first were converted to Islam
in the eleventh century, when installation ceremonies included
presenting to the new ruler a sword, a shield, and a copy of the
Qur'ān said to have been sent from the caliph at Baghdad as an
insignia of office (Hunwick 1966:197). Islam then became the official royal religion although the mass of the populace remained
pagan with a largely pagan court ceremonial. The politics of succeeding rulers, some of whom gave preference to Islam, some of
whom tried to return to traditional Songhay religion as a support
for power, reflected the delicate balance between Songhay religion and Islam as political bases of high authority. The situation
culminated in a military takeover in the fifteenth century by a
high-level Muslim commander, Askia Muhammad Ture, when a

THE AUTHORITY OF DISTANT KNOWLEDGE

firm attempt was made to Islamize state rule (Hunwick 1966:296–304; *askia* is a military title and honorific of succeeding Songhay rulers).

Soon after assuming power, the askia went on a two-year pilgrimage to Mecca. As Trimingham states it, "the sole foundation, apart from right of conquest, upon which the first askia could base his authority was Islam and he performed the pilgrimage to Mecca to obtain divine approval and acquire new symbols" (1959:144). The new symbols included presentation by the sharif of Mecca of a green *qalansuwa* (a form of headgear), a white turban, a sword, and appointment as deputy (Khalifa) over western Sudan. "Strengthened by this authority and the 'magical' blessing (baraka) which was ascribed to pilgrims, the Askia could return to rule his kingdom without fear" under the guise of a "pilgrim-king" with Islamic baraka as chief ritual support of kingly authority (Hunwick 1966:307). In addition, the askia appreciated the system of magic and spiritual power (baraka) expressed in charms, talismans, and divination, and relied on the advice of Muslim clerics and the usefulness of literacy. Ultimately, as a basis for Songhay practical authority, Islam turned out to be very problematical for the askia's successors, for Islam remained largely an alien religion of foreign and elite groups. For our purposes, however, the attempt to bolster or sanctify state authority through reference to the spiritual and political power of a geographically as well as ideologically wider world is the relevant point.

Since Islam in West and also in East Africa was largely a religion for nobles and chiefs, there are many examples of the conversion of native rulers or the adoption of Islam by ruling dynasties in order to reinforce, enhance, and extend established authority. In many cases, even in courts that were not fully Islamized, the very significant ideological and ritual component of traditional chiefship was enhanced by adoption of Islamic regalia and Islamic rites of royal installation in the pursuit of mystical blessing for the support of the king (Lewis 1966; Adamu 1978:41–42). Even unconverted native rulers, including the august Asante monarchs, used Muslim greetings, hung Quranic charms around their bed-chambers, and made public appearances from time to time in robes "studded all over with Arabic writing in various colored inks" (Wilks 1966:333).[5] Many royal lords, like Mutesa I of Buganda, being deeply concerned about the political and economic significance of increased foreign contacts, undertook genuine and serious intellectual study of the holy books of Islam (Southall 1979:217–19). Chiefs who were not literate, because they were not Muslims, still took part in Islamic festivals and adhered to certain Muslim practices (Goody 1968:212) or adopted Muslim dress as ceremonial garb, as certain chiefs of North Ghana adopted the burnūs, the highly decorated hooded gown of a Muslim scholar, and kings of the Volta Basin adopted the embroidered gowns or *alkyabha* robes of the Hausa for formal public appearances (Adamu 1978:60–61, 75).[6]

The acceptance by local ruling elites of the "official" ideology of a major outside polity or civilization can be readily illustrated in Asia as well as in parts of Africa. The spread of Hinduism, Buddhism, and Sanskrit in court circles of South India and Southeast Asia provide cases in point where validation of authority was sought by association with elite political ideologies from a geographically "distant" realm, just as sub-Saharan African rulers accepted the power and status proffered by Islam. Thus the upper strata of Dravidian society in South India was receptive to Aryan influence, although indigenous culture remained dominant in the rest of society. Kings assumed high titles, some derived from northern usage, and Sanskrit and brahmans arrived. In the words of Thapar, "as keepers of [Vedic] tradition they [brah-

---

[5] Tribal polities could appreciate the power of foreign association, too Adamu notes that whenever the Tiv appointed a new chief they brought him to the Hausa settlement at the town of Katsina-Ala to be blessed by the Hausa, and a song commemorating the first such visit was said to be still used by the Tiv paramount chief (1978:45).

[6] "In some communities which have apostasized, the staff and the burnūs of an ancestor have been enshrined and so worshipped as sacred objects" (Wilks 1968:170). Comparable validation of rulership through association with a more powerful distant realm is found in the *Popul Vuh*, an ancient Quiche Maya hieroglyphic book, in which is recounted how the descendants of lineage founders in the highlands acquired additional "marks" of legitimate lordship by traveling on pilgrimage to the court of a great lowland king, where they acquired canopies, thrones, jewelry, and possession of the *Popol Vuh* itself (Tedlock and Tedlock 1985:125).

mans] were venerated in the south and found their supporters in the kings of the peninsula who, like most royalty, anywhere, sought the highest respectability available by conforming to tradition, in this case the tradition as interpreted by the brahmans, whether through the performance of Vedic sacrifices or through liberal grants to those familiar with the Vedas. No doubt the kings felt that to conform with the Vedic pattern would bestow a higher status on them. The brahmans' claim to being in communication with the gods, and their supposed ability to manipulate the unseen powers, was more convincing to the Tamil kings than the claims of the indigenous priests" (Thapar 1966:184–85).

Like Islamic trader-scholars, brahmans in South India, as symbols of an outside high culture, enjoyed royal support and prestige in high circles as religious leaders and were involved also in commerce and with trading castes (ibid., pp. 211–12). They also were leading figures in the development of Indianized royal courts in Southeast Asia. In Indian literature of the early centuries A.D., Southeast Asia is depicted as "an eldorado beneath the sunrise; in Sanskrit texts it was Suvarṇadvīpa, the Golden Island, and in Pali Buddhist writings it was Suvaṇṇabhūmi, or the Land of Gold" (Wheatley 1975b:232), a half-legendary land to the east where precious metal allegedly could be picked up from the surface of the ground and where spices and aromatics were available for foreign traders (ibid., p. 233; Coedès 1968:19–20). Conversely, in the eyes of Southeast Asian chiefs whose lands provided the aromatics, drugs, woods, and minerals desired by Indian long-distance merchants, India (particularly South India and Ceylon) was a new world that offered new models for defining the nature of kingship and legitimizing royal status, and provided the ceremonial regalia and other chiefly perquisites that were necessary to visibly bolster that model. "In the course of time he [the Southeast Asian chief] would have ceased to be, as the Malay proverb has it, a frog under a coconut shell . . . , his ecumene bounded by . . . a single river valley, and have become instead a cultural broker on the expanding frontier of a great civilization" (Wheatley 1975b:238).

The major means for legitimizing chiefly authority according to Indian models of royal government was the brahmanic installation rite by which a local leader could be inducted into the Hindu ruling class as ksatriya, adopting Sanskritized titles of authority appropriate to the Hindu model of divine kingship. This form of legitimation, as Wheatley points out, might well have facilitated economic interaction between elites and foreign representatives (both Indian and Chinese) while increasing the social and ideological distance between rulers and ruled in Southeast Asian polities (Wheatley 1975b:239–40). Consecration as king on the Indian model required in turn the presence of brahman officiaries, and thousands of brahmans came to reside at Southeast Asian royal centers to direct Hindu–Buddhist ceremonies and rituals as court chaplains and to act as royal advisers and literati, "devot[ing] themselves solely to study of the sacred canon . . . and practic[ing] piety ceaselessly by day and night" (third century Chinese envoy, quoted in Wheatley 1975b:242).[7] By the sixth century A.D., "epigraphy and literature both bear unequivocal witness to the role of brahmanas at the royal courts of Southeast Asia as purveyors and conservators of the *siddhānta* (esoteric knowledge) necessary for stable government" (Wheatley 1975b: 244). Esoteric knowledge was expressed in magical consecratory rites, Hindu magical and religious formulas to acquire kingly power, mythological genealogies of ruling houses, Indian iconography, epic characters and plots, and the complex ceremonial character of Indian court life (Wheatley 1961:186; Christie 1964: 55–57). In addition, brahmans came also as merchants "to seek wealth by serving the king, with whom they are in high favor" (Wheatley 1961:243, 245).[8]

Although some degree of Hindu–Buddhist "Indianization" gradually moved beyond court circles into society at large, nonetheless, the focus for our purposes again rests on the broader as-

[7] Some rulers apparently were also trained in a royal court of India (Wheatley 1961:289). In light of examples from Africa of foreigners from high civilizations founding royal lines, it is interesting to note, too, that traditional chronicles in Southeast Asia also recount tales of kingdoms founded by culture hero-princes or adventurers who came directly from India (Burma) or from beyond the sea (Java) and who ascended the throne through marriage with a queen (Cambodia) (see Wheatley 1975b:241; 1961:186; Christie 1964:59–61; Coedès 1968:37).

[8] Regarding brahmanic travel to Southeast Asia in light of Hindu concepts of purity and prohibitions on overseas travel, see Wheatley 1975b:244; 1961:189.

sociation of ruling lords with countries, high-status representatives, and political ideology from afar. These associations were reflected in Southeast Asia in the emergence of numerous centralized states based on Indian concepts of royalty and rule in which Southeast Asian ksatriya kings with Indian titularies and the aid of brahmanic dignitaries ruled according to Hindu principles of kingship in royal temple-centered city-states (*nāgara*), where the sacred language of Sanskrit was the language of government and higher bureaucracy (Wheatley 1975b:246–50; Geertz 1980; but compare Bentley 1986:288).

As is well known, political elites on the frontiers of traditional China have long been affected by a parallel experience of Sinicization. Ever since the emergence of the Shang civilization, the territories of permanent Chinese dynastic authority to the north, west, south, and east were bounded by peripheral states somewhat within the ambience of Chinese culture, while beyond them lay numerous independent tribes, chiefdoms, and emerging states whose leaders nonetheless confirmed their local authority and sought other benefits by investiture according to Chinese political ideology (Wheatley 1971:58–59, 114–15; Yu 1967:66–78; Ch'en 1968; Toby 1984). When, for any number of reasons, a frontier ruler sought the favor of the imperial throne he requested (indeed, often demanded) basic provisions, coinage, and symbols of political-ideological status of a sort we have encountered before, including silken garments and thread, a golden girdle and a robe of state in many colors, a Chinese scholar to act as his resident adviser and educator, copies of the Chinese classics, or all of these things. He also requested a handsome wallet in which his ambassador (perhaps a son or younger brother) could carry the official token needed for proper identification and reception at the Chinese capital when tribute would be offered to the throne in return for resounding honorary titles ("king, marquis, or the like") and the valued royal gifts that would outweigh tribute-gifts in value. Here again, while the Chinese interpreted their influence as evidence of cultural and imperial supremacy (based on the Confucian code of conduct, the use of the Chinese ritual calendar and written language, and the rare and precious tributary products amassed from afar) over frontier "barbarians" dwelling on the wild periphery of the civilized world of which China was the center, the barbarian lords valued and aggressively sought this influence as a legitimizing political-ideological contact with prospects for further economic and political benefits (Schafer 1963:26–27; Lattimore 1968:381; Fairbank and Têng 1941:137–41; Yu 1967: 41–43, 78, 142, 144, 194–95, 207–8, 210; Fairbank 1968:1–14; Toby 1984).

As would be expected, given the pattern of political and ideological center–periphery contacts between traditional empires and border polities described above, native rulers on the northern periphery of Rome and her empire also looked to the imperial center far from their own realms as a distant, elitist *axis mundi*. While to those within the empire the frontiers were important as defensive political and military zones, to those outside it, the empire held a fascination (as Wheeler has put it) like as to a promised land, an El Dorado of wealth and of knowledge. Such wealth and knowledge could serve well the Germanic chiefs attracted to it both before and after the formal end of the empire. To take but one example, in the early era of Roman–Germanic relations, Maroboduus (a Germanic ruler mentioned by Tacitus), king of the Marcomanni in Bohemia, had been to Italy when young and (like so many other northern "barbarians"), may have served in the Roman army. Later, during his official contacts with the empire as "king" he evidenced skill in Roman diplomacy and applied Roman training to the organization of his own kingdom. Tacitus notes that this ruler and others who, like him, were friendly to the empire, depended upon the authority of Rome for might and power, and were supported with money and "artisans of every trade, both peaceful and warlike . . ." undoubtedly to enhance chiefly prestige as well as to create machines of war (Wheeler 1955:10, 19, 20; Wallace-Hadrill 1971:5–7; Dyson 1985:64–74, 81, 132, 144, 159).[9]

[9] Roman recognition of an earlier so-called *rex Gallorum*, a certain Cincibilis, included not only overt political support but prestigeful gifts, including money, torques of gold, vessels of silver, horses, horse trappings, and armor, along with permission to buy horses in Italy and transport them over the Alps. Roman titles were also granted to local leaders, a practice that both conferred honors and drew such chiefs into the network of Roman frontier administration (Dyson 1985:70–72, 170).

In later centuries, after the political collapse of the Roman empire, contact with Rome and Romanized provinces (including employment of educated Romanized statesmen, notaries, and churchmen in high offices as advisers) helped to strengthen and legitimize militant Germanic kingship by the adoption both of Roman Vulgar Law and of sacral and "imperial" concepts of authority. Christianity was directed primarily toward chiefs and kings, and learned Christian ecclesiastics, who sought to educate militant non-Roman rulers to fit a particular model of Christian kingship, emphasized that eventual divine judgment as well as secular power and achievement defined the quality of rule (Collins 1983:18, 20–24, 29, 32; Wallace-Hadrill 1971:8–9; 1966:31–32; Jones 1971:385–86).

Whatever their religious preferences, however, kings and chiefs who grew in prominence also expanded their contact with the wider world. The Merovingian Childeric, a very successful and widely experienced fifth-century Frankish ruler in northern Gaul, may have traveled to Constantinople. His son, Clovis, ably manipulated both his own heritage as a great Germanic warlord and protector of traditional gods and his recognition by the emperor in Byzantium and the bishops of the Roman church as Christian ruler of a Roman province as symbolized by an imperial coronation ceremony complete with purple cloak, diadem, diploma, and high title (Wallace-Hadrill 1971:17–20; 1966:69–73). As the usefulness of Christianity and the influence of Christian ecclesiastics and scholars for barbarian rulers increased, and as ambitious Germanic lords sought to emphasize their association with the greater, distant sacred power, the bishops of Rome (who were emerging to political primacy within Rome and Italy and were just as eager to control Germanic rulers) found two themes that were especially attractive to the aggressive Germanic kings: warfare, now in the name of Christ, and obedience to St. Peter.

The cult of St. Peter, first bishop of Rome, was the most potent of all medieval Christian cults, and engendered a special prestige. "In a world of holy men and relics, all efficacious for kings who knew how to make use of them, none was more efficacious than St. Peter" (Wallace-Hadrill 1971:68; 1966:30–31). Relics of the Roman martyrs, especially those of St. Peter and St. Paul, were

145

appropriate gifts for north European rulers (ibid., pp. 68, 89), especially those whose pagan ties were still strong and those, who,
old and tired at the end of their reigns (or prudently resigning the
crown while still politically ahead), resolved to make pilgrimages
to Rome as final, Christian acts of attrition, piety, and sanctity (a
practice peculiar to Anglo-Saxon kings of the seventh to ninth
centuries; see Stancliffe 1983). The allure of the Holy City for foreign rulers was clearly its setting as the Christian *axis mundi*,
partly because, in the eyes of those who made pilgrimages there,
the pope was master of it, and partly because of its major saint,
obedience to whom (through the papacy) was a condition of a
prosperous reign and also an extension of power (Lot 1931:306).
"Through St. Peter, Rome was the mistress of kings, and by St.
Peter alone could they gain access to the kingdom of heaven"
(Wallace-Hadrill 1971:88; Sumption 1975:228–29). "God has
granted me," wrote the English King Canute in 1027, "the privilege of praying within the city of Rome. And this privilege I have
sought because wise men have told me that the apostle Peter has
received from God the power of binding and loosing, and carried
the keys of Paradise" (quoted in Sumption 1975:227).

Through St. Peter's Church (and to some extent at its insist-
ence) northern Europe's early medieval kings also came to be
strengthened and legitimized in their earthly realms, pragmati-
cally and spiritually, both by the magically felicitous ritual of
unction[10] and, through the efforts of scholarly Christian clerics
and "wise men" who served as royal advisers and foreign diplomats, by encouraging literacy and learning, as Wallace-Hadrill
notes, not as "mere hobbies," but as "conditions of survival" for
royal government (1966:99; 1971:101; 1975:181–200; Ganz 1983).
Charlemagne, in keeping with his time, combined military
prowess with the role of Christian champion; he is probably the
most famous ruler (though not the only one) who exemplified
both approaches to the ideology of kingship. He was annointed
by the pope and strove particularly to establish scholarly production and instruction in biblical, liturgical, and secular matters as a

[10] The rite of unction led certain Frankish kings to identify themselves as new
versions of God-created Old Testament rulers, such as David.

matter of state policy and security. In the insightful words of Wood (1983), Charlemagne "had seen that the realities of early medieval power demanded their ideal dimension. To maintain an *imperium* a king needed not only military force, but also councillors in kingship and ritual, technicians of the sacred, craftsmen, illuminators, poets and scribes, a 'think tank' of *gesceadwise men* in constant attendance on him" (1983:251). Not only was esoteric knowledge (especially literacy) now a necessary tool of government, but more particularly under Charlemagne's instigation, monastic and cathedral schools trained literate Christian clergy both to live among still pagan frontier populations and to control the more settled regions of the Frankish world. Preparation of such churchmen-cum-state agents, in turn, required access to books, scholars, and artists from the centers of Christian–classical learning in Italy and its educational outposts in England, and fueled the so-called Carolingian renaissance of the eighth and ninth centuries (Wallace-Hadrill 1966:99–104; cf. Stancliffe 1983:175; Wood 1983).

Visible evidence of royal association with Christian learning and with Christianity's Holy City and its power continued to be found in holy relics, generally acquired in Rome or Constantinople. Immense private collections of relics were gradually accumulated over the centuries by rulers and high churchmen, who spent much money and energy on enlarging their holdings. Relics were objects of political pride and the guarantors of political prestige and spiritual authority. A region, a city, an individual ruler, or high ecclesiastic acquired new status and new evidence of association with the temporally–spatially distant sacred history of the holy cities and the sanctity that still emanated therefrom when a valuable relic was obtained (Sumption 1975:29–31). The relics themselves were not mere mementos or souvenirs, but were imbued with power and holiness. In addition, they were associated with gems and metals, since antiquity considered the greatest "riches of the earth" not so much because of their material value but because of the magical and mystical (god-given) powers long associated with various types of precious stones and metals (e.g., protection from physical harm, curatives for disease

147

and troublesome dispositions, association with moral qualities and virtues) (Evans 1922; Sumption 1975:24).

As saints' shrines and reliquaries came to be heavily decorated with precious stones, precious metals, and rich textiles, so they also became repositories of the powers associated with these rarest and most exquisite materials and showcases for the delicate crafting skills that brought out their inner beauty and therefore illuminated their puissance. In a sense, as Sumption notes, this wealth was a form of savings intended to be used when needed, as in emergencies, by ecclesiastical and royal patrons (1975:153–56). Yet, such material expression of cosmic–Christian powers and "untold riches" also correlated with concepts of spiritual grandeur that, by definition, rose above the mundanely familiar of this earth (ibid., p. 156). Consequently, the bejeweled and tapestried shrine can be seen as a tangible recognition and encapsulation of the supernaturally charged power of the Christian universe as represented in the saints whose remains were so honored, in the shining wealth and the potent, glistening riches with which it was encrusted, in the delicacy and uniqueness of the craftsmanship that controlled and enhanced the beauty of the materials with the astonishing skill of human hands and intelligence. All this accrued to the ecclesiastical lords and royal rulers whose domains contained the sacred repositories that attracted such sacred wealth, whose courts employed such craftsmen, and whose authority thereby evidenced a measure of control over the sacred as well as secular powers that ultimately emanated from Rome.

Knowledge, Power, and Foreign Affairs

In the previous section examples were given of the association of elites, particularly rulers of centralized societies, with geographically distant places or peoples, as evidenced in mythical tales or historical episodes in which rulers or ruling dynasties were derived from external sources. We also reviewed situations where kingship was at least partly legitimized by association with foreign political ideologies derived from outside polities, particularly complex civilizations with sacred centers of their own. In both types of situation the external circumstances producing or legitimizing rulership also stressed foreign customs and advisory personnel, ceremonials and regalia, sacred writings, holy cities, and even foreign gods. These associations can not help but further emphasize the separation or contrast between elites and commoners in the home society, and thus enhance the power and authority of high office.

There are also many other situations, however, where, even though political leadership may be firmly rooted in native origins and legitimized by traditional ideology, political-religious specialists are still associated with external phenomena deriving from geographical domains beyond the range of most members of society. Such circumstances may augment the status of leadership or serve as expression of the qualities of leadership, may derive from active attempts to expand geographical contacts or at least to associate with foreigners, or may simply fall within the range of responsible leadership rather by default.

In this latter situation foreign persons or goods may come under the authority of the rulership simply because, being foreign, they are not associated with any local social or kinship unit. Thus, for example, the Maori *ariki* had rights to sea mammals and to products of the ocean—flotsam and jetsam—washed ashore because he was entitled to things that were nonordinary and exceptional (Goldman 1970:509–10; see also Handy et al. 1965:187 concerning comparable rights of Hawaiian chiefs).[11] Similarly, in Tahiti it was considered appropriate that canoes whose occupants were strangers would be raided and stripped of their cargoes and the strangers of their personal belongings, much of which property apparently ended up in the chief's possession (Ferdon 1981: 226–27).

Conversely, the kings of early medieval England and Ireland entertained similar rights to foreign materials in the form of responsibilities to protect strangers to their shores, a practice which yielded Saxon kings material benefits associated with long-distance merchants whose persons and goods fell under their protection—and their tolls—but yielded Irish kings only the gratitude

---

[11] One cannot help but wonder, too, whether products of the sea were also the prerogative of the *ariki* because of symbolic connotations associated with the sea.

CHAPTER 4

and prayers of holy but impoverished pilgrims and exiles (Sawyer
1977:150–51, 153, 157–58). Alur chiefs also held chiefly prerogative over persons or groups found wandering or searching for
asylum (Southall 1953:196), and certain Ashanti kings extended
protection to "priests of all nations, but more especially to those
who came from Egypt, or any part of the Holy Land," in this case
because they were Muslim (Wilks 1966:330). Indeed, the association of Muslim trader-clerics with elites in pagan Africa not infrequently was made possible by the protection accorded such
strangers by chiefs (Skinner 1963:308–9). Comparable politics of
royal protection were extended to Jewish communities in medieval Europe for similar reasons (Roscher 1944). In like fashion, a
Bantu chief, such as among the Tswana, generally not only
served as a representative and spokesman of the tribe in external
relations (as many political-religious specialists traditionally have
been expected to do, worldwide), but visiting strangers had to be
reported to him, and his permission was required before tribesmen could travel abroad themselves (Schapera 1956:69; see also
Lawless 1975:28 regarding Kalingan chiefs' attempts to restrict
travel by nonelite members).

Chiefly knowledge of foreigners can also result from necessary
privileged access to strangers, their services, or their valuables because high status demands it, regardless of the risks, as part of
proper chiefly behavior. For example, in an intriguing paper on
relationships in Fiji, Tonga, and Samoa, Kaeppler recounts how,
for certain high-ranking Tongan elites, the sacredness of their
bodies requires services of foreigners, particularly Samoans, for
tasks which no Tongan dare perform. "In an aristocratic system
where the persons of certain individuals are considered sacred or
even dangerous for ordinary mortals to touch, it is useful, even
necessary, to recruit outsiders to perform certain tasks, not only
for the safety of one's subordinates, but also to conserve and pre-
serve respect for one's *mana* (or supernatural power)" (1978:248).
The services in question included tattooing Tongan chiefs, cut-
ting their hair (the head of a Tongan chief is extremely *tapu*), and
preparing their bodies for burial. The attendants suited for these
tasks were members of a special group of ceremonial servants
(*matápule*) brought from Samoa, although some matápule were

said to have originated in Fiji or (note) in the sky (ibid., pp. 248, 250).

Quite a different task of privileged access was assumed by Yucatec Mayan elites after European contact, when Yucatec nobles felt it was their right and privilege to have access to European religious knowledge, and their duty and responsibility to control its dispersal among commoners. According to Clendinnen, the Maya regarded the Spanish intruders as uncultured and unmannerly but as bearers of new and useful knowledge (cf. Chapter 5). High Maya chiefs were quite prepared to discuss finer points of religion with Spanish friars, just as Nachi Cocom, formidable chief of Sotuta, was ready to talk with Diego de Landa and to show the young friar one of the sacred hieroglyphic books of his lineage, "not in submission, but as part of an exchange between men of special wisdom versed in high matters" (Clendinnen 1980:384). In the same spirit, "native lords who obstinately persisted in traditional rituals also readily set up illicit schools and churches where they pretended to teach Christian doctrine," even to baptize and marry. To them, such duties seemed rightly to fall within their traditional role as custodians and administrators of knowledge and authority (ibid., p. 385). To the puzzlement of the friars, however, native elites also tried to protect commoners from the apparent mortal dangers of baptism (for those ailing souls whom the friars most urgently rushed to baptize generally died), and yet they "submitted themselves to it [baptism] again and again, to test and augment their own spiritual force" (ibid.). Apparently the learned Yucatec men of power felt it fitting that they themselves should have privileged access to potent new knowledge, but that commoners had to be protected from the same dangerous power.

Rasmussen recounts a somewhat similar, though more pleasant, circumstance of "privileged access" among the Netsilik Eskimos when, on a trip to collect amulets, he spent an evening in the company of a highly respected and famous old shaman, who justifiably regarded Rasmussen as an equally learned man from afar. Settling down to talk on the sleeping bench the two discussed "the gravest religious problems." In Rasmussen's words, "he [the shaman] was not long in realizing that I was just as well

versed in the mysterious forces of life as he himself. For preference I dwelt upon the miraculous powers of amulets, and was able
to tell him of experiences quite novel to him, observed during my
sojourn among distant tribes. Thus, we parted in mutual esteem
as colleagues of equal merit" (1931:41).

As we have seen in previous examples, however, the capacity
to cope ably with foreigners, their realms, and their powers not
only need be a matter of privileged access to foreign power and
danger, but can also be a measure of the power of a leader, and as
such can be actively sought as an expression of leadership abilities. Wealthy Afghan landowners in almost any village built guest
houses and entertained travelers, invited or uninvited, for just this
reason. "The [landowner] met people from all over the country,
sometimes useful contacts in the future; he was the first to get
news of the city or the capital; he might buy or beg rarities off the
guest which would be unique in the village. These advantages
tended to increase his personal power and assure his position as
village chief. Anyone who thought he could afford it could build
a [guest house] and entertain travelers. If the house was not well
provisioned, the neighbors ridiculed the host. If he outspent the
current [landowner] in his hospitality, he could usurp the prestige
first, and then the power of the [landowner] for himself. The
[guest house] was therefore both a symbol and a means of the
[landowner's] power" (Chaffetz 1981:158).

Another way to seek foreign experience as a measure of leadership is to actively travel to foreign places. The Yao of East Africa, famed as long-distance traders and travelers, seem to exemplify this point (see also Fernandez 1982:419 regarding journeying and leadership among the Fang). According to Alpers,
Yao trading activity grew out of the travels of a particular Yao
clan that specialized in smelting and forging iron and traded
their products. From this base Yao began to exchange iron and
other local products for coastal goods, and by the seventeenth
century undertook long trips to the East African coast to do so.
A man who had traveled in this way was highly regarded, and
such prestige opened the possibility of wider leadership roles
within Yao society. As the Yao would say, "he who knows foreign parts is a man worth knowing," and a man who knew other

countries was always listened to with respect, "the people hanging on his words delighted, all of them gazing at him sometimes with awe, saying 'Good Lord! You are a wonder! Eh! but you have travelled!' And the people would believe anything he told them." A man who had not traveled would sit silently, without saying a word, laughed at as a fool and a stay-at-home, as a man who knew nothing, a pounder of grain (Alpers 1969:406–7). As trade opportunities grew in succeeding centuries success in organizing long-distance caravan trade became an increasingly important way to attract followers (perhaps replacing hunting in this way to some extent), and coastal trade eventually became the monopoly of chiefs (ibid., pp. 409–11).

In quite a different part of the world, Maya elites apparently not only were involved in the operation of long-distance acquisition but also traveled actively as long-distance specialists. Prominent lords of Chichen Itza may have gone to Honduras on trips yielding cacao, feathers, and other goods (the son of the last Cocom ruler of the Yucatec center of Mayapan was in Honduras at the time of the fall of that city) (Roys 1972:51, 59, 116). The long-distance professional traveler-traders of highland Guatemala were also members of the elite (Feldman 1971:72), while in the exchange center of Acalán the wealthiest merchant was also the lord of the polity (Scholes and Roys 1968:4). A ruler of the Bay Islands offshore from Honduras apparently was a long-distance merchant, too (Davidson 1974:26–27). Yet here, as elsewhere when elite travel was encouraged, the benefits of such activity may well have derived from the knowledge and experience gained by visiting distant places as much as from the acquisition of potent exotic goods.

Success in dealing with foreign things and the acquisition of esoteric knowledge and goods thereby, also seems to be an important factor in the emergence and recognition of political leaders in at least some Melanesian societies involved in the kula or other long-distance exchanges. As is well known, kula success and the resulting spread of personal fame is a goal of all kula participants, but at least in the Trobriand Islands, opportunity for and extent of kula activity may fall more to persons of rank whose fame is all the more enhanced. Malinowsky comments that in the Trobriands not everyone can carry on kula transactions and that the number of partners a man has varies with his rank and importance—a commoner would have only a few partners, whereas a chief would have hundreds, not all, to be sure, overseas (Malinowsky 1922:91–92). Uberoi agrees that differences in rank among persons and among villages or districts in the Trobriands correlates at least to some extent with kula activities, such that the higher rank between two districts or villages "would belong to the one which was more proficient in the *kula*, and had the more advantageous external affiliations" (Uberoi 1971:124). Likewise, members of descent groups claiming the high rank titles of "Tabalu" are leaders of overseas expeditions, regardless of whatever other level of economic success, power, and privilege they have attained (ibid., pp. 125–26, 130, 132). Brunton has extended Uberoi's argument to suggest that the emergence of rank and chieftainship in Kiriwina district in the northern Trobriands relates to effective competition for limited positions allowing overseas activities. Low-ranking persons in Kiriwina have very limited participation in kula activity or none at all, while political success has come to be based largely on success in the kula (Brunton 1975:549, 553, 555).[12]

Finally, Bradfield associates rank in the Trobriands not only with acquisition of kula valuables but also with the associated renown. One of the marks of particular ranks is the right to wear particular kula valuables as ornaments, some of which are so prestigious that only a chief may own them. The ability of kula valuables to confer prestige on those who own them, in turn, may be related "to certain beneficent properties believed to reside in them. . . . Whatever the origin of the [renown]-conferring powers of [kula valuables], the belief that they possess such powers lies at the root of the communal trading expeditions (*kula*) which the islanders undertake to get hold of them." Such expeditions

[12] Brunton also suggests that controlled access to valuable boar's tusk ornaments by leaders in Wogeo, off the north coast of Papua New Guinea, may play a role in the existence of higher leadership there. "Rank is bound up with boar's tusks," and only hereditary leaders (*kokwal*) wear the ornaments which are obtained from the mainland through infrequent trading trips initiated and controlled by the kokwal (Brunton 1975:555).

were originally restricted to men of rank and those closely connected with them (Bradfield 1973:237). If Scoditti is correct, the "beneficent properties" associated with kula armshells and necklaces, at least on nearby Kitava, may be associated with the quest for knowledge. Armshells and necklaces are circular, as, ideally, is the movement of kula resources along a chain of islands and villages and as is the design painted on the cheeks of kula transactors on expedition. In kula ideology, "the circle stands for complete knowledge of the cosmos, realisable but never actually attained by men, given that only they have the capability of knowing the world through travel, diving under the sea, exploring the terrestrial underworld of caves, climbing mountains . . ." (1983:271–72); i.e., knowledge of the horizontally distant as well as vertically distant (above and below) wonders of the world. (Malinowski offers a rather cryptic but perhaps not unrelated comment regarding the intellectual value of contact abroad in his brief description of a headman of Sivaketa who, though "a queer old man, spare and lame . . . is renowned for his extensive knowledge of all sorts of magic, and for his long sojourns in foreign countries, such as the Amphletts and Dobu"; see Malinowsky 1922:197.)

The personalized expression of such a knowledge quest will appear in the fame and renown given to one's name as it, too, circulates around the kula path, a fame that increases with age if not with (or in addition to) rank. Munn relates how, among the Gawa (and also in a sense among the Trobriands) knowledge of the proper spells and operations for successful kula expeditions is held not by junior men but by senior men who, as they have become older, have developed "internalized" sources of the knowledge or power that magically animates successful kula trips. Through kula voyages, this internalized power can then be "exteriorized" or "extended" out in space much farther than the still limited power of the young can be expressed (Munn 1977:50). Personal power, in other words, has a spatial component that is expressed in the ability to animate outside contacts, just as personal fame derives from successfully completing transactions within the external, inter-island world. Both personal power and overseas fame—which also confers major political value on

Gawa—accrue with age to the point of achieving the highest possible personal and social prestige for those whose names circulate the farthest. For those kula participants whose names also become linked with prominent shells so that they may hope to achieve ultimate prestige through immortality, circulation in distant space can become transformed into preservation in ultimate time (Scoditti 1983:272).

The thought, to be sure, is hardly unique to ambitious Melanesians. It is implied in every recitation at any time and place of royal titles claiming dominion over universal domains that lie between the encompassing seas, or on which the sun does not set, and in every cosmology that locates ancestors at the ends of the earth.[13] It is implied, too, in more manageable actions designed to associate royal renown with its spread over exterior space and geographical distance. So the Asante king, considering the matter of hospitality to foreign traders to his capital, explained that "some traders are kings' sons and brothers, and great captains: I must not say to them, give me gold, but I must give them gold and provisions, and send them home happy and rich, that it may be known in other countries that I am a great king, and know what is right" (Osei Tutu Kwame, quoted in Wilks 1966:326–27). Melanesian big-men would understand the situation well, even though they may act within a more restricted setting, for the personal and political goals—and the risks—involved in the extension of exchange transactions into larger and larger networks of relationships are the same. "Expanding the personality by . . . increasing the range of his interactions with others, an ambitious man put his integrity at risk and increased the opportunities for rebuffs" (Burridge 1975:89).

Such big-men (or managers, as Burridge prefers) are also required to face risks of a different sort as they manipulate the expansion of their fame. "Well travelled because he had a far-ranging network of affines, friends, and trading partners, a manager had to be capable of accepting the considerable risks from sorcery

---

[13] The complement to seeking an increase in prestige by increased extension of one's fame in distance is, of course, the granting of greater prestige or power to famous shamans, hermits, and rulers who live far away. In both cases the element of distance enhances reputations.

and ambush that travelling entailed" (Burridge 1975:101). It is not unlikely that part of the personal leadership capacity sought and expressed by a manager was evidenced by his courage and ability to face and overcome (manage) these outside dangers or obstacles, too. Little is said in the ethnographic literature of the political or religious significance of the capacity for successful travel in supernaturally and/or secularly dangerous territory (though we have seen a few examples of the rituals associated with such success), but surely this "skill" both expressed and strengthened the aura of distinctiveness and uniqueness accruing to a leader.

Thus, for example, in Alurland where prior to colonial pacification one did not travel far, an exception was recognized for chiefs, who were "credited with traveling vast distances among potentially hostile peoples, often with very few companions" (Southall 1953:194). Similarly, in West Africa learned Muslim trader-scholars enjoyed relatively safe travel even through troubled areas both because of the need for trade and because of the religious prestige and supernatural aura associated with their persons (Curtin 1984:39). Alternatively, the dangers of travel could be allocated to subordinates (aided perhaps by carrying a piece of royal regalia that provided protective powers by extension) or to agents, as Aztec emperors allocated them to the pochteca, who gained appropriate glory for their expertise in overcoming the risks of long-distance travel (via linguistic facility, disguises, armed escort) while the emperor safely enjoyed the political rewards associated with contact with distant lands.[14]

The active expression of elite concerns with geographically distant peoples and places has also been noted in the context of foreign education, whereby young men and especially future political-religious specialists could spend time away from home

[14] It is also interesting to note the general association that can be made between rulership and travel or journeying as a special condition or attribute as, for example, is suggested by the apparent assignment of members of the traveling curers (the Callahuayas) of the Andes as special litter-bearers of the Inca (Wassen 1972:16), and by the metaphor of Maya rulership as a burden to be carried, as expressed by the symbolism of the tumpline There is also clear association in various Mayan linguistic forms between the symbolism of rulership as a burden carried on a journey and the time span of an official reign as a measure or length of distance (Rice and Foley 1983).

learning the language, songs, ceremonies, and other customs of foreign peoples. The training of young people in Yakutat Tlingit society and expertise acquired by the Germanic king Maroboduus while among the Romans were briefly mentioned above. It was also the custom among pre-Islamic princes of Dagomba, in West Africa, to "go to other places to learn the arts of warfare and government and then return home to face the struggle for the throne" (Adamu 1978:69). In one particular situation, a future culture hero king was sent by his father to Hausaland to train with a Muslim from Timbuktu. In the course of his education he traveled as a trader to Timbuktu, Kano, and Zaria (compare the Yao travelers and Mayan elite traders mentioned above). Once the throne was secured with the aid of trade profits, Hausa traders, clerics, and artisans were encouraged to settle in Dagomba, too (ibid., pp. 69–70, 72).

The detailed documentation available concerning the training of Kuna political-religious elites allows a closer look at some of the concepts involved in such practices. Following a tradition that may have pre-Columbian origins (Helms 1979, Chapters 4 and 5), the most renowned political-religious specialists (*neles*) among the Kuna Indians of eastern Panama traditionally have sought extensive education "abroad"; "[religious specialists] tend, in order to enhance their position in society, to wrap themselves in a cloak of mystery. They undertake long journeys to broaden their learnings" (Nordenskiöld 1929:157). More specifically, Kuna elites traveled to northwest Colombia and to select locales in eastern Panama to study (sometimes for several years) with distinguished specialists in traditional medical, historical, linguistic, and political skills and lore; topics which included learning the lives of famous chiefs of the past, the history of Kuna dealings with non-Kuna peoples, and the governmental systems of non-Kuna societies, meaning present-day Colombia, Panama, and the United States. Holloman, who has recorded a detailed case study of one such chiefly educational career, notes the "open" nature of this educational pattern, which encouraged a man of knowledge specifically to explore the ways of "foreigners" both by traveling to their realms and by studying with others who had been there, for the ability to deal with foreign, non-Kuna political leaders is a quality, or hallmark, of a good Kuna leader (1969:63–64, 233, 237, 418, 441).

Yet the importance of journeying to distant places to acquire knowledge carried significance beyond that of an individual's quest for a good instructor. Howe explains that the Kuna student–teacher relationship also involves a distinct context of relative ranking with the student subordinate in status to his instructor. Given the strong tendencies for status competition among Kuna village leaders, a man, perhaps already of some prestige, who wishes to learn a particular song or chant, may not wish to place himself in such a position vis-à-vis a village peer who knows the chant, but elects to study with a teacher who lives at a distance with whom the status relationship may present less of a problem. Indeed, if the teacher is a man of high reputation, association with him may enhance the student's own prestige. As a man's reputation grows, he seeks ever more knowledgeable and famous teachers, until eventually, in some cases, chiefs decide to end their studies, "not only because of personal limits to their ambition and interest but also because after a certain number of years as chief they feel that there is almost no one with whom they can study without loss of face" (Howe 1974:163). In addition, "learning at a distance has a special prestige . . . and it offers opportunities to acquire specialties unknown in one's own village. . . . Furthermore, by learning a somewhat distinct variant of a chant far from home, one makes it more difficult for local critics to suggest that one has mislearned it" (Howe 1974:232–33; 1986:83–84; see also Helms 1979:129–32, 137–38, 141–42).

The Kpelle of Liberia pursue a comparable program of foreign education, though with adjustments to take into account the changing nature and locale of esoteric "power" (Murphy 1981). Ritual specialists among the Kpelle hold top rank in the hierarchy of secret societies by virtue of their ability to convey the impression that they have privileged access to mysterious, dangerous, powerful, hidden esoteric knowledge or supernatural secrets. Knowledge of this sort derives from association with equally mysterious, "dark," private, "remote" places that contain hidden or secret power. The forest that surrounds the open, public, visible village clearing is one such locale, and knowledge of the dangerous supernatural forces primarily associated with the forest underlies traditional ritual specialists' claims to power as mediators between forest and village. Today, however, the new city of Monrovia is viewed as a comparable place of mystery and remoteness where powerful and dangerous "civilized matters" exist. "Civilized matters" now constitute the secrets of the new "forest" such that "in most Kpelle villages knowledge of civilized matters has eclipsed in political value knowledge of the mystical affairs in the traditional forest," and "Monrovia is the geographical entity replacing the forest as the locus of mysterious and remote knowledge" (Murphy 1981:674). Concomitantly, contemporary "knowledge specialists" are trained to deal with this new source of power through the traditional institution of wardship, whereby a child is reared for part of his early years in a household other than his natal one. In this case, the child is given to an American–Liberian family in the city to be raised with an awareness of city and national customs, to learn English, and, eventually, on returning to his traditional community, to act as a new form of ritual specialist and mediator, a cultural broker between village and city, often in the role of schoolteacher or principal and perhaps even as chief (for a comparable situation among the Canelos Quichua of Ecuador, see Whitten 1976).

Contrasts between the mysteries of the countryside and the mysteries of the city, or between the magic of the wild and the power of the sown, or the dangers of the hills and forests and the safety of the plains (or vice versa) are, of course, as old as urbanism, even as old as village life, and the Kpelle example is but a recent illustration of contrasts that have long required the mediating skills of knowlegeable specialists. That which lies without, in whatever direction, being different and therefore dangerous, has long contained power, and those with greater knowledge of these realms and regions have long been recognized for this distinction. Such simple contrasts, of course, tend to veil the fascinating social, economic, and perceptional relationships that in fact link such contrasting domains. Marlowe has ably illustrated this point in the context of relationships between Sqaw Karen and Khon Muang or Northern Thai in southeast Asia. In the eyes of the Khon Muang, the Karen of the hills appear as a necessary frontier extension of their own life as civilized plains people, while in Karen perception the plains people are but a necessary lowland extension of the Karen hill world; "wild" and "sown" seem to melt into each other even while remaining distinctive (Marlowe 1979:193–205; cf. Lehman 1979:243). Yet there are points where extension reaches its limits, not only geographically but also conceptually, for the Khon Muang believe the Karen to have greater supernatural powers based on their intimate relationship with the "spirits of the wild," while the Karen credit the lowland Khon Muang with greater mystical powers because of their possession of Buddhist written texts on which to base their formulations and divinations (Marlowe 1979:205–7).

The Karen–Thai relationship, and especially Karen attitudes toward the greater power of the wider Thai world, are comparable to those described by Lehman for the Kayah and the Shan of Burma. The Kayah, too, generally feel that the wider Shan–Buddhist world is a place of wisdom and power, and that they should be cognizant of what "wiser heads" from outside have to say, especially if a man comes among them acting as a leader of men should act, i.e., a man with charisma who bears superior knowledge (Lehman 1979:243–44). In mythical-historical times such men appeared as knowledgeable charismatic outsiders from the Burmese–Buddhist world who founded religious-political cults and political entities among the Burmese Kayah (ibid., pp. 224, 226). There is, however, another version of this history among Thailand Kayah; a tale not of a charismatic leader who arrived from outside, but of one of their own who chose to leave, "who separated himself, his godliness, and his basically foreign, cosmopolitan wisdom from the Kayah once and for all," calling out derisively, as he and his house platform rose into the sky, that he was disgusted with their ignorance of how to treat him properly and therefore would not stay (ibid., p. 244). In either case, it would appear, greater powers and greater leaders lie without.

In a very literal sense, cosmopolitan wisdom has extended the horizons of learned leaders *within* many societies, too. "It appears that the Incas possessed more knowledge of the extent of the world than the commoners. . . . Their actual horizons [went] as far as northern Argentina and Chile on the one side to the middle of Ecuador on the other and from the sea to the Amazonian jungle . . . the limits of the Empire. The common people, except those who served in the army or as colonists, had apparently very little idea of the extent even of the Empire except from hearsay and kept to their own small world—their own valley, puna, or bit of table-land" (Mishkin 1940:232). Bhardwaj's study of Hindu places of pilgrimage in India suggests a somewhat different type of "cosmopolitan wisdom," but one that also has connotations for relative awareness of the world. He notes that ritually high trading castes and brahmans form a high proportion of pilgrims and that there is a distinct preference and tendency for mercantile castes and for brahmans in particular to visit the more sacred, higher-level, Sanskritic, pan-Hindu pilgrimage shrines (rather than more regional ones), which are correspondingly less popular among ritually lower castes (who predominate at regional shrines) (1973:167, 186–87). It is also generally the case that ritually low, scheduled castes travel shorter than average distances to sacred places, while mercantile castes are the most mobile, perhaps because of relative wealth and the nature of their occupations (1973:191).

The skills of a good Nambikuara chief in the Mato Grosso of Brazil also require exceptional regional awareness, not necessarily, it would seem, in the sense of having knowledge of more territory (though that may also be implied), but in the sense of having more complete knowledge of the entire region at all times. The chief "must have a perfect knowledge of the territories haunted by his and other groups, be familiar with the hunting grounds, the location of fruit-bearing trees and the time of their ripening, have some idea of the itineraries followed by other bands, whether hostile or friendly. Therefore, he must travel more and more quickly than his people, have a good memory, and sometimes gamble his prestige on hazardous contacts with foreign and dangerous people. He is constantly engaged in some task of reconnoitering and exploring, and seems to flutter around his band rather than lead it" (Lévi-Strauss 1967:55).

In a somewhat different context, the Mayan Chamula of the highlands of southern Mexico associate leadership with far-flung time-space associations as exemplified in types of animal soul companions. The most powerful shamans and political-religious leaders are typically associated with large animals and particularly the jaguar as soul companions. The jaguar, in turn, is associated with great antiquity and the totality of human experience and wisdom (having existed since the very earliest of several creation cycles). Along with great size, he also has great supernatural strength, and, in addition, is associated with the farthest reaches of geographical distance, i.e., the hot tropical lowlands, situated at the very edges of the earth, far away from the cool Chamula highland home at the center of the world. The jaguar (and other animals-cum-soul companions associated with at least moderately successful people, including ocelots, coyotes, weasels) is also infrequently seen and nocturnal, that is, "distant" in the sense of being "out of sight" in the highlands. In contrast, less powerful and smaller animal soul companions (e.g., rabbits, possums, skunks) associated with ordinary poor and humble people were created in later creation cycles and thus do not have as much "temporal experience" (meaning, cumulative wisdom) as the jaguar. They are also generally found closer to the Chamulas' highland home and, therefore, like ordinary people themselves, are regarded as more numerous and more visibly mundane (Gossen 1975).

The Emperor's Zoo

Generally speaking, political-religious specialists are acquainted with powers and with distance, geographically as well as supernaturally defined. Their intellectual and experiential horizons extend beyond those of ordinary folk. They may travel farther, perhaps with greater safety. Their fame and reputations are more widely flung. Their knowledge of the customs, languages, and religions of outsiders is more complete. Their chiefly compounds and royal courts receive both strangers and official visitors, whose news and stories contribute to the repertoire of knowledge of afar, even as their gifts and tribute add to the wealth of foreign goods on hand. Their messengers and agents may venture into distant lands while learned priestly scholars and travelers with foreign skills, and therefore greater wisdom, offer them advice and revelatory insights into cosmic mysteries. Their ultimate goal is greater understanding, greater power, and greater control over the fateful mysteries of the universe; understanding, power, and control that will support, legitimize, and enhance special statuses at home by attesting to the greater wisdom, sanctity, and esoteric knowledge that attends those who become familiar with the unfamiliar.

To experience that which lies without and to express these insights through activities with relevance at home; to attract, obtain, and gather up the power that exists and is expressed in the curious, rare, exceptional things and creatures of the earth, whose curiousness and rarity and exceptionality are directly enhanced by distance from home and by the symbolic significance accorded such distances; these are at least some of the factors behind the tendency for political-religious elites to be interested in and relatively better informed about the geographical world around and beyond their realms, and to seek tangible evidence of these associations.

Tangible evidence can take a variety of forms. Foreign advisers from distant realms may bring new magico-philosophical systems and sacred repositories (amulets, books, and texts) and new technical (crafting) skills (from literacy to clocks) that also evidence exceptional powers. Foreign tribute-payers or traders or agents of the polity itself (perhaps in turn serving as tribute payers to an outside realm) may bring exquisitely crafted goods or highly valued and symbolic natural "riches" of the earth. Official symbols and regalia of rank or of office may include foreign ornaments, accoutrements, or robes, and great effort may be expended on exotic collections of holy relics, foreign wonders, strange plants, curious animals, or even human beings, such as foreign slaves and entertainers, which graced temple precincts and royal courts, or were housed in royal zoos and aristocratic gardens in (for example) ancient Egypt, pre-Columbian America (Cuzco, Tenochtitlán), the ancient Near East, and the capital of imperial China (e.g., Soustelle 1970:124–28; Yu 1967:192, 196–97). Far from being mere curiosities (though some collections may have been, at least to some extent; see Casson 1974:238ff), these animate and inanimate exotics from the ends of the known earth or from its most sacred centers were repositories of power and symbols of the distant, potent regions known to, and "controlled" by, the lords of the realm. The royal garden of the Chinese Emperor Wu, for example, was a "concentrated universe" where, among other wonders (including models of sacred mountains), "all the beasts of the air, of the water, of the earth, thronged in his fish-ponds and his parks. No species was wanting in his botanic garden . . ." (Granet 1958:393–94). ". . . precious articles like shining pearls, rhinoceros horns, tortoise shells and emeralds overflowed in the inner palace, four best kinds of horses filled the palace gates, and giant elephants, lions, fierce dogs, and big birds were fed in the Imperial garden. In short, rare things of various places came from all directions" (quoted in Yu 1967:142), a plenitude due largely to the symbolic value long accorded strange plants and animals as rare and precious tribute-objects to the imperial throne. Similarly, centuries later, after Cheng Ho's expeditions overseas acquainted China with East Africa more directly, "Egypt distinguished itself when its ambassador brought lions, tigers, oryxes, nilgaris, zebras, and ostriches for the imperial zoological garden in the emperor's capital" (Mirsky 1964:256–57).[15]

In a sense, far-fetched though at first it may seem, royal collections of the strange and the sacred such as these can be considered as vastly elaborated expressions of the power-filled medicine pouches of tribal shamans, filled with potent bits and pieces of unusual minerals, wood, flora and fauna replete with (and symbolic of) cosmic power, or of the small personal "pods" prepared by young men in Canelos Quichua society to enhance their social and intellectual development and the acquisition of personal power, pods in which they place various magical substances such as beetle wings, balls of hair from a tapir's stomach, tree bark, certain leaves, bird bones, etc.[16] Whitten describes how prepara-

[15] In comparable fashion, it is very likely that the mature specimens of anaconda and caiman from the Amazonian tropical forest presented to the Inca for a menagerie in highland Cuzco held considerable religious significance, considering the symbolism accorded these animals in Andean and Amazonian ideology (see Lathrap 1973:181–82).

[16] In directly comparable manner sacred enclosures were maintained in villages of the Ika of the Sierra Nevada de Santa Marta in Colombia, in each of which was

tion of his pod involved the young man in discussions with older people about meanings, metaphors, and power, and how, in addition, "he often must travel to distant areas, trade with people he does not know, and also learn more of the jungle environment. Substances and some articles from other peoples are readily incorporated into his mixture as the [young man] tries to learn transcultural as well as intracultural secrets" (Whitten 1976:143). It is likely that the emperor's natural history collections attested to the same interests and the same goals, though on a considerably larger scale. The emperor's zoos and botanical gardens, like the shaman's pouch, contained bits and pieces of the animate cosmos, power-filled natural wonders, examples of the rare, the curious, the strange, and the precious—all expressions of the unusual and the different attesting to the forces of the dynamic universe that by definition lies outside the (again by definition) controlled, socialized, civilized heartland.

Since it is the primary duty and obligation of all political-religious specialists to mediate in some manner or other between society's controlled heartland and the wider world, it is a primary responsibility of all such specialists to become as widely informed as possible of the characteristics of this powerful world and of means to manage and control this power, both for society's protection and benefit, and (not so incidentally) as personal or official expression of political-religious expertise. The powers of the universe are expressed in many dimensions and forms and can be approached through many dimensions and forms. I have been concerned with that dimension that can be seen to exist in the horizontal plane or level of geographical space and especially distance, and I have argued that the types of ethnographic evidence relating rulership to geographically foreign phenomena are, in fact, data attesting to the symbolic significance that such phenomena hold for political-religious specialists (symbolic significance that need not obviate more secular political or material value).

Substantiation of this point requires that we recognize the sym-

planted (so far as was possible) a specimen of every bush and flower growing in Ika country "so that it symbolizes the whole world" (Attenborough 1976:60).

bolic significance or value associated with maintaining foreign advisers and diviners at royal courts, acquiring natural materials or crafted goods from afar, living with foreign peoples as part of proper elite education in order to learn foreign arts of government and ceremony, traveling to foreign realms to acquire prestigeful foreign products, accepting ownership of the flotsam and jetsam of the seas, offering hospitality to strangers and foreigners, etc. The particular contextual significance attributed to such activities may be expected to vary cross-culturally, and the few examples that have been offered are not intended by any means to completely cover the range. The common factor in all these situations, however, is that they associate rulership with foreign things and people, with phenomena that derive from a geographical distance. The virtue attached to geographical foreignness from the point of view of political-religious specialists in turn is predicated on the fact that foreignness ("distance") is by no means a neutral concept but correlates strongly with expressions (symbolisms) of universal sacrality and energy, helpful or harmful, awareness of which can be a valued part of the total package of knowledge that political-religious specialists seek to acquire.

The foregoing comments have also rested on the assumption that in traditional societies most people tend to stay at home, or closer to home, so that those who do travel or who have knowledge of outside places may be distinctive by virtue of the act of travel or the experience of knowing itself, as much as by the content of that experience. In this sense, closer personal association of political-religious specialists in general with travel or with agents who travel or with foreigners or with foreign products may be a valuable "honorific" factor identifying and legitimizing their status and their power again largely because of the associations of exceptional power and/or danger or at least esotericism accorded to geographical distance and the things and peoples "out there."[17] There is, however, at least one very important ca-

[17] The honorific or status factor is important in understanding the value of long-distance experience for political-religious specialists, since this element distinguishes their activities from those of certain other types of "long-distance experts," particularly traveling peddlers (as, for example, in China or the ancient Mediterranean) whose long-distance experience yielded more obvious economic

veat to this position. Although in previous pages a considerable diversity of ways and means have been illustrated in which the geographically distant world may be utilized for political-religious goals, there has been no intention to imply that knowledge of geographical distance is inevitably a necessary attribute of political-religious specialists and leadership. On the contrary, particularly in light of the various "dangers" associated with geographical distance and with foreigners, many political-religious leaders are *not* geographical long-distance experts. Some ritual experts seek to protect themselves against such outside dangers rather than to exploit them, or, if they do delve into geographically foreign elements, do so with circumspection. Thus in the early days of Islamic penetration into Tanzania ritual leaders among the Gogo deliberately kept away from strangers, fearing physical harm and danger to ritual peace (Rigby 1966:280–81). Similarly, Pueblo Indian ritual leaders were reluctant to venture too far into dangerous areas outside the pueblo (Ford 1972:44). In other situations, as we have seen, the world outside is recognized as dangerous (unpredictable, uncontrollable), but usable if ritual precautions are taken or risks are accepted.

In some societies the tasks of exploring unknown worlds are divided between those experts who are concerned with peoples and places of geographically situated worlds, the "horizontal" dimensions of space-time experience, and those who are concerned with "vertical" dimensions of religious experience or with dimensions "internalized" in extraordinary psychological states or in symbolic separation from active society. Native societies of Indonesia provide examples of this type of duality. Among the Mambai of Timor leadership is distributed between two authority positions: passive, introspective, ritual figures who are symbolically confined to sacred knowledge; and active, energetic, worldly executive figures who uphold the jural order and the ac-

---

profit but whose activities were seen as the very opposite in social value and whose social position was at the lower end of the social scale (see Wheatley 1971:283–85). We can perhaps modify Polanyi's well-known paradox regarding long-distance trade ("he who trades for the sake of duty and honor grows rich, while he who trades for filthy lucre remains poor") to suggest that he who deals with distant phenomena for the sake of duty and honor grows rich, while he who deals with distant phenomena for filthy lucre remains poor (Polanyi 1975·137–42).

tive expression of rule and who symbolically patrol the "outer realm of space," observing and regulating the ongoing course of everyday affairs. Here, as in other Indonesian ritual systems, the higher form of knowledge is that involving ignorance of worldly concerns, and the center or inside is therefore judged superior to the exterior or outside (Nordholt 1971:412; Geertz 1980:107–9).

In a somewhat similar situation, cognizance of the geographically outside world may be only one of a considerable number of specialized tasks for which influential men may receive recognition. Among the Mekranoti of central Brazil, as we have seen, individuals may gain recognition and prestige for expertise in hunting, crafts, body painting, warfare, and trade with outsiders, and may gain reputations for their special knowledge of foreigners, Indian customs, ceremonies, or the ancestors. Although there is significant overlap in individual areas of expertise, "knowledge of civilized ways" is an area of prestige least likely to be associated with other prestige areas, i.e., the men who know about civilized ways are not likely to be the same men as those who are shamans, songleaders, orators, or authorities on the ancestors (Werner 1981:265–66).

In short, although this essay has focused on knowledge of geographically distant peoples and places, I am assuming that this avenue provides only one of a number of possible sources of exceptional political-religious power and esoteric knowledge. The means and extent to which this particular "fund of power" will be tapped by political-religious specialists may be expected to vary considerably cross-culturally. Similarly, even among elites of a given society, interest in what lies toward or beyond the geographical horizon may be expected to differ individually, even as shamanic expertise is known to vary greatly according to personality, individual skills, and other attributes. Individuals may show a considerable range of skills or of interest in dealing with foreigners, in their adaptability to dangerous travel or to living conditions in distant places, in their ability to learn foreign languages, and even just in general curiosity. Not all political-religious elites need share the nostalgic yearning of the Emperor Trajan, who, in his last years, standing on the shore of the Persian Gulf and watching a ship sail away to the East, purportedly wished that "above all things would I have passed over to India, were I still young" (Wheeler 1955:135).

Intriguing questions remain to be investigated. What cultural circumstances encourage one type of geographical long-distance contact over another for political-religious specialists? It would appear reasonable to expect to find greater visibility given to long-distance associations in general as polities become more centralized and political-religious statuses hierarchically more focused, restricted, and publicly enhanced with sumptuary laws and elaborate regalia. Yet long-distance associations can benefit individual political-religious statuses as much as ranked positions. Shamans or lineage headmen or band leaders of more egalitarian societies, also being specialists in political-religious affairs and therefore also separated from society as ritual and knowledge experts, may be expected to pursue long-distance geographical contacts, too, and for essentially the same reasons.

Do long-distance associations increase proportionately according to increases in cultural complexity, i.e., does a more complex society entrust a relatively greater proportion of its centralized political-religious legitimacy to visible long-distance contacts than does a simpler society, or might the reverse be true? Does degree of centralization affect significant differences in type of "goods" acquired from long-distance settings, i.e., do political-ideological specialists in more egalitarian polities emphasize intangible forms of foreign knowledge (songs, languages, curing skills) more than tangible ones, while political-ideological specialists of highly centralized polities put greater emphasis on tangible material goods as expressions of this knowledge? Would such contrasts (if they are valid) correlate with a greater likelihood that shamans, lineage elders, and other men of influence in more egalitarian societies may personally undertake foreign travel to a greater extent than chiefs, kings, and emperors of more complex societies, who rely more heavily on other types of long-distance specialists (scholar-traders, diplomatic agents) to undertake the physical acts of travel on their behalf?

Existing ethnographic and ethnohistoric literature may help answer such queries and future fieldwork may provide new data. On the other hand, difficulties in comparing scope and scale or relative impact of distant associations cross-culturally have been enhanced by the effects of European and other industrial societies on simpler forms of traditional society. Long-distance contacts and activities may well have been among the earliest casualties of European expansion in many areas of the world, and therefore have gone unrecorded in the general ethnographic literature. On the other hand, as Chapter 5 illustrates, European contacts may also provide excellent primary data on native concepts regarding distant peoples and places.

5

Gods or Devils or Only Men

Ancestors and Mythical Heroes

The "mysterious white-winged object passing along the surface of the ocean like a gigantic pelican" appeared abruptly
on a day in late autumn before certain people of the Dulingbara
who were foraging on the beach front. Observing it more
closely, as they followed its course along the beach, they saw people moving on it. Finally, they watched the *Endeavour* disappear
from view in the direction of a dangerous shoal (called *Thoor-
vour*).

> These strangers, where are they going?
> Where are they trying to steer?
> They must be in that place, *Thoorvour*, it is true,
> See the smoke coming in from the sea.
> These men must be burying themselves like the sand crabs.
> They disappeared like the smoke.

The lines of the corroboree composed to commemorate the
sighting also express metaphors of death and burial (traditionally,
for the people of Fraser Island, in the sand, like crabs) and the re-
lease of the spirits of the dead over the sea to the sky country (accompanied by a smoky fire to prevent their return). Since everyone's spirit went to the same place in the sky country, and since,
apart from their own homeland and the lands of other tribesmen
they knew, no other places existed, it was clear that the brief appearance and disappearance of Cook's ship, with its passengers
and bit of smoke, was a "fleeting spiritual manifestation or, perhaps, a portent" (Evans and Walker 1977:39–41).

Initial interpretations of and reactions to Europeans by native
observers can provide excellent ethnographic data relevant to traditional indigenous perceptions of people and things from afar,

172

particularly in the case of nonliterate egalitarian and rank societies. Descriptions of *initial* contacts and reactions are particularly
useful because they relate to that usually brief interval when native interpretations of Europeans are most likely to have been
genuine reflections of traditional cultural perceptions, and before
the more disastrous consequences of an inherently unequal con-
test began to appear.

In his brief essay *Der Fremde* (*The Stranger*), Simmel noted that
the stranger in a group "imports qualities into it, which do not
and cannot stem from the group itself" (Wolff 1950:402). In as-
sessing the general interpretation most frequently imparted to
Europeans by native hosts on their first acquaintance, this assessment appears valid, for Europeans almost invariably appeared as
manifestations of some aspect of the unregulated "power outside," suddenly and often inexplicably made manifest and intrusive into regulated society. On the other hand (and departing
from Simmel's apparent intent), interpretations of the outside
world as a place of power, and of Europeans as expressions of
such power, do derive directly from the group itself in the sense
that traditional cosmographies and cosmologies define the cosmos and its power, assign particular symbolic significance to its
parts and manifestations, and differentiate between the qualities
associated with the cultural center or heartland of socialized community life and the extraordinary, power-filled supernatural attributes of realms that exist beyond and far off. Consequently, we
find that initial native reactions to Europeans were virtually identical to the various reactions to things from afar described in previous chapters.

The first Europeans arrived either out of the sky or from the
horizon that stands across the sea or the river or at the far end of
the trail, and were given the only identification that could be attributed to beings from vertical or horizontal distance, i.e., they
had to be ogres or demons or spirits or ancestors or gods because
such were the types of animate beings "inhabiting" distant locales. As such, Europeans by definition were embodied expressions of universal *mana* and contained supernatural powers for
good or for harm.

As we have seen, to the inhabitants of Fraser Island, Europeans were spirits or ghosts of the dead returning in a reincarnated form for some portentous reason. Not only did these beings eventually land on the sands, with which burial was associated, but they were also found to be light-skinned, like aboriginal corpses prepared for funeral ceremony, and "their whiteness was symbolic of death, mourning, and apprehension" (Evans and Walker 1977:41).[1] In the early years of European contact, when "ghosts" on Fraser Island were few and appeared sporadically (generally from shipwrecks or as escaped convicts), if a native recognized "it" as reincarnated kin, acceptance into the tribe (and survival) was assured, but if no such identification were made, the "spirit" was destroyed as dangerous (ibid., p. 42; Broome 1982:23).

Inhabitants of New Guinea and islands of Oceania recognized Europeans as returning ancestors or relatives, too (see also Braudel 1984:434 regarding West Africa). Speaking of groups along the Gulf of Papua, Williams mentions several cases where a European was warmly greeted by one of the natives as his parent. "A certain young man of one of the smaller Vailala villages when walking in the bush encountered a white man, in whom, after a close scrutiny, he recognized his father. The father and son sat down and wept together for a long time, until at last the former rose, cut some bananas, and, leaving them with his son, disappeared . . ." (Williams 1977:342; Mannoni 1964:82, n.1). If the newcomers were not ghosts of deceased relatives, they must be spirits or demons for, as Codrington noted, if brief acquaintance shows that the white visitors aren't ghosts it doesn't necessarily follow that they are men. Spirits or demons were powerful but, unlike ghosts, also mischievous and prone to bring disease and disaster. In such circumstances it was best to drive them away before there was any chance of trouble (perhaps to the genuine puzzlement of a peaceful missionary who knew of no reason to anticipate difficulties), and since they were not men, the arrows couldn't do much harm (Codrington, in McAuley 1960:73–74).

The natives who greeted Francis Drake in California had a similar interpretation of the newcomers. According to Heizer's anal-

---

[1] In preparation for final disposal a corpse would be "painstakingly stripped of its outer layer of dark skin, exposing the 'cutis vera or true skin . . . perfectly white' beneath" (Evans and Walker 1977:41).

FIGURE 5.1
Wooden ship model from the Nicobar Islands, first half nineteenth century, showing Europeans wearing top hats and sports cap amidst other sailors. From J. E. Lips, *The Savage Hits Back*, p. 64, figure 12. Published by Yale University Press, 1937.

ysis of the ethnohistorical accounts, judging from the doleful shrieking, weeping, crying, and laceration of the flesh that suddenly erupted at various times after the Indians' first visit to Drake's ship, the English (and particularly the younger sailors) were regarded as anything but mortal beings, and probably as returned ghosts or ancestors for whom the usual mourning observances were now being performed (Heizer 1947:263, 265, 271, 273). In addition, "the Indians showed the English their infirmities, aches, sores, and wounds, and it was made clear that if the English would but blow upon them they would be made well" (ibid., p. 271).

In Polynesia, the obvious origins of the strangers again declared their status. Remembering that the sky touches the horizon and that the horizon extends behind or beyond the sky's edge, it was understood that white men and their vessels had broken through the heavens from the other side or had come from

175

behind the sky through a hole in the lower part of the sky (Williamson 1933a:90–91). The terms commonly applied to Europeans in parts of Polynesia included not only the concept of "sky," but also that of "father" or "ancestor" or sometimes "chief;" hence, white travelers also carried the connotation of chiefs or reincarnated ancestral spirits from the sky beyond the western horizon (Williamson 1933b:74–75, 101, 292–93).

Europeans (Russians) came to the Yakutat Tlingit in a similar way, from an opening ("cloud hole") in the horizon (the hole that fish come through), since they arrived from far out under the clouds and must have lived there, near the edge of the world (de Laguna 1972:794). To the Netsilik Eskimo, the high masts of the great ship seen early one winter in the middle of a bay indicated it was a great spirit, and, fearful that it might destroy them if not dispatched first, a group of Arviligjuarmiut set out with harpoons and bows. They discovered that the great spirit contained strangers, the famous white men of whom they had heard so much and who were said to have derived from the offspring of an arrogant and disobedient woman of their own country and a dog. The Eskimos then visited the ship and received precious gifts of things they could not otherwise obtain, including nails, sewing needles, and knives. In addition, the white men had an amazing abundance of wood—a highly valued item very hard to acquire. "Indeed, however incredible it may sound, they lived in a hollowed-out floating island of wood that was full of iron and everything else that was precious in their own country" (Rasmussen 1931:25, 28, 127).

The supernatural status accorded Europeans as strangers from afar is particularly well attested to in situations where the unusual foreigners were accorded a definite place in the mythical history of the polity. The association of Cortés with the Aztec myth of the culture hero-deity Quetzalcoatl, who disappeared over the water to the east (or was transformed into the morning star) promising to return to claim his rightful rule, is well known. According to one account, as the high white sails of Cortés' ships floated over the sea, looking like temples on the water, the emperor Moctezuma, faced with an event of potential cosmological as well as political import, sent gifts, including beads and biscuits, to Cortés to see if the stranger would recognize them and eat the food. The Spaniards did eat the food and made a return presentation of beads and biscuits to Moctezuma, who regarded them as divine gifts from Quetzalcoatl. "He ordered his priests to carry [the biscuits] to the city of Tula with great ceremony and bury them in the temple of Quetzalcoatl. . . . Hymns appropriate to Quetzalcoatl were sung and the biscuits were buried with great pomp at Quetzalcoatl's temple in the ancient city." At Moctezuma's order the beads were similarly buried at the feet of the god Huitzilopochtli because they were divine objects (Durán, quoted in Carrasco 1982:200, see also pp. 30, 42, 198–200; León-Portilla 1969:149).[2]

Godship, or at least great honor as exceptional beings by virtue of association with sacred realms or traditional myth, was attributed to Spaniards in other parts of the New World, too, at least for a while. According to Clendinnen, the Spanish intrusion into Yucatán seemed to fit an expected cyclical pattern of local disorganization followed by orderly government by foreign lords of exceptional wisdom. Such a cycle had occurred centuries before when semihistorical invaders of Mexican origin, the Itza, under the leadership of one or more culture heroes called ("titled") Kukulcan (Quetzalcoatl) established rule at Mayapan and, with the guidance of esoteric knowledge kept in sacred books of hieroglyphs known only to them, initiated a period of harmonious government that eventually collapsed. The local Maya lords now identified the Spaniards with the Itza, recognized them as men of special literate wisdom, and apparently expected another period of temporary but orderly foreign domination and the eventual return of legitimate rule to indigenous leaders (Clendinnen 1980:383–84; Roys 1972:77). In similar fashion, in Peru, the Spaniards who appeared over the ocean were initially identified by the Incas with the return of Viracocha, the culture hero creator-deity who had traveled across the land to the coast and then disappeared over the waters, and according to the journal of Christopher Columbus, in the Greater Antilles the admiral and

[2] Note the burial of things from afar at temple perimeters as described in Chapter 3.

his ships and men were honored as having come from the heavens (Columbus 1960).

The burden of mythical history and of godhood fell particularly heavily on Captain James Cook, for he was killed at Kealakekua Bay in Hawaii in order to keep the accuracy of a myth crucially intact. The story is analyzed in detail by Sahlins (1981). In effect, it concerns two gods (and two theories of government), Lono and Ku, one of whom (Lono) is associated with peaceful rule by inherent right, benevolence, and productivity, while the other (Ku), the deity of the incumbent line of Hawaiian rulers, supports rule by more violent usurpation and indulges in human sacrifice. Each year recognition of the two gods was ritually alternated with a series of ceremonies which first introduced a period of rites associated with fertility and with Lono, at the end of which the god suffered a ritual death and returned to the invisible, distant land beyond the horizon (or the sky) whence he had come, and the god of human sacrifice, Ku, and his earthly representative, the ruling chief, superseded and became predominant for another year.

Cook was identified by the Hawaiians as a personification of Lono, while the chief with whom he dealt, and who ritually required his death, was the personification of Ku. Cook's identification initially stemmed from the fact that the British had appeared, god-like, from the direction of the invisible ancestral lands beyond the horizon. Thus Cook's first visit to Hawaii was considered as a divine appearance. His second visit, however, coincided with the festivals marking the annual return of Lono, which definitely established his identity with the god. His eventual demise represented the fulfillment of the prescribed sequence of ritual events which included the death of the god (Sahlins 1981:10–11, 18–21). Actually, Cook's ships coincidentally did set sail from the islands at the appropriate time in the native ritual calendar when the god Lono should leave for his distant homeland and the god Ku and his chiefly representative become supreme. Unfortunately, a few days later the *Resolution* sprung her foremast, and the ships returned to harbor. The new return of Cook–Lono was a clear contradiction to myth and to the appropriate sequence of "political theory" by which "Ku" now held power. In the ensuing confusion of native reaction to this apparent impropriety of the "gods" and British retaliation against the improprieties of the "natives," Cook was in effect ritually murdered ("sacrificed") basically because the god could *not* be allowed to return if the ideological legitimacy of current chiefship (Ku) was to continue. Cook's remains were apparently accorded ritual treatment appropriate to the enshrining of a deceased chief as an ancestral spirit, and his bones thereafter reappeared in annual rites associated with Lono (ibid., pp. 22–25). By these procedures Cook in effect became a divine guardian of the ruling chief, and through this guardianship, expressed by the appropriation of Cook's bones, the *mana* of the kingship of Hawaii also became British.[3]

Fortunately, in other settings Europeans could be placed into traditional myth-histories with less dramatic consequences even if the assignments were not always as complementary. Among the Lugbara, Europeans were associated both with mythically (temporally) ancient beings and with socially (and territorially) distant nonhumans. As we have seen, for the Lugbara the known world is categorized spatially and temporally such that as one moves outward in space from Lugbara territory people become more evil and more prone to magic and sorcery, while the most distant creatures fall entirely beyond decent social constraints, are hardly human in appearance, walk on their heads, and are cannibalistic. This spatial zoning corresponds with temporal depth in that the earliest (most distant) created beings also were not yet socialized and behaved very badly, while later ancestral heroes became more or less socially acceptable, although still somewhat superhuman. When Europeans ("red" people) appeared in Lugbaraland, they were readily fitted into these pre-existing cate-

---

[3] Captain Cook's final fate is reminiscent of that which befell Magellan long before him. Magellan's final days in the Philippines were spent preaching Christianity, curing a sick man, and befriending the king of Cebu with promises of the greater power that would be his as a Christian and ally of Spain. Attempts to extend such information to other chiefs led to a battle in which Magellan was killed. The victorious chief refused to return the body of Magellan, saying that they "would not exchange him for the greatest riches in the world but that they wanted to keep him so that they would not forget him." Magellan's remains were never recovered, and we can only speculate as to the powers believed associated with such a learned curer from afar (Anderson 1976.394).

gories. "Red" people were given an ancestor related to Lugbara ancestors, but since Europeans themselves originally had lived outside Lugbara territory they also had to belong initially to the most "distant" and least socialized or inverted category of beings. Thus, the first Europeans were considered to be "exceptional" or non-normal in a number of ways. They were said to be cannibals and were believed to disappear underground, to walk on their heads, and to be able to cover vast distances in a day by that means. The first (earliest) district commissioner in particular, a Mr. Weatherhead, could travel at fantastic speeds. In addition, rather like early heroes (who were at least on the way to becoming human), he walked among the people unarmed and was said "to have had greatness of personality, courage and sympathy that could have been due only to magic and heroic qualities" (Middleton 1960:234–35).

An appreciation of similar forceful personal attributes sometimes underlay the successful initial reception accorded Europeans in other settings, too. The first Europeans to visit the southern Madang District in New Guinea, the Russian scientist N. N. Mikloukho-Maclay and a Swedish sailor, were identified as deities and to some extent as spirits of the dead. After a slow start, Maclay in particular came to be not only highly respected but also venerated as more than merely human, partly because of his calculated show of disinterest in sex, partly because of his "quiet courage and unfailing courtesy." He always traveled unarmed and met very unsettling demonstrations of hostility with complete nonchalance. This impressive sang-froid, plus his fair skin, his clothing, the huge ship in which he arrived, the strange things in his house (scientific equipment, guns, a primus stove), and certain events that transpired, made it obvious that he was superhuman. As such, Maclay was approached (culture hero-like) for material things—tools and new plant seeds—and for advice, for he was seen "as a source of not only wealth but also superhuman knowledge" (Lawrence 1964:66, 64–68; Webster 1984:94–97, 101).

Even under less hostile circumstances Europeans could be accorded some of the attributes of powerful "wise strangers," particularly those who married into families of local elites or those who became progenitors of their own lineages. There are a number of such situations on record, particularly from Africa.[4] We have noted above examples from the Nyakyusa-Ngonde area of traditions in which chiefs or priests arrived as strangers and benefactors, or in which powerful medicines came from afar or the best doctors were derived from foreign descent. Although Nyakyusa-Ngonde attitudes towards Europeans were ambivalent, the newcomers were fitted into the category of chiefs who had brought benefactions, often in recognition of the greater pacification deriving from white administration. It was also assumed that whites had powerful medicines, and any white, regardless of how ignorant of medicine, was expected to provide treatment for general ailments. Other particular skills were admired, too. A Scottish mission doctor was celebrated as the man who first taught Nyakyusa boys to read music, and the ability to knit socks was also highly prized.[5] In short, "[Traditional wise strangers] brought fire to people who ate their food raw; iron to those who used wooden hoes; cattle to cultivators; the institution of chieftainship to those who lived unorganized, in scattered villages. . . . The whites brought cloth, literacy, medicines, the gospel" (Wilson 1977:178, 167).

Sometimes, in their capacity as "wise strangers," Europeans themselves became local chiefs in ways similar to those described in traditional accounts of a foreign hunter or curer marrying the daughter of a local chief and founding a dynasty, or as a result of association with local chiefs in the capacity of powerful and knowledgeable men from afar. European chiefly power sprang from superior weapons, superior skills or organizing ability, and useful trade contacts with the outside world that gave access to cloth and other foreign goods. In addition, "sometimes they were credited with supernatural power, particularly control over rain.

---

[4] See also Nordholt (1971:173–75) regarding the Portuguese in Timor, and Ruby and Brown (1975:144–45, 169) regarding white traders and Chinook elites on the northwest coast of North America.

[5] Almost everywhere in traditional societies musical talents rank high among the special skills that reflect extraordinary, and thus supernatural, powers and abilities; thus the introduction of musical skills can be an appropriate and appreciated task for a foreign "culture hero." Knitting presumably was seen as a type of weaving—again, a distinctive and distinguished "gift."

Often, they formed an alliance with an existing chief, giving aid in war, acting as an advisor, providing 'medicine', and cementing the friendship by marrying a daughter of the chief" (Wilson 1958:59; see also 1979:53, 57–58 for the cases of John Dunn, Henry Francis Fynn, Coenraad de Buys).

People of Power

It is by now a truism that, in the mix of reactions to the coming of Europeans, one of the major attractions of these newcomers was their exceptional technical skills and the products produced thereby. The material benefits of contact can hardly be denied, but to be properly appreciated, it is useful to bear in mind the underlying concepts that were accorded in traditional societies to exceptional crafting skills and to certain types of material goods, particularly unusual or foreign ones. Basically, exceptional crafting skills reflected exceptional personal powers, powers that could only be derived from a special relationship with the spiritual world (see Chapter 3). It is easy to lose track of this point in recounting the exploits of European trader-explorers with native leaders and elites, all of whom seemed intent on maximizing material benefits by whatever means possible. For example, when Chief Comcomly of the northwest coast Chinook married one of his daughters to a leading Astorian trader, McDougall, and then took advantage of his father-in-law status to make frequent visits to the European fort and its blacksmith shop for forged weapons and tools, the motive seems obvious. But Comcomly's interest may have been based on a deeper appreciation of the skill of blacksmithing and the tools produced thereby. Traditional belief credited a compassionate deity with teaching the first people how to be skilled in eye and hand and how to make basic tools—canoes, paddles, and nets. But "when it came to iron objects, Chinooks had received no similar instructions from their deity; they would have to depend on earthbound Astorian smithies for such things" (Ruby and Brown 1975:144). Both McDougall and Comcomly were wily rascals and the most pragmatic of men, and it is not my intention to declare the Astorian traders to be gods, or even culture heroes. But it is also not unlikely that Comcomly appreciated the skills of the smith in a way the Astorians did not, and it is that appreciation that merits our interest.

In traditional societies the same type of exceptional skills, revealing the same abundance of exceptional power, underlay talents not only in material craftsmanship, but also in the less tangible fields of music, curing, literacy, divination, general intelligence, and understanding of esoteric knowledge. In this sense, the Europeans' superior weapons and their access to seemingly unlimited trade goods, as well as the teaching of music, knitting of socks, and instruction in the skills needed to read the bible, all attested to the same superabundance of powers and related intellect with which Europeans were endowed.[6] Exceptional skills and derivation from distant places frequently combined to identify Europeans either as latter-day culture heroes or as contemporary demons; in any case as beings with powers and therefore with control over life, death, and the riches of the earth. Lienhardt expressed the matter succinctly:

> *Juok* is usually said to be the supreme being of the Shilluk, to be spirit. . . . what the Shilluk cannot otherwise account for, they account for by this concept. So, for example, the creation of the world and of life is the work of *juok*, and he may also be an explanation of sickness and death. *The presence and powers of the foreigners are explained with reference to* juok, *for those who are specially gifted are supposed to be so by virtue of the stronger flow, in them, of the being which created and animates the universe* (Lienhardt 1954:156, my emphasis).

Generally speaking, Europeans' exceptional power, either for good or for evil, was recognized both in terms of quantities and qualities, that is, in their excessive and seemingly inexhaustible supplies of foreign material goods, especially trade goods, their command of writing and literacy, their apparent control over life and death via the extraordinary power in medicine and guns, and

---

[6] Speaking of the reaction of the Samoans to their first Europeans, Burridge notes that the European artifacts that the Samoans soon began to covet were connected not so much with the abilities and the capacities of the Europeans themselves, who at least initially were considered inferior, unhealthy, and smelly, as with Europeans' beliefs and assumptions about power (1969:22).

FIGURE 5.2

European official studying his book and seated on a throne. Mid-nineteenth century Javanese *ciré-perdue* bronze. From C. A. Burland, *The Exotic White Man*, figure 15. Verlag Anton Schroll, 1968. Reprinted by permission of Werner Forman
Archive.

their extraordinary knowledge. "White people could kill a man
with thunder that sent invisible spears to tear a hole in his body
and spill his blood in the sand," so testified Australian aborigines
(Reynolds 1978:66). In Africa, "though the Europeans were usually at first so few in numbers, their miraculous firearms, their
lavish personal supply of clothes, their elaborate domestic equipment even under camping conditions, the technical wonder and
variety of even their trivial trade goods, and the unlimited wealth
suggested by their supplies of cotton cloth, all gave the quality of
a unique marvel to their first appearance among any African people. To the latter the newcomers appeared to have a complete

184

FIGURE 5.3

British teacher with his book. Yoruba carving, ca. 1930. From C. A. Burland, *The Exotic White Man*, figure 12. Verlag Anton Schroll, 1968. Reprinted by permission of Werner Forman Archive.

mastery over the material world, and a degree of control over life and death through their medicines and their firearms, which was genuinely terrifying. Even after the first shock had worn off, the indelible impression of a master of fantastic forces of unknown extent remained. This induced many African peoples to submit to the establishment of European administration with little opposition . . ." (Southall 1953:230; see also Fernandez 1982:68–70 and Rasmussen 1931:127–28 for very similar interpretations of white men by the Fang of Gabon and by Netsilik Eskimos, respectively).

Regarding literacy as an aspect of foreign power, "many Africans felt that mere possession of the Bible or acquisition of the skills of literacy was effective in warding off misfortune or promoting temporal success" (Strayer 1976:3). Thus, attendance at Christian worship services and the eagerness to read could be highly gratifying to resident missionaries, who, of course, knowing the Bible and being literate, were themselves potential sources of religious power, a position they sometimes encouraged, particularly in pioneer days, by trying to find and eradicate witches or by praying for rain or by presenting reading as a magical art in order to evidence the virtues of the new religion in competition with tradition (ibid., pp. 4, 6). The reactions to these powers, however, could work two ways, while still acknowledging the presence of superior power. Thus, concerning the Fang of Gabon, Fernandez has reported that "whereas earlier there had been a tendency to assimilate the Europeans, with their manifest material superiority, to the ancestors or to some other kind of supernatural status, there now appeared a tendency to assimilate them to the power of evil, and in various myths, to ascribe their superiority to trickery and duplicity" (Fernandez, quoted in Strayer 1975, p. 5; Fernandez 1982:71–72).

One of the more enticing qualities of Europeans was their tremendous wealth. They seemed literally to surround themselves and fill themselves with riches. To the Netsilik this was apparent in the hollow wood islands full of iron in which their first white men arrived. To Hawaiians just meeting Cook's sailors, the foreigners themselves seemed made of wealth: "they have doors in the sides of their bodies [pockets] . . . into these openings they thrust their hands, and take thence many valuable things—their bodies are full of treasure" (Dibble, in Sahlins 1981:18). In addition, there was the even more curious fact that whites apparently did not have to work to acquire their material goods. They simply made marks on slips of paper and huge stores of these items came to them in ships and aircraft from a distant place.

The implications of this extraordinary evidence of power (which seemed so frustratingly unavailable to natives) underlay much of the well known "cargo cult" movements in Oceania. Since it was generally accepted in traditional Melanesian ideology that all forms of wealth and prosperity ultimately derived from

proper ritual manipulation of the spirits, the key to the material prosperity of the whites had to lie in knowledge of the correct ritual that Europeans used to direct their deities to bring about such results. Quite a few daily activities of the colonial Europeans were interpreted in this light. Reading and writing seemed one of the more important ritual acts, so that here again achieving literacy in English became vitally important and "book learning assumed the characteristics of ritual knowledge." The happy gathering of Europeans for a mild celebration when a ship or plane arrived with often essential necessities also appeared ritual-like to native observers inclined to view it that way. So did the daily raising and lowering of the flag at government stations and similar types of behavior (Read 1958:283; Lawrence 1964:248–49; Lindstrom 1984:303–4).

As powerful or power-filled strangers from a distant place it was also logical that Europeans should be expected to display unusual personal attributes indicative of their unusual status. The question of their mortality was not always immediately obvious, particularly for returned "gods" or "ancestors." In sixteenth-century Puerto Rico, native *caciques*, uncertain whether they faced immortal celestial sons of the Sun to be revered or mortal men to be attacked, held a Spaniard under water to see if he would die (Fernandez de Oviedo 1852–53: Bk 16, Chapter 8). Three hundred years later, Herbert Baldus was also questioned about mortality when he visited Tapirapé villages in Brazil. He knew that Tapirapé recognized that whites had power and "riches," but "what was to me a true revelation, transporting me into a world completely different from our own, was the fact that, in 1935, they questioned me about whether we, the whites, would have to die, too. When a human condition like death is not known to be universal, I think it is justifiable to speak of different worlds, thus characterizing the profound difference in views of the totality of natural and supernatural things." For the Tapirapé, it was not an idle question, for whites undoubtedly were well versed in magic: ". . . they never doubted my shamanistic qualities since, by analogy, they believed that a society as powerful as that of the whites could not exist without shamans. They believed in my ability to travel great distances in dreams" (Baldus 1974:386).

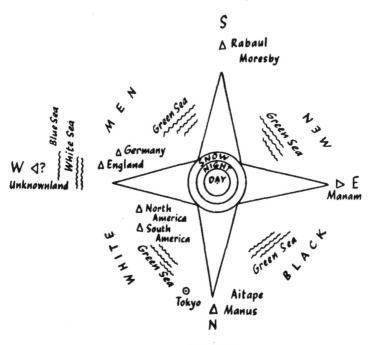

FIGURE 5.4

Sand drawing by a Manam Islander, Melanesia, depicting the center land of God's creation surrounded by cardinal points and the Green Sea, where various distant European places are located. The "unknownland" in the very distant west was the source of all knowledge and good things, and possibly was associated with the Seventh Day Adventists. From K. Burridge, *New Heaven New Earth*, 1969, p. 58. Basil Blackwell, Ltd., publisher. Reprinted by permission of the author and the publisher.

Rasmussen's special powers were dealt with in a different, yet entirely consistent manner, by the Netsilik Eskimos. After careful discussion with a respected shaman of the theological implications of his intent, Rasmussen induced the Netsilik to part with prized magical amulets in exchange for equally prized sewing needles, files, tobacco, matches, and similar wonders. The shaman then shrewdly pointed out to Rasmussen that amulets, being sacred property, should be replaced by sacred property. Furthermore, he went on, since Rasmussen had emphasized his wide travels and experience among innumerable tribes of both white men and Eskimos, it was obvious that he (Rasmussen) possessed "a special quality over life" that made this expertise possible. The part of a person with the greatest life-giving power was the hair, and thus Rasmussen should give a lock of his hair to all who had sold amulets to him. Accepting this logic, but concerned about the practical effect of baldness in Arctic conditions, Rasmussen agreed to give tufts of hair (hacked off with a blunt hunting knife) to those who had given the most valued amulets, but gave pieces of personal clothing (bits torn off a fur jacket and a shirt)—also recognized as useful for amulets—to the rest (Rasmussen 1931: 43–44).

That whites were believed to be part of the powerful, "natural" order of the cosmos is well evidenced in other New World native societies. Fowler, discussing Arapahoe concepts of the universe and its operation, notes that personal and social problems in general, apparently including problems brought about by contact with white society, could be alleviated by proper relationships with the supernatural. "While Sun Dance vows are most commonly vows for the recovery of a sick relative, it is not unheard of for an individual to participate so that a relative will be released from prison" (1982:258). The parallel of illness, presumably caused by intangible harmful "powers," with imprisonment as a problem situation sufficiently similar to require Sun Dance vows, implies that the latter condition (prison) was also caused by harmful "powers" (i.e., foreign whites).

Among native communities of Mesoamerica and the Andes, where the powers of white foreigners have been felt in most unequivocal fashion, Spanish-speaking ladinos or mestizos or other figures of European extraction who are rich, foreign, and/or urban (including missionaries· or even anthropologists), have been equated very directly with the powers of the universe. Not infrequently such foreigners have been interpreted as new physical manifestations of power-filled traditional entities who, as "owners of the earth" or "lords of the mountain," also controlled access to the "riches of the earth" (Taussig 1980a:184–87). Vogt put the matter succinctly in his description of the Zinacantecos of highland Chiapas, who recognize the sacredness of various types of geographical features (mountains, rocks, trees), including "holes in the ground" (a limestone sink, a cave, a waterhole, a spring or a ravine). All such holes into the earth are conceived as "openings to the domain of the Earth Lord (Yahval Balamil, literally, 'Earth Owner'), who dwells beneath the surface of the ground and . . . is always described as a large, fat Ladino (mestizo) who possesses vast quantities of money, herds of cows, mules, and horses, and flocks of chickens. At the same time he has the attributes of thunderbolts and serpents. He owns all the waterholes; he controls the lightning and the clouds . . . and he claims all the products of the earth as his own" (Vogt 1981:126; see also pp. 140–41 for additional discussion of why "earth lords" and ladinos resemble each other).

Consider, too, the description accorded to mountain deities, the Wamanis, by residents of the Andean community of Chuschi in highland Peru. The Wamanis, the most powerful indigenous deities of the Pampas region and the "owners" of all plants and animals, live in the highest region of the tundra, in the highest mountains and puna lakes, that no one approaches alone. The various individual Wamanis preside over particular territories, and have an organizational hierarchy similar to that of provincial government structure in which the particular status, position, or "office" each holds is fixed according to the height of their respective mountain peak or lake. Wamanis are described as tall, white, bearded men who dress elaborately in Western costume and are rather like doctors, lawyers, and politicos. They, too, are associated with the earth's "riches." "Their palaces, located inside the mountains and lakes, are sumptuously furnished in gold and silver" (Isbell 1978:59, 151; Taussig 1980a:161–68, 184–86). Isbell also describes how, to the Quechua-speaking villagers, non-Quechua "foreigners" in the community are similarly associated with the "threatening outside world," and are also believed to be, by definition, rich and knowledgeable.[7]

The powers of the lords of the mountains are also well known to the laborers in Bolivian tin mines, who honor images of the Devil or Tío (Uncle) that are placed in the main shafts at each level

[7] The local soccer teams are divided between Indian "comuneros" and mestizo "vecinos" who call their team "amanta," the learned ones (Isbell 1978:73).

of the mine. Tio is the "owner" of the wealth of the mines, of the minerals buried in the mountain and now being extracted by his permission (for he reveals the veins of ore only to those he chooses) by miners who are careful to give thanks for this largesse by giving offerings of liquor, cigarettes, and coca to the image. The images are always shaped from minerals, using clay from the mine, bright pieces of metal, and bits of glass or crystal, and convey a complex symbolism of life and death.[8] But basically "the *Tio* is a figure of power; he has what everyone wants, in excess. Remains of coca lie in his greedy mouth. His hands are stretched out, grasping the bottles of alcohol he is offered. *Some have described him as a "gringo"* (a term applied to any foreigner with blond hair or fair complexion whether from Germany, the United States, or elsewhere) wearing cowboy hat and boots" (Nash 1972:225, my emphasis; Taussig 1980a:143–48, 185–86).[9]

The Acquisition of European Power

Since it is the rightful duty of political-religious specialists in traditional societies to comprehend and then to come to terms with or "control" the powers of the universe as they are variously expressed, so it is reasonable to find native elites interested in trying not only to understand the nature of Europeans' power but also to utilize such powers both in the fulfillment of their expected duties and as a source of supernatural support for their own statuses and offices. As with any manifestation of exceptional power, initial approaches were made with circumspection. When European officers (*kiaps*) first settled near their region of the western highlands of New Guinea, the Kuma were understandably cautious. "Some leaders who were more than usually brave went to find out personally what they could about the pale-skinned strangers. . . . Others sent men of no account to visit the kiaps and re-

[8] It is tempting to also consider in this context the ancient symbolism of metals and minerals in Andean traditions as described by Reichel-Dolmatoff (1981); see Chapter 3.

[9] See Taussig (1980a) for a fuller discussion of the complex political-ideological symbolism and associations involved in correlating foreign ownership and exploitation of natural and social resources with traditional concepts regarding control of and access to natural resources.

FIGURE 5.5

Tribesman from Lake Kopiago, Papua New Guinea. From P. Snow and S. Waine, *The People from the Horizon*, p. 10. Published by Phaidon Press, Ltd., 1979. Photo by Mike Holmes. Reprinted by permission of Phaidon Press, Ltd.

port back to their groups if they ever returned from this risky assignment. In particular, they wanted to know how the white men derived their power over people and their power over things" (Reay 1967:203).

In considering what seemed to be an almost overwhelming desire among native elites (and later the general population) for foreign material goods, it is easy to lose sight of the equally pressing desire for access to the esoteric knowledge commanded by Europeans. It was a wish for this understanding and insight that impelled the Netsilik shaman to work with Rasmussen and to treat him as an equal, that encouraged the Maya lords of Yucatán to reveal their treasured hieroglyphic codices to the Spaniards and to press for further understanding of the magic involved in reading and writing, and that filled the mission churches in many places with genuinely eager seekers of new foreign truth. It was an equally compelling interest in turning this new knowledge to useful political-religious gain that prompted elites in particular to associate with white foreigners and to try to master—and openly express—this new association in order to add a new power source to their political-religious basis of operation.

Before missionaries had permanently settled in eastern Canada, certain band leaders of the Cree-Ojibwa legitimized their positions not only with reference to traditional supernatural powers but also via their new statuses as heads of the Christian church in their area (Rogers 1965:272). At the other end of the scale of political complexity, but very likely with similar goals in mind, Mutesa I, kabaka of Buganda, courted first John Speke and later Henry Stanley, "white-skinned, highly skilled stranger[s] from a far-off country" (Bridges 1970:125). In a move suggestive of the attitude of Hawaiian chiefs after Cook's death, "it is said that he [the kabaka] interpreted the first visit of a white man to Buganda as a sign that he was the rightful king," that in the presence of the European he had at his command a more powerful influence than supported other Bugandan chiefs and priests (a point made when Speke and Mutesa visited the shrine of one of the most important traditional lake gods where the kabaka treated the god's medium with considerable contempt). "Bana, I love you because you have come so far to see me and have taught me so many new things," so Speke reports the king said to him (Bridges 1970:127, 129).[10]

Supporting the kabakaship with the power of Europeans also

[10] Predictably, chiefly members of the court aristocracy were jealous of Speke's influence with the kabaka, which, as we have seen (Chapter 3), is not uncommon when learned foreigners achieve high prestige and influence for their esoteric knowledge and skills.

CHAPTER 5

led both to the predictable request for guns and to Mutesa's interest in the Bible. Henry Stanley, thirteen years after Speke's visit, assisted Mutesa with both. The kabaka had by now become a serious student of the Qur'ān and a practitioner of Islam, and eagerly added Christianity to his growing awareness of the powers of a wider world. As Southall (1979) notes, the descriptions in Stanley's diaries of gun-induced battle carnage interspersed with biblical instruction during lulls in fighting may sound bizarre, but both guns and the Bible attest to the kabaka's concern with the new sources of power that were available through his learned European teacher and adviser. The general context is expressed by another passage written by Stanley: "the causeway [part of a battle tactic] is progressing, Scripture is being translated, and we touch now and then upon the wonders of nature, the Heavens, the air, the nature of rocks, etc., all of which is hailed with wonder by the Sultan and his people" (Stanley, in Southall 1979:218).

A different aspect of European powers was tapped by the Kuna Indians of Panama, who appear to have associated European power with the power of both harmful and helpful spirits. In Kuna epic tales, Spaniards and other outsiders (missionaries, soldiers, various oppressors) play parts similar to those of horrible animals and spirits in Kuna curing songs. Kramer has suggested that historical attacks by Kuna on Spanish forts during the colonial period as described in these epics provided a model for struggles between shamans' tutelary spirits and spirits of sickness described in curing songs in which the spirit "troups" of the shaman invaded the forts or strongholds of the evil spirits and freed the soul of the patient (Kramer 1970:81, 119). In actual curing rituals the curer places several carved wooden figures or "stick dolls" (*nuchus*) under the hammock of the sick person and discusses the problem with the beneficent spirits represented by the dolls, instructing them how to deal with the evil spirits who have caused the illness (Sherzer 1983:111). Although nuchus may be carved in various animal forms, some of the dolls known from ethnographic collections were carved to represent colonial-era Europeans; men dressed in top hats and older style coats or figures wearing religious garb (Figure 5.6; Wassén 1940:76–79). The exact nature of the association is not clear, but it seems apparent that

194

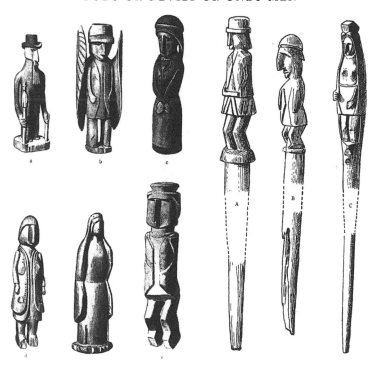

FIGURE 5.6

LEFT, wooden *nuchus* carved with European representations from the Kuna Indians of eastern Panama. From E. Nordenskiöld, *An Historical and Ethnological Survey of the Cuna Indians*, Comparative Ethnographical Studies No. 10, 1938, p. 425, figure 26. Reprinted by permission of the Göteborgs Etnografiska Museum. RIGHT, wooden curing sticks carved with European representations, from the Kuna Indians of eastern Panama. From H. Wassén, An Analogy between a South American and Oceanic myth motif and Negro influence in Darien, *Etnologiska Studier*, No. 10, 1940, p. 78, figure 2. Reprinted by permission of the Göteborgs Etnografiska Museum.

Europeans were accorded significance in curing symbolism not unlike that accorded various other expressions of "outside" natural power carved in the form of curing dolls (including the various types of animals depicted and the kinds of wood utilized).

The ceremonial garb and regalia used by political-religious specialists have always bespoken the avenues employed to acquire or associate with cosmic powers. A necklace of quartz crystals, a headdress of red and yellow feathers, an armshell, a beautifully embroidered imported robe not only identify rank and status but also tangibly express the wider world of extraordinary qualities and outside contacts that are the stock-in-trade of political-religious specialists. The adoption of European clothing, table manners, house styles, and other symbols of association by traditional political-religious elites represented the same concepts and accomplished exactly the same effect, for such adoptions served to associate the wearer (or the acquirer) more closely with the aura of the foreign Europeans, just as a quartz crystal pendant associated him more closely with the energies of more traditional forms of cosmic forces. It was not a matter simply of imitating a "superior" people, as so many colonial Europeans chose to believe, but more one of respectful association with a power-filled people.[11]

Thus Mutesa I, a proud and powerful monarch in his own right (who, as Rotberg puts it, sometimes regarded a foreigner like Speke in a light similar to that in which the court of imperial China examined envoys from the West; 1970:9), not only studied the Bible, adopted guns, and obtained Speke's opinion on the nature of rocks, but also took to sitting in a chair and wearing trousers and a hat like Speke's (Bridges 1970:129). Noble Hawaiians did the same, adopting European names, clothing, and domestic arrangements of housing and cooking as means of expressing the association and identification they felt with the new chiefly invaders from ancestral lands overseas.[12] "Great chiefs of the Islands never tired of asking early European visitors if King George lived as well as they, or vice versa" (Sahlins 1981:30–31).

[11] This is what Mannoni seems to mean when he says, with reference to Madagascar, that "the European . . who has always something of an inferiority complex, interprets the value set on knowledge of his ways as a valuing of himself; he takes it as a tribute to his immense superiority. But the really typical Malagasy takes an interest in the white man, and even unconsciously identifies himself with him, without actually making any comparison between himself and the other, or feeling inferior, while at the same time adopting a dependent attitude" (1964:80).

[12] During Vancouver's visit to Hawaii, King Kamehameha sent a personal servant to the ship's galley to learn British techniques of cooking and requested a complete set of plates, cutlery, kitchen utensils, and a bed.

Among Tahitian nobles, elaborate English clothes became the trend and European table manners and eating paraphernalia (cutlery, tables, chairs) learned on board ship were duplicated, not only when entertaining Europeans but also as a matter of elite prestige. European ships themselves were copied, or at least an attempt was made to make a European sailing vessel. European music was more successfully achieved—again by chiefs, who took to having their arrival preceded by a band of musicians (Ferdon 1981:280, 302–6). After association with British and French advisers, foreign music (that ubiquitous skill or gift of the gods) was appreciated by Radama I of Madagascar, too, along with the rest of the accoutrements expected of a traditional prince attempting to emulate the trappings of European monarchy:

> In 1816, King Radama was sitting on the floor, clad in a traditional loin cloth of raw silk, eating off silver plates. A few years later he was presenting himself as a princely hussar, attired in a military hat, red tunic, blue pantaloons, and green boots, giving formal European dinners on silver and crystal. . . . A band played English and Scottish music, and afterwards European country dances were sometimes performed. His new palace . . . built by French and Réunionnais architects, was a place of exquisite beauty; Napoleon was his hero. . . . in 1818 he asked [James] Hastie [a British agent and intimate associate], 'Am I not becoming an English Monarch?' (Southall 1979:221–22).

Chief Comcomly of the Northwest Coast Chinook would have appreciated the feeling. He, too, expressed identification with the king of England and received in return from an English ship's captain "an old flag, a laced coat, a cocked hat, and a sword" with which he appeared the next day on his own ship dressed in full British uniform and with the Union Jack flying in the breeze (Ruby and Brown 1975:148–49). A comparable identification was expressed by the so-called "kings" of the colonial era Miskito of eastern Nicaragua, who gloried in titles such as "governor," "admiral," and "king" bestowed along with commissions at formal coronation ceremonies held by English authorities in Jamaica or Belize. Titles, commissions, and coronation procedures helped legitimize these positions of local leadership and were apparently accompanied by appropriate, brightly colored British officers' uniforms and royal scepters. Not surprisingly, Miskito "kings" were also proud of their ability to speak and write English, and were avid students of European missionaries, activities which again directly identified them with the political-ideological power and mystique of European foreigners (Dennis and Olien 1984; Olien 1983; Helms 1986b).

To the Arapahoe Indians of North America, as for many other native peoples, prestigeful evidence of European association was found not only in dress but also in letters and medallions received from whites. Yet, interestingly enough, the most sought-after symbols of leadership soon came to be a trip east to meet with United States officials (Fowler 1982:25, 26). "A visit to Washington signified to the Arapahoes that the government was impressed by a council chief's reputation and his ability to influence his people's behavior. Council chiefs brought back from these visits gifts that in the Indian view signified the special relationship between the president and the chief. Medals were routinely presented at such conferences. On several occasions . . . both Black Coal and Sharp Nose, claiming that their medals had been stolen, successfully petitioned the agent for ceremonies in which new medals were presented. . . . Black Coal had a special outfit that he wore when he confronted federal representatives on behalf of the tribe: a broadcloth suit and watch and chain presented him by the secretary of the interior, a white felt hat with an eagle feather stuck in the crown, and his medicine on one of his fur-wrapped braids. Sharp Nose, who had the distinction of being Crook's head 'soldier', often wore his army uniform" (Fowler 1982:79).

That such visits to the distant center of European (United States) power may have attested to more than diplomatic niceties is suggested by Fowler's discussion of the benefits to the Arapahoe of becoming army scouts, an experience that included building *béétee, béétee* being "a pervasive power or life force [which] . . . invests the universe" (ibid., p. 257). "Scouting offered a man opportunities for the war exploits he needed to build a reputation for success and for *béétee*; yet in forming personal friendships with army officers, in making 'brothers' of them, the chiefs

tapped resources they could use to buttress their positions as intermediaries. The scout's uniform worn with the accessory traditional emblems of success in battle—personal medicine, feathers, paint—was a mark of both a man's influence with white
officials and his prowess in overcoming his enemies" (ibid., p.
289). We may also venture the interpretation that the scout's uniform with traditional accessories, like the medals acquired by
council chiefs on visits to Washington and the culturally mixed
suits and accessories worn on these occasions, marked the relationship between a man's influence with outside distant "powers"
in general (with whites and/or with enemies) and the resulting
growth of his *béétee*.[13]

Generally speaking, elements of foreign power traditionally
could be acquired by accepting foreign visitors or by traveling
oneself to distant power sources. Both approaches were used to
tap the powers of Europeans. Visiting European missionaries,
explorers, early colonial administrators, and traders brought new
magical skills, particularly literacy and firepower and metal
working, as well as new funds of esoteric knowledge and new
gods (or seemingly new tangible expressions of traditional
knowledge and traditional gods), new political-religious regalia,
and legitimizing coronation ceremonies to many, many local
elites, just as itinerant Islamic scholar-trader-advisers introduced
to West African elites the potent magic of literacy and the power
of the Qur'ān, the benefits of foreign material goods, and the
symbolism of foreign royal robes and installation ceremonies, or
as Hindu brahmans brought new learning and new symbols of legitimacy to Southeast Asian chiefs. Alternately, many native

---

[13] In comparable fashion, in discussing the general correlation among wealth,
kula eminence, and high rank and between rank and good foreign connections in
the Trobriands, Uberoi also suggests that new exploits (such as pearling) made
possible by whites could provide wealth and prestige comparable to that acquired
by the traditional kula. . . . "If more material were available the old foreign affiliations via the *kula*, as well as the new foreign affiliations via the whites, could be
shown to be intimately bound up with the rank of a Trobriand local lineage at
home" (1971:116). He also notes at least one case where a community turned
completely to pearling and gave up kula expeditions (ibid., p. 118). If we assume
that the motivation to develop one's fame and name have not substantially
changed, then activities involving interaction with foreign whites must carry
symbolic association comparable to that associated with the traditional kula.

elites, like the Arapahoe chiefs, eagerly sought opportunities to travel themselves (or to send agents) to Europe or to European settlements. In this context, first-hand experience with European countries and especially with European heads of state or their representatives can be seen as directly comparable to a first-hand visit with a renowned shaman in a distant land or to a pilgrimage to a distant, higher-level *axis mundi*. The Arapahoe chiefs' trips to Washington can thus be considered comparable to the trips taken by West African chiefs to Mecca, or by northern European early medieval kings to Rome, or by the rulers (or their envoys) of frontier Asiatic tribes to the imperial court of traditional China. All such journeys can be seen to fall within the wider context of elite responsibility for acquiring knowledge of the dynamics of the universe by close acquaintance with foreign power-filled domains located either on vertical or horizontal axes from the homeland, and reached either by trance or other altered states or by physical travel to a geographically distant place.

The Miskito "kings" of eastern Nicaragua, whose legitimacy may have been particularly dependent on European support, seem to have considered foreign education as essential. For two hundred years (mid-seventeenth to mid-nineteenth centuries) Miskito "kings" traveled either to England, Jamaica, or Belize (the last two under British authority) for education and/or commissioning or crowning as "king" (Dennis and Olien 1984:734). According to one historian, a Miskito "prince" in the mid-seventeenth century spent three years in London and was reportedly a great favorite of Charles I, "from whom he met with the most gracious reception [and who] had him often with him on his private parties of pleasure, [and] admired his activity, strength, and many accomplishments" (Sorsby, quoted in Olien 1983:203).[14] A century or so later, the heir of the then Miskito chief, "George I," who was to become "George II," spent a year or so in England

[14] A later Miskito chief, "George I" (many, indeed apparently all, Miskito chiefs took English names), visited Jamaica and reportedly, in 1774, sent a barrel of Miskito shore soil to his "brother king, George III of England," along with a promise of 5,000 Miskito warriors to help with any problems that might develop in the North American colonies (Olien 1983.211). Since Miskito men served as mercenaries for Britain in the Caribbean on a number of occasions, such an offer probably seemed quite reasonable in Miskito terms.

where he was baptized and given his English name, and where he and his entourage learned to speak some English. They were apparently quite taken by the British system of titled nobility, perhaps because of its usefulness for politically ambitious leaders at home (e.g., the future "king's" uncle adopted the title of "Duke of York"; Olien 1983:211–13).

Farther to the south, among the Kuna of eastern Panama, for whom travel to foreign places has been an expected activity for both future and current political-religious practitioners for centuries (perhaps even in the pre-Columbian era), we have an intriguing account of a trip made by a learned native chanter, Ruben Pérez Kantule, to Sweden in 1931 under the patronage of the well-known ethnologist, Erland Nordenskiöld, who wished his services as an assistant in translating Kuna texts and manuscripts and preparing commentary for a catalogue on museum holdings of Kuna ethnographic items. Nordenskiöld remarks that Pérez showed little noticeable interest in Swedish life except for questions having to do with nature or the plant world. Nor did he show much interest in museum displays and materials other than those dealing with the Kuna and Panama. He was, however, very interested in an illustrated paper showing the stages in the life cycles of butterflies and energetically copied old writings about the isthmus in order to lecture on them when he returned home (Nordenskiöld 1938:xiii–xxii). Considering that knowledge of flora and fauna, history, and the "origins" of things is a fundamental aspect of traditional expertise not only among the Kuna but for many learned men of many native societies, Pérez' areas of interest seem understandable. Perhaps they carried additional import because he acquired this information while resident in a distant land (Sherzer 1983:117; Helms 1979:196–97, note 12).

It seems likely that a similar quest for esoteric knowledge as expressed in European traditions, including literacy and craft skills, provided at least one motive underlying requests by native elites of various societies to have their children educated by Europeans. (Pre-contact traditions encouraging the educational value of foreign experience undoubtedly facilitated this practice, too.) Ruby and Brown, for example, relate how the Chinook chief, Comcomly, offered to send his young grandson to the Anglican Missionary Society School at Red River in Winnipeg (where missionaries had their own reasons for wanting to educate the sons of native elites), a request which in this case was denied because the boy was too delicate for the long journey to Red River (Ruby and Brown 1975:170).

A continent away in southeast Madagascar, the circumstances surrounding the initial contacts between Portuguese Jesuit missionaries and the king of the Antanosy people were not dissimilar. King Tsiambany agreed to give his eldest son to the Portuguese to take to Goa to be educated in Roman Catholicism and Portuguese culture with the understanding that the Jesuit priests would remain in Antanosy as hostages. Unfortunately, by the time the Portuguese were ready to leave, the king had had second thoughts and refused to let his son leave, offering to send another young man instead. The Portuguese, feeling insulted, kidnapped the prince but treated him well in Goa, apparently educated him in Portuguese and Christianity, and brought him home two years later hoping (in vain as it turned out) that he would help with the further conversion of his countrymen (Southall 1979:214–17). Several centuries later, in the Madagascar hinterland state of Imerina, where King Radama I enthusiastically sought to emulate the sumptuary laws associated with European monarchs, the king also enthusiastically encouraged foreign education, particularly for elites, an education they apparently were eager to acquire. "In 1820, ten Merina men, most of them nobles, were sent to Mauritius to learn carpentry, goldsmithing, jewelry, ironwork, painting, and cobblery. Ten former slaves went there to learn music, and women were sent to learn house management. Fifty more Merina were learning navigation on British ships. One noble offered Radama 3,000 piastres to have his son chosen for training. . . . In 1821, nine Merina men, including a prince, were sent to England with the London Missionary Society, first to attend school in London and then to be apprenticed in Manchester" (Southall 1979:223).

To Radama I and his nobles the British must have appeared to be a rich storehouse of skills and knowledge, a veritable treasure trove of intellectual wealth available for those who sought to learn. It was on a much smaller scale and in different forms but in the very same context that Hawaiians believed British sailors, with their wealth-producing pockets, to be virtually filled with treasure, that the Netsilik marveled at the superfluity of wood and iron with which "their" first white men surrounded themselves, and that the hopeful adherents of cargo cult movements sought the wealth of manufactured goods, power, and knowledge available to Europeans, and hopefully to themselves, from a land of plenty "far away and beyond the seas where everything could be learned and the good things of this world obtained" (Burridge 1969:57–58).

There is no way we can know what thoughts passed through the minds of the nine Merina men who went to England, or of the Antanosy prince who went to Portuguese Goa, or of the Miskito "king" while visiting the court of Charles I, or of the many other individuals from native societies who accompanied European explorers and missionaries back to Europe or on further exploratory voyages. The experience must have been in some senses unique, and yet must have been placed within already existing contexts of geography and cosmography. Similarly, those who made such trips (and survived them—see Foreman 1943) must have become "exceptional" individuals, for better or for worse, in their home societies, and, indeed, we know that such was often the case. It was no accident that the initial instigators ("prophets") of various cargo cult movements in Melanesia and Polynesia often were individuals with wider travel experience and knowledge of the white man's world, some of whom even traveled in European ships to distant European settlements (e.g., to Sydney, Australia, sometimes associated with heaven; see Burridge 1969:22, 50, 52, 72, 156–57; Lawrence 1964:77).

The account of the travels of Bichiwung, a Makusi from British Guiana (Guyana) in South America who introduced to his region a semi-Christian cult called the "Hallelujah" religion, gives us some idea of how such trips may have been perceived, and also provides an excellent example of the congruence of geographical distance with sacred distance in native cosmologies. Briefly, after missionaries arrived in Georgetown in the mid-nineteenth century, the interior Indians became interested in the new god who lived with his spirit-helpers in a sacred place called "Engiland"

and wished to meet and talk with him, "just as their own shaman priests always made journeys to the other world to speak with the gods there and to obtain advice and guidance from them" (Blackburn 1979:70–71). Consequently, about the turn of the twentieth century, a man called Bichiwung apparently was taken to England by a parson returning home. According to accounts of Bichiwung's trip later recorded from adherents of the cult (and with allowances for elaborations), as he approached the strange coastline of "Engiland" low mists, a sort of cloud, hung down from the sky (an unusual phenomenon for someone from Makusi country) making it seem as if the sky came down to the sea at the horizon. Bichiwung saw a space in the horizon ("sky base") like a door, and the steamer went through this door to England which lay beyond, the place where the parson came from, and the place where the sky met the sea. While in England, Bichiwung apparently was baptized and also may have had a trance experience in which he believed that he personally visited God, who gave him songs, a small bottle of special "medicine," a piece of paper (interpreted by Hallelujah adherents as a new kind of "bible," i.e., a source of sacredness), and some cultigens to take back home. When Bichiwung returned to Guyana with his experience, his "medicine," a gun, and several chests of material wealth, he introduced the new cult, and both it and his fame spread. With his fame and his productive garden, his hospitality, and his new knowledge, Bichiwung unfortunately attracted the attentions of a jealous sorcerer who, after several unsuccessful efforts to kill him (which were foiled by the power of the new medicine), ultimately succeeded. The cult then fell upon difficult times, but it survived and eventually spread among a number of other Carib-speaking groups (Butt 1960; Blackburn 1979:70–73).

This account of the origins of the Hallelujah cult contains practically all the necessary ingredients of a traditional "origin" myth, i.e., a shamanic journey in the form of a visit by a selected individual to a distant sacred place where the deity is consulted and where, culture hero-like, new knowledge, useful plants, and material goods (tangible signs of the trip) are acquired; a brief period of successful enjoyment of new benefits; and a decline from the original "golden era" after the good hero loses a competition with an evil competitor. Clearly not all trips to Europe undertaken by natives under the auspices of the new foreigners had such immediate and extensive results or were so well remembered and "idealized," but some amazement, some elements of the general context of Bichiwung's journey to a very special, power-filled place, surely were part of all such experiences at least on an individual level even if society-wide ramifications did not always result.

In considering the advent of Europeans in native society as essentially an event of cosmological portent, members of traditional societies identified Europeans themselves as superhuman beings, as wise strangers with exceptional power, much of which was expressed and evidenced by their access to quantities of unusual material goods and by their technical ("magical") skills and capacities. As we know, material goods in traditional societies offer tangible expression of a range of political-ideological concepts. The natural materials from which goods are crafted and the unusual characteristics of the manufactured objects, including those strange and rare creations acquired from distant places, may contain and convey universal powers themselves and, in addition, attest to the acquaintance with this same dynamic field by those who acquire them or who craft them.

Generally speaking, these dimensions and characteristics were attributed to European goods as much as to traditional goods in native society. The natural materials out of which European goods were made could convey supernatural associations, their curious forms and purposes could attest to the extraordinary power contained in the product and reflected in the skills of the manufacturer, and the acquisition of such goods by natives could attest to the privileged association of select individuals or of entire groups with this new source of power and to the potent insights derived therefrom.

Knowledge of the universe could be revealed not only by the magic of Europeans' books but also by Europeans' magical (scientific) instruments. "Cortés quickly discovered that the Indians regarded his navigation charts, and particularly his compass, which he frequently referred to, as the instruments of a hidden art, and that they confirmed native beliefs that nothing was hid-

FIGURE 5.7

Wooden Kongo statue of a white man and his dog. The figure is festooned with magical emblems and was probably used in curing. From J. Blackburn, *The White Men*, p. 36. First published by Orbis Publishing Ltd., 1979. Collection Musée de l'Homme, Paris. Reprinted by permission of Musée de l'Homme.

den from him" (Brotherston and Ades 1975:296). Life and death could be regulated with a new and stunning directness by European medicines and guns. Even lowly glass trade beads could assume cosmic significance. Hamell has discussed the symbolism accorded glass beads and other European trade "trifles" within the context of North American Great Lakes and Eastern Woodland native ideology, noting that Indians were initially interested in European implements as ornaments—natives of the New York coastal area even tried to wear iron axes and hoes around their necks until they were shown their correct (European) use. Scraps of copper trade kettles, glass beads, and fragments of European glasswares and glazed ceramics were similarly valued. Hamell (1981) proposes that in the sixteenth and early seventeenth centuries European trade goods of glass and copper were considered analogous to crystal and siliceous stones, shell, and native copper and other free-state minerals (silver, galena, meteoric iron), all of which were valued in traditional societies for their magico-religious properties and their supernatural significance as tangible metaphors of life, light, intelligence, esoteric knowledge, and divination, and all of which were often worked into what we call "ornaments," i.e., gorgets, pendants, and beads.[15]

Hamell suggests that in the early years of contact the symbolic functions and supernatural powers associated with these native valuables were transferred to glass trade beads and other glasswares, to glazed ceramics, and to brass trade kettles and European copper. Europeans were consequently viewed as purveyors of supernatural power; power which they had in tremendous quantities. "We may imagine something of the initial metaphysical excitement . . . which native contact with the Europeans and their material culture must have precipitated. From a native perspective, not only did Europeans possess so much "power" in terms of these "powerful" substances, they even fashioned them into "everyday" utilitarian artifacts. Not only that, the Europeans seemed so willing to trade so much of this "power" for so little; the Indians' animal skins, the source of their everyday clothing

[15] Beads also could be conceptually regarded as spirit forms of "berries" or "seeds" signifying material abundance and well-being.

and home-furnishings" (Hamell 1981:25; 1982; Miller and Hamell 1986).

The aura of Europeans and of European goods can linger long. In Hawaii, even after Europeans were recognized as human, their humanity was still of a distinct variety: they were British or American—not Hawaiian, and they still existed outside the established Hawaiian order and were exceptional. "No doubt that Europeans from the 1790's onward were not Hawaiian gods, but the goods and capacities they possessed embodied a *mana* superior to things Hawaiian. On that account European goods were still Hawaiian necessities, especially for chiefs" (Sahlins 1981:55).

The advent of Europeans was often a shock and tremendous surprise, but at least initially the newcomers were placed rather easily within existing cosmological frameworks with interpretations that attest to native understandings of the nature of things from afar. Particularly in the early days of European contact, when the colonizer first appeared as a stranger, as a guest, and not yet an enemy, the esoteric knowledge, learned skills and crafts, and ideological efficacy offered or at least represented by explorers, missionaries, and colonial administrators opened another realm of outside forces to local power seekers; a realm that was readily accommodated within the cosmological framework that associated things and events of the geographically (and supernaturally) distant world with exceptional powers of the universe.

Ultimately, the fundamental difficulty underlying European–native relationships was simply that most Europeans were unaware of the roles they played and the places they were assigned in native cosmologies and cosmographies. "They were not to know that their position of dominance was due to the fact that in the network of dependencies they occupied roughly the same position as the dead ancestors" (Mannoni 1964:87). Consequently, Europeans generally failed to behave in ways that extraordinary beings with an abundance of universal *mana* should behave. They could not be "controlled" by the usual means by shamans, priests, and chiefs; they did not recognize the mutuality of expectations between themselves as manifestations of the natural forces of the cosmos and local representatives of the societies of already "cultured" or "civilized" people they met. They appeared more like

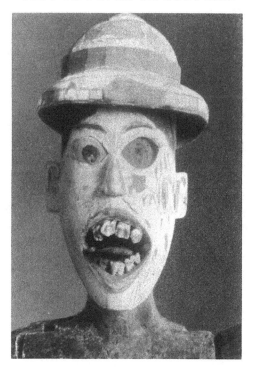

FIGURE 5.8

Head of a carving of an Englishman, from the Nicobar Islands, used to drive away evil spirits from home or fields. The complete figure stands with legs apart on a round base and is portrayed as wearing white trousers and shoes, a pink coat, and tropical helmet. From J. E. Lips, *The Savage Hits Back*, p. 104, figure 56. Published by Yale University Press, 1937.

destructive tyrants than as reciprocators. The disenchantments and frustrations that inevitably erupted in native societies were not so much reflections of indigenous peoples' dislike of powerful foreigners, as expressions of their confusion and resentment that these awesome beings did not behave appropriately. Exceptional power they could understand; misuse of such power, especially on such a scale, was a new and cosmologically upsetting phenomenon.

It is this paradox that underlies the perplexity expressed by

Taussig when confronted by the very deep antipathy of Andean Indians towards whites on the one hand, and on the other, the fact that the spirit owners of the mines and mountains who are accorded characteristics of hated whites are also revered as lineage ancestors and protectors of life (1980a:190). The association of powerful strangers from distant places with ancestors of distant times and with the forces of nature is in full accordance with tradition. It has been the attitudes and behaviors of the foreigners themselves that have appeared to misuse and abuse these forces, that have belied and betrayed this rightful association, and, in consequence, have earned the deep antipathy and sometimes outraged disappointment of those who, like the mountain people in Kipling's insightful story of *The Man Who Would be King*, eventually discovered that the skilled and seemingly learned strangers-cum-deities from afar were "neither gods nor devils, but only men" (Kipling 1963:179–219).

6

The Outer Realms of Christendom

Wilderness and Paradise

Although Europeans approaching over the horizon initially appeared as spirits of the dead or as returned ancestors to native societies, Europeans in turn did not accord as highly valued status on the indigenes they encountered. The medieval cosmography influencing Europeans of the Age of Exploration did not people the cosmographical frontiers with feared or revered ancestral spirits, but with strange and fantastic legendary creatures whose points of contrast with "normal" society ultimately lay more in the realm of the physically and/or morally deformed than in the realm of the deified. But this was not always so. Depending on the direction and the era, the cosmological periphery could lead to paradise as well as to wilderness, could exemplify great good as well as evidence great evil. Thus the symbolic significance of geographical distance for traditional Europe had much in common with that of the non-Western traditional world.

In this chapter I present a general assessment of European views of distant peoples and places within the context of European cosmology, particularly as it relates to interpretations of the discoveries and "inventions" of faraway places that marked the era now known to us as the Age of Discovery. Understanding the dynamics of this age is, of course, a monumental undertaking that has been approached from a number of scholarly perspectives and has yielded an immense literature. In this discussion I intend no more than brief consideration or affirmation of a particular viewpoint, one that I have found helpful in trying to understand the basic rationale behind the general reactions of Europeans to indigenous populations prior to the Enlightenment, and one that complements the preceding discussion of the political-ideological

significance of geographical distance and faraway places in traditional non-Western societies. The ultimate conjunction between
this chapter and the preceding one, of course, lies in our continued contemplation and comprehension of why the two worlds
that ultimately met and intertangled produced such a roughly
textured weave. The following overview, though brief, greatly
simplified, and sacrificing intriguing nuances and much useful
detail, will nonetheless suffice to establish (or remind us of) a few
particular points.

The central heartland of the classical cultural geography of antiquity (the Greek *oikoumene* or Roman *habitatio*) and its immediate hinterland (e.g., Roman Europe), were bordered by geographical (latitudinal) zones that were considered generally
uninhabitable because of either extreme heat or extreme cold.[1] In
the majority view, to the south heat increased to the point that at
the torrid equatorial zone no life could survive. To the north, and
to the extreme south, the polar zones also obviated the possibility
of life. Three additional and habitable land masses in more temperate zones to north and south between the equatorial and the
polar zones were postulated by some to lie opposite to the oikoumene: one to the south of the equator and the oikoumene, and
two on the "other side" of the globe (*ge*), opposite to and coun-
terbalancing the Mediterranean world and the land to the south
of the equatorial zone. All were separated and bounded by two
encircling oceans, one running east–west in the fiery equatorial
regions and the other north–south at right angles to the first (Casson 1974: 59–61, 122–25).

When Judeo-Christian ideology redefined and contracted classical cosmography in the Middle Ages, the oikoumene came to
be focused and circumscribed somewhat differently. The nature
of the world became a spiritual rather than "empirical" assertion,
and thus the domain primarily of theologians. The "maps of the
world" (*mappae-mundi*) that have come down to us from the earlier medieval centuries (obviously symbolic and not intended to
be as utilitarian as the later portolan charts) reveal a circular reli-

[1] I am considering the classical heartland to include the Mediterranean area including North Africa to the Sahara and the Nile Valley, the Levant and Asia Minor, the Black Sea, and Asia to the Indus Valley.

gious field on a stationary earth that some church fathers and scholars held to be spherical, but which others held to be flat. On such maps, Christ's cross essentially formed the east–west and north–south axes. Jerusalem, with its pre-eminence in both the Old and New Testaments, stands at the center as the *axis mundi*. The two longest rivers of the known world, the Don and the Nile, mark the north–south line, meeting the Mediterranean, which runs from west to center. The east (which stands at the top of such maps) is marked by the head of Christ or/and terrestrial paradise (Figure 6.1). The possibility of additional landmasses was debatable and their habitability even more so if scriptural authenticity was to be maintained. Again, as in so many "tribal" world views, the ocean bounded and limited the outside periphery (Wright 1925; Sanders 1978: 9–10; Kimble 1938: 11, 182–88; Penrose 1952:2–3).

In medieval cosmography, as the mappae-mundi imply, the east–west axis, and especially the east, appears to hold primary symbolic significance. More specifically, "The Orient . . . held a peculiar charm for both classical and medieval men, being associated in their minds with fantastic wealth, natural wonders and magic" (Penrose 1952: 10). From the perspective of this essay, the East expressed conditions of symbolic extremes that contrasted with the controlled and civilized Christian heartland just as the "abnormal" contrasts with the "normal," as the more purely supernatural (both the very good and the very evil) contrasts with the mundane, or as the uncontrolled and unblessed wilderness contrasts with the sanctity of the settled plain. In other words, the medieval Christian view of the East associated geographical distance with supernatural distance and the untrammeled expression of universal powers in many dimensions. Thus, Asia, and especially India, were the setting of a great body of myths and fiction, including fabulous and marvelous tales of curious, inverted animals and monsters, of pygmies and giants, of men with feet turned backwards and eight toes on each foot, of headless creatures with eyes in their stomachs, of people who lived by the smell of food alone, and a variety of other anomalous beings.[2]

[2] These stories were collected by ancient Greek writers and figure prominently

FIGURE 6.1

The Turin map of the eleventh century. From C. R. Beazley, *Prince Henry the Navigator*, p. 77. Published by G. P. Putnam's Sons, 1923.

In accordance with the words of Genesis (II:8) and as the mappae-mundi frequently show, the terrestrial garden paradise, with the tree of immortal life (both of which were inaccessible to mortal man) was placed by many at the easternmost limit of the world "beyond all known land" at the edge of the ocean, thus associating the geographically distant east with the temporally distant past and with the origins of human time and conditions. Medie-

---

in the Romance of Alexander and in other medieval encyclopedias and collections of animal lore and legend.

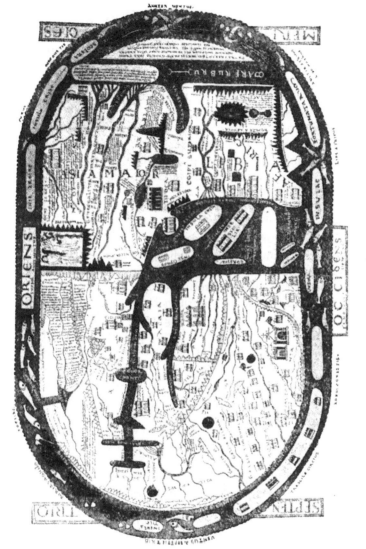

FIGURE 6.2

St. Sever Beatus map. East is at the top. From J. K. Wright, *Geographical Lore of the Time of the Crusades*, p. 69. Published by the American Geographical Society, 1925. Reprinted by permission of the publisher.

val tradition also located Gog and Magog, the savage tribes whose apocalyptic emergence at the Last Day would bring destruction to the world, in Asia, thereby associating the distant East with the finality of future time, too. To some medieval writers, the East, particularly India, was a land filled with the riches of the earth, abounding in gems and gold, minerals filled with magical powers as well as temporal wealth in the medieval view. To others the Orient was a place of poisonous animals, polluted waters, and death. Sometimes the images of the powers of the universe were combined, as when paradise is depicted as surrounded by a savage, trackless waste, infested with wild beasts and serpents (Wright 1925:71–73, 211–12, 261, 278; Kimble 1938:24–25, 30, 184–87; Penrose 1952:10–11; Manuel and Manuel 1971; Evans 1922).

Much of the fantasy and many of the fables of the East focused on the adventures of ancestral heroes who (like ancestral heroes of numerous non-European peoples) ventured into its extraordinary and supernatural domains; a related genre, also very popular, purported to tell of "actual" journeys by pious monks and other ordinary mortals to paradise (Wright 1925:263–64). The depictions of the head of Christ and the paradisiacal Garden of Eden on mappae-mundi set the stage, in a sense, for associations of extraordinary men known for great and sacred deeds with the supernatural East. The legend of Alexander the Great (particularly in his role as traveler and conqueror at the limits of the known world), was largely set in India and was given a Christian slant appropriate to the age by having the hero visit paradise. Far to the northeast, Alexander also enclosed the terrible Gog and Magog behind great walls and even dealt with Satan himself. The legend of St. Thomas the Apostle was also situated in India where the saint had "a shadowy but glorious career" as missionary and martyr (Penrose 1952:11). Prester John, famed as superlative king and Christian priest, superior in wisdom, wealth, and power to all other monarchs of the world and almost Christ-like in his personal piety, allegedly dwelled somewhere in the East in an immense domain whose rivers ran with gold and silver and jewels; the search for his miraculous and paradisiacal realm was a preoccupation of Western clerics and kings for centuries. A real-life, though still legendary, potentate whose domain again was situated at the farthermost east of the inhabited world was the Great Khan and the enticing city of Cambaluc (Peking), which replace the figure of Christ and the Garden of Eden on the Catalan Atlas of the mid-fourteenth century, reflecting the impact of medieval travelers to the Far East (Manuel and Manuel 1971:118; Baudet 1965:11–17, 43–45; Penrose 1952:11–13; Sanders 1978:11, 13–15, 40–43; Lovejoy 1948:99–135; Marshall and Williams 1982:173, 175).[3]

Until the discovery of the New World, the West seems to have received somewhat less attention as a distant place of extraordinary powers, perhaps because its land areas were concealed in the realm of encircling and limiting ocean and were known to be islands (the term also referred vaguely to any distant and remote land that could only be reached by a long sea voyage; see Ramsay 1972:111–12). Nonetheless, western islands contained their share of medieval cosmographical wonders, which also frequently fell within the general theme of paradisiacal conditions, though without the full weight of Biblical connotations and expressing more classical pagan attitudes. For all its wonders and riches, the East in the medieval mind was a fearsome place—immense and wild, a place of an Edenic paradise forever lost to man, and a place from which ultimate destruction would rage forth in the final apocalypse. Western islands, in contrast, though still the domain of the miraculous, the strange, and the curious, were generally envisioned in far gentler terms, as blessed settings for peaceful health and happiness that might be sought and even possibly obtained in a future characterized not by chaos but by perfected utopian existence.[4]

---

[3] China would acquire an extraordinary aura once again in the late sixteenth to eighteenth centuries when Western philosophers lauded the excellence of its moral and philosophical codes and institutions of government.

[4] The far northern reaches of Europe also entered the realm of fable with which all the most distant reaches of the known world were associated. Northern Scandinavia was inhabited by dwarfs, bearded women, Amazons, and monsters; and the "stiffened ocean" of the far northern seas was made menacing by great whirl-

CHAPTER 6

Myths of enchanted and enchanting islands derived from the
Greeks on the one hand and from maritime northern Europeans
on the other (e.g., the Celtic paradise of Avalon in the western
sea). The great submerged island of Atlantis had been the subject
of speculation since Plato, and the carefree life of the Fortunate
Islands or "Isles of the Blessed" were part of a general Hellenic
theme of a golden age that included the Elysian Fields, the death-
free, comfortable retreat for heroes that Homer located in an
ocean setting "at the end of the earth," but which Hesiod identified as an island (Manuel and Manuel 1971:87). To Isidore of Se-
ville, the Fortunate Islands, "in the Great Sea, . . . near the end of
the west" as the Catalan Atlas describes them, were so-called because they were filled with good things—grain, fruits, trees, with
food available without labor and a temperate and pleasant climate
(Sanders 1978:32–33).

Yet the most famous and most influential medieval island legend, probably entangled with that of the Fortunate Isles, involved
the Irish abbot, St. Brendan (Brenaind), a legendary hero of sorts
for the Western realm as the Eastern realm had its heroes (Figure
6.3). St. Brendan journeyed among enchanted isles and fantastic
seas to the west of Ireland until he reached the paradisiacal saints'
Land of Promise, a broad, spacious, and fruitful country where
night was unknown, to which the saint allegedly returned after
his earthly death and which was still placed on maps as late as
1755 (Ramsay 1972:77–81, 90; Wright 1925:212, 233–35, 262,
350–53, Babcock 1922; Penrose 1952:14).[5] Here too, as with the

pools and by islands of giants and loathsome monsters and spirits (Wright
1925:329, 248–49).
    [5] Consider, too, the legend of the seven bishops who fled from Moorish Spain
and discovered a beautiful island in the Atlantic on which they settled and built
seven cities; also the tale of the Island of Brazil (Breasil, Bersil, etc.), the most fertile and beautiful land on earth, though with tendencies to disappear once discovered (Babcock 1922:922; Ramsay 1972:90–91; Newton 1926:162–63). One of the
more fascinating aspects of the medieval view of islands was the long-existing
(from ca. A.D. 1000 to 1500) papal doctrine that argued that all known islands be-
longed to St. Peter's patrimony (a stance reminiscent of native chiefs' rights to
products of the sea). Therefore, the pope had the right to possess and dispose all
known western islands, generally referring to those in Northern Europe and the
Mediterranean close to and part of European settlement. This doctrine was ex-

218

FIGURE 6.3

An old German engraving depicting St. Brendan and his crew celebrating mass on the back of a gigantic fish between the Fortunate Isles and the Isle of St. Brendan. From E. and J. Lehner, *How They Saw the New World*, Table of Contents page. Published by Tudor Publishing Co., 1966. Reprinted by permission of Amiel Book Distributors Corp.

Fortunate Isles, is a land without care that bears considerable resemblance to the Paradise of Eden, but which associates the West with an emphasis on a fresh, fertile, and generous nature, in contrast with the harsh, forbidding, though gem-filled magic of the East. Similarly, as the East appears in medieval Christian thought as the place of origins and the place of final apocalypse, associated with the time of the beginning and the time of ending, so the idyllic islands of the West are places seemingly devoid not only of

panded to the Atlantic proper with the beginning of the great oceanic discoveries, when the new world of America was still viewed by Europeans as only a group of islands near the Asiatic landmass (Weckmann-Muñoz 1976:202–207).

death but also of time and of the changes and imperfections, the challenges and complexities caused by time. (It is useful to remember at this point that the utopian societies of the sixteenth and seventeenth centuries, such as Harrington's *Oceana*, More's *Utopia*, and Bacon's *New Atlantis*, were located to the west in distant seas; see Baudet 1965:32–35).

Although they differed in characterization, supernatural lands and some form of paradise could be reached by traveling either east or west. Of the two directions, the East, situated significantly at the top of mappae-mundi, though vast in scope, was a definitely more fixed, more stabilized, and more definitive symbolically charged direction and locale in medieval thought. The West was more elusive, literally veiled in mists. The East, though equally invisible over the horizon, was much more substantial and certainly attracted more attention. The East was more of a power-filled *place*; indeed, it was the best recognized geographically distant, supernaturally charged realm. As such, the East was also the place to be visited by identifiable heroes and the place that yielded real and tangible gems, spices, and silks, as well as intangible fables, monsters, and sacred settings. In addition, the East was substantially linked by land to Europe, and both were in a sense encircled by and bound into a common cosmic setting not only by European (and Asiatic) thought, but also by the ocean waters.

The West, in contrast, was more a symbolically significant *direction*, a direction that immediately left the orientation and stability of terra firma, though one that, if pursued, could also lead eventually to supernatural peripheral island end points (which, however, were basically elusive and had yielded little tangible evidence of their reality). The obvious logic of Columbus's voyages, as every schoolchild knows, lay in combining (pinning down?) the directionality of the West with the "placement" of the East, but it was a rationale that not only followed geographical and cartographical reasonings but also recognized traditional cosmological logic in which, if one, hero-like, sought distant sources of riches and power ("paradise"), the best *place* to reach was the Orient, which, at least in this "paradisiacal sense," is now devoid of directional significance and contains only the symbolism of its placement in geographically distant space.[6]

The same can be said, of course, of the mystical islands set somewhere in the Western Sea; they, too, were supernatural places "somewhere" in geographically distant space, an uncertain somewhere that logically might approach the most definite, best known placement in distance, that of the Orient, as some medieval writers in fact indicated (Weckmann-Muñoz 1976:202). Thus the identification of where one was, after traveling oceanward, could be either Oriental, or insular, or both, as, of course, was the initial assumption of the first hero-explorers to successfully venture to those places by that direction.[7]

In this context, the Orient does not really reassume a directionality for its location until it is realized that the places contacted by western ocean travel were indeed not Oriental but separate and distinct; i.e., until Columbus was replaced by Vespucci (Quinn 1976:639–40, 651). Only then does the westerly direction lead to a distinctive western locale that, ipso facto, reassigns the Orient, or better said, the significance of the Orient, to its own directional East. At the same time, European cosmography was faced with the necessity of symbolically absorbing and defining these newly recognized distant "places of the West," a culturally unique task which, in effect, required not only the recognition but the creation or invention of a new spatially and perhaps temporally distant supernatural domain in the geographical-cosmological

[6] "Columbus always insisted that his 'execution of the affair of the Indies' was a fulfillment of prophecies in Isaiah and not a matter of mere reason, mathematics and maps" (Manuel and Manuel 1971:119) It is also pertinent to remember that even though it was generally agreed that paradise was in Asia, it was not a universal belief, nor was there much uniformity concerning its location even in Asia. Throughout the Middle Ages alternative opinions were offered placing paradise beyond the encircling ocean to both east or west, or perhaps beyond the torrid equatorial zone, or on an island *beyond* the easternmost limits of the habitable world. Its exact whereabouts was not necessarily a crucial issue (see Wright 1925:262).

[7] Consider the initial identification of Caribbean islands as close to the Asian coast and the assumption that portions of the mainland (Florida, Yucatán) were islands, as well as Columbus' conviction, elaborately argued with all the appropriate fine points of medieval cosmology, that he had found the site of paradise on a high point near the Orinoco (Weckmann-Muñoz 1976, Manuel and Manuel 1971:118; Quinn 1976:636–39).

periphery of the European cosmos (Quinn 1976; O'Gorman 1961). In this process, of course, Europe redefined itself. "It is not the mere existence of unknown lands—timeless, from any human viewpoint—nor even the theoretical recognition of their existence, but the irresistible impulse to tear these lands from their obscurity at just that particular moment which defines the Age of Discoveries as a historic turning point" (Goldstein 1976:32). [8]

This newly discovered and created domain also placed Europe strongly in the center of a cosmography that now had a peripheral symmetry of *both directional* West and East and *locational* West and East. This concentricity of center and peripheries came to replace, at least for a while, the polar positioning of sacred heartland (Europe) versus supernatural hinterland (the Orient) that prevailed in medieval cosmology. This medieval polarity is reflected in the format of the mappae-mundi which, though apparently focused on the center (the European *axis mundi* of Jerusalem) seem to give equal symbolic recognition to the top (or East), defined by the powerful symbols of paradise or the head of Christ. With the creation of the "New" world, the East and the Center were joined by a definite West, and at times both East and West held important symbolic significance. (Lovejoy 1948; Baudet 1965:43-44). Ultimately, however, a new polarity would emerge as the East began to be relegated to a symbolic backwater in which it would be increasingly viewed as the setting for bizarre and fanatic religions and as representative of cultural stagnation and conservatism (Marshall and Williams 1982:94, 113–15, 128–31), while the West would shine forth as the major supernatural hinterland balancing the sacred European heartland. [9]

Not surprisingly, the initial attempts to fashion and design this new supernatural realm assumed the character of a work of intel-

[8] "Geography in the Renaissance was not a discipline separate from chronology, astrology, theology, mathematics, and astronomy" (Johnson 1976:616).

[9] A theory of an east–west movement was also expressed by some writers in the Middle Ages, who argued with an apocalyptic view that the order of cosmological-historical time and place moved in series such that civilization flowed from east to west. Thus when the movement of civilization from the East (Biblical era) to the Greeks, to the Romans, reached the uttermost limits of the West, the human race would meet its end, just as the "light of heaven" moves from eastern origins to western decline (Wright 1925:233–35).

lectual *bricolage* as a diverse assortment of classical, Biblical, and medieval concepts derived from the original characterizations of the Western isles and the supernaturally well established Orient were roughly fitted together to form a cosmographical-philosophical structure with many loose fittings and rough edges that are still reflected in the variety of interpretive approaches taken to the perennial subject of the "meaning of the New World in European perspective." Ultimately, as cosmological construction continued, the prevailing view, though still greatly mixed and varied, seems to have hoped to combine the more beneficial aspects of both the medieval East and West, for the New World was soon expected to offer a combination of tangible riches and utopian existence (not excluding the destruction of perceived evils necessary to achieve this).[10] In a sense, it was expected to combine the wealth and wonder of medieval India with the alleged beneficent ease of the Fortunate Isles. Simultaneously, the emerging Renaissance culture of Europe developed an expanded sense of space as its western horizon achieved a greater clarity and definitiveness and receded to a greater distance from the homeland or, perhaps better said, acquired a *definite* distance from the homeland (Goldstein 1976:31). In addition, the passage of the caravels through this once timeless space now became not only an adventure of physical duration but also a progression into a state of cosmological time.[11]

Attempts to identify the cosmological time of the new Western world were an important variable determining the interpretation and significance accorded by Europeans not only to the landscape and material resources of this land but also to its inhabitants. Or perhaps the reverse position is more accurate, i.e., the interpretation and significance accorded by Europeans to this new cos-

[10] As Baudet (1965) and others have repeatedly emphasized, the highly influential myths of the glorification and "noble savagery" of the Indian that "covered the distant earthly paradises with a veil of enchantment through which they were seen as the home of the blessed and the elect" formed no hindrance to, and could exist comfortably alongside, an accompanying wholesale destruction and ruthless exploitation of these same indigenes.

[11] The ocean had now become a link between places, no longer a limiting boundary; see Goldstein 1965; Johnson 1976:624–26; O'Gorman 1961:67, 131–32, 145.

mological world determined the identification of the cosmological time attributed to the new locale. For in the era of initial contact, exploration, and identification (which is the era of interest here), "time" to Europeans was still part and parcel of a particular European cultural tradition rooted in classical antiquity and Judeo-Christian sacrality. Time in European culture had not yet been neutralized, generalized (separated from meaningful events), secularized, or universalized; time was still a specific part of Judeo-Christian sacred history, just as time is conceived as a culture-specific variable in each of the diverse "sacred histories" of non-Western traditional societies. This kind of time, as Fabian has emphasized, was still a means of celebrating select mythical and historical events and circumstances; of recounting chronicle as well as chronology (1983:2, 13).

In medieval Christian cosmology the East was heavily imbued with sacred time; it was the source both of the origins of man and of the anticipated final extinction. The medieval West, with its idyllic islands, was essentially without time, a temporally floating realm characterized solely by the cultural-environmental contrasts afforded by comparison of an idealized natural paradise with realized social living. In creating a new cosmological world in the newly substantiated Western locale, even though characteristics of the Orient as well as of the West were applied, the major emphasis lay again in establishing cultural-environmental contrast with European reality, whether in terms of abundant tangible riches, or extreme social and moral conditions of great goodness or great evil, or a hoped for personal immortality (the fountain of youth syndrome). Where these contrasts (and, thus, the New World), were situated temporally could vary so long as the temporal situating itself was also contrastive, i.e., was not in the here and now of the European present. Thus we find that the distant Western realm (not unlike the East) is accorded a considerable range of extraordinary identifications, some of which are set in temporal situations associated with past conditions, and some in temporal situations associated with anticipated future conditions.

As a place of "paradise existing" the New World and its inhabitants represented a life prior to the Fall from Grace that was "not yet" corrupt and "still" in ideal harmony. As setting for "paradise to come" (utopia) the New World was a place "not yet" perfect but anticipating ideal harmony (Baudet 1965). As a place also of savage wilderness beyond the pale of any form of paradise, the New World provided a glimpse of ancient and primordial savage rudeness as did the fabled wildmen of medieval Europe who also lurked and crept in the uncontrolled wildness beyond the borders of settled life. In more specifically temporal terms, as exemplifying idyllic life before the Fall the New World existed *before* sacred time, i.e., prior to the beginning of the truly human time (origins) of fallible man. As exemplifying idolatrous and pagan life beyond (bereft or ignorant of) Christianity, the New World also stood *beyond* sacred time, i.e., distant and apart from the moral and spiritual enlightenment and salvation that Christian sacred time marked and celebrated. As exemplifying satanic and tabooed existence (e.g., cannibalism) the New World even stood *against* sacred time, i.e., opposed to the respectable order and progressive improvement (salvation) of the Christian universe defined by sacred time (Bucher 1981:54, 63, 77, 79).[12]

If position in time was variable, and not in itself an immediate or crucial identifying factor for the cosmological creation and identification of this new geographically distant domain, the cosmological environment was of greater interest, and the earliest observers of the American world became very involved with the business of identifying the characteristics of its animate and inanimate setting. Here again both classical antiquity and the Judeo-Christian medieval heritage supplied the basic guidelines. Fundamental were concepts of paradise and wilderness, both of which depicted strong contrasts to settled medieval Christian (European) life, both of which had been identified with the geographically distant and supernaturally potent East and with a

---

[12] The recognition of a range of temporal associations that can be applied more or less simultaneously has continued to be characteristic of Western views of the Western Hemisphere. There has been, on the one hand, the frequent emphasis on native inhabitants and their customs (whether still existent or not) as replication of concepts associated with past or ancient time. On the other hand, particularly as the continent becomes devoid of native inhabitants and is increasingly colonized by Europeans, cosmological time becomes that of the future, even as secular or historical time and the "course of Empire" move west, too.

temporally earlier Mediterranean and Biblical heritage, and both of which, though they may seem at first to be antithetical, are replete with the symbolism of supernatural power in its purest or most refined forms (the blessed and the cursed, the divinely good or divinely evil, the haunt of God or the haunt of the Devil, the place of beasts and the place of saints; Williams 1962). As we have seen, a form of paradise already held Western connotations prior to the discoveries, but the attribution of wilderness and its qualities to the West was new and clearly part of the effort to create and identify a new cosmological locale. Similarly, the creatures who inhabited the wilderness in traditional belief and experience provided prototypes for identification of New World indigenes. Indeed, from the perspective of the fate of natives, the wilderness perspective is the most important, although the paradisiacal view of the New World strongly influenced the ideology of European colonization.[13]

As is well known, Mediterranean and European cosmology traditionally defined the territory beyond the oikoumene somewhat in the manner of zones inhabited by beings evidencing varying degrees of physical and behavioral contrast (inversion) with settled and civilized life. To the writers of the Greek and Roman worlds of classical antiquity, as well as to compilers of medieval encyclopedias and chronicles, the most distant frontiers (generally inland and interior) that lay beyond the oikoumene and its

[13] Since both wilderness and paradise were expressions of the extremes of universal power as it is expressed outside the borders of ordered, controlled, and settled society, it is not really contradictory to find them in close juxtaposition and applied to a common setting. Traditional Eastern and European interpretations already did so. In the medieval East the Garden of Paradise was thought to be surrounded by harsh and forbidding trackless wastes, while in the Biblical origins of Judaic myth wilderness is a potential paradise or a paradise lost, and must be endured before entry into a new form of Promised Land can be achieved. Punishment and desire can go hand in hand (see Williams 1962). Similarly, the interpretation of the characteristics of indigenous New World inhabitants could derive from several perspectives that, though seemingly opposite or contradictory, in fact are parallel or conjoined and, like the paradise/wilderness constructs, could be simultaneously entertained (Jaenen 1982). Seeing these perspectives as conjoined or juxtaposed rather than opposite or contradictory goes somewhat counter to the usual emphasis on a single or "clustered" theme or on opposed themes for understanding the New World and its inhabitants (see Jaenen 1982:44 for a summary of prevailing views).

most immediate hinterland were, because they were remote, places of fable and the habitat of beings that were definitely "non-normal," being either physically or morally deformed (lotus-eaters and cannibals, cyclops and dwarfs), and of creatures that were definitely "non-natural" (ants alleged to be bigger than foxes, griffins; Wright 1925:37–38, 257, 329; Casson 1974). Those "barbarians" who lived closer to the oikoumene or its territorial outskirts were human, but considered "below normal" in the sense that they lacked the moral and organizational attributes of settled and lawfully ordered society (*Romanitas*). They were deemed instead to be warlike and predatory, ferocious and treacherous, unpredictable and cruel, the incarnation of perfidy and savagery, and indicative of the worst in human life.

As Catholic Christianity became established as the ideological underpinning of the later Roman Empire and the early Middle Ages, the contrast held religious connotations: barbarians now were pagans or members of Aryan Christianity, which had been declared heretical by the Catholic Church (Jones 1971). In the later Middle Ages the religious connotation diminished somewhat and the term reverted to meanings closer to the classical emphasis on ferocity and/or unrefined conduct. Yet the most familiar barbarians of the thirteenth and fourteenth centuries were the Tartars of the East who were not only awesomely ferocious but also pagan and posed a cosmological and physical threat to civilized Europe likened to that of Gog and Magog, and thus of the Devil himself, who, though vanquished and disarmed "in the most important and puissant places of his kingdom . . . hath retired himself into the most remote parts" wherein he still rules (Acosta 1588, quoted in Taussig 1980a:169; see also Jones 1971:399–400; Pagden 1982:24).

Fabled deformed creatures of the very distant lands, being so far away and beyond expectations of direct contact with the oikoumene, served mainly as markers for "other worlds" that had little direct bearing on the known world of Christian European human beings. They posed no direct threat and were of no direct importance other than identifying by symbolic inversion (deformity and exaggeration), the "extreme" conditions and absence of "control" that correlated with far distance. In contrast, in the experience of classical and medieval Europe, conditions and contrasts posed by barbarians definitely posed more of a direct problem or carried a more immediately significant message, since barbarians, unlike deformed monsters or super creatures, were closer geographically and were in direct interaction with established society. Simple observation and incredulous amazement were not enough; something had to be done about them.

Particularly in the earlier medieval centuries, barbarians were considered as direct moral and physical threats to established life that required several kinds of active attention. On the one hand, barbarians could serve as vehicles for demonstrating the benefits and moral salvation of civilized life if they could be remade ("saved") to be trustworthy, peaceful, and believers in the true faith. Barbarians thus provided moral and territorial testing grounds for the rightness and righteousness of ordered Christian life. On the other hand, if these attempts failed, barbarians could be legitimately regarded as permanently retarded infants or as sources of invincible diabolical evil and placed permanently beyond the cultural pale either to be pitied and tended in a resigned manner or to be marked for permanent enmity and, if possible, destruction (Jones 1971:397–99; Pagden 1982:15–21).

Barbarians as fields for *testing* the validity of moral, ordered society also contrast with the traditional wild men of medieval European myth, literature, and credulous peasant belief, for wild men, although also outside of civilized life, simply provide a *contrast* with its virtues and expectations. Wild men were portrayed as content with their own habitats in the most remote and uninhabited areas of forested mountain or desert wilderness, yet they and their wilderness were viewed intellectually as falling within the interstices of settled life, and in this sense were part of the overall established order. Wild men themselves were believed to live in a primordial and unsocial manner, without the benefit of hearth and home and kinsmen, yet did not directly threaten social order. They were not as actively warlike and destructively intrusive as barbarians (although they could be disruptive tricksters), either in legend or in the cases of those unfortunate outcasts who fit the description in real life (Bernheimer 1952:16). Nothing needed be done about them, although those who, in myth or legend, ventured into their domains could expect unpleasantness or, alternatively, find oracular and magical insights if the wild and raving man of the wilderness was also regarded as a prophet (ibid., p. 13; White 1972:21; prophecy, of course, has long been one of the attributes of hermits and others who have made the wilderness their home).

Wild men were said to be nude and hairy in appearance, lacking speech and reason, and living on raw meat, acorns, and berries, and provided the antithetical or inverted image of "nature" and "natural beast," or of "one without God's grace," for society's thesis of "culture" or "civilized (socialized) man" or "blessed man" in an overall symbolic imagery that acknowledged the validity of both natural and cultural, wild and civilized, in the order of things, and could contain both. Barbarians, on the other hand, though possibly salvageable, stood closer to genuine evil as an active opposition to society's genuine good (Pagden 1982:21–22; White 1972). Both were anomalous, and thus power-filled: wild men were not fully human, yet neither were they fully animal; barbarians were certainly not fully good nor were they judged hopelessly, irredeemably, and fully evil without strong cause. Both could be seen as containing expressions of exceptional supernatural power, of partaking of the wild, unknown, unblessed, and therefore demon-filled realms beyond that world already sancioned by the Christian God's plan of salvation.

If fabled creatures, barbarians hovering somewhere between potential good and probable evil, and wild men defined ambiguously as neither cultured man nor natural animal but partially both (natural man or cultural, e.g., tricky, beast) inhabited the far distant realms, frontier regions, and desolate wildernesses, respectively, of the classical and medieval geographical and cosmographical world, then such are the likely interpretations to be accorded to inhabitants of the new Western geographical and cosmological realm, particularly in the first century or so of its discovery, exploration, and "creation" prior to the Enlightenment. As Boon has recently emphasized (1982), Enlightenment interpretations of geographically distant places and peoples of the New World differed significantly from those of the pre-Enlightenment era. In Boon's analysis, the pre-Enlightenment medieval and Renaissance perspective essentially interpreted the diversity of behaviors and conditions evidenced by the New World as part of the same pattern of sacred–secular life as existed in Europe without "territorializing" or considering geographical distance as a significant independent variable. Conversely, the Enlightenment perspective emphasized geographical distance and "natural" remoteness and "otherness" as essential to the definition of the New World as an exotic antithesis to European culture, which was viewed as an entity in itself (1982:34–44; see White 1972:31 regarding the "fictionalizing" of the concept of wilderness).

The dichotomy between Enlightenment and pre-Enlightenment interpretations recognized by Boon is crucial for a general understanding of relationships between Europe and the West (see also Chaunu 1979:vii, 205). Though I am in general agreement with him, I would prefer to describe the conditions of the dichotomy somewhat differently. In the pre-Enlightenment era, I suggest, the New World was accepted conceptually as part of the cosmographically real world of European Christendom in the same sense that the Orient or far distant realms such as Scandinavia or Russia had traditionally been accepted as part of the cosmographically real world, i.e., because they were faraway lands where, as a reflection of their distance, demons or fabulous creatures lived ("The strange, the fantastic, and the unreal were familiar and to that extent real," Quinn 1976:636). In other words, the Orient and the West (and other distant domains to the north and south) formed a single entity with Europe because the symbolism accorded them was a direct result of their geographical distance from the European heartland. In the Enlightenment view, as Boon notes, this entity was divided into two parts: the single reality of the European heartland and the remote "other," which was not characterized as a "real" geographically distant cosmographical setting as much as it was created and utilized by social philosophers and political commentators to serve as a locational commentary on the problems of European society. From this point on, geographically distant lands and their inhabitants began to lose sacred cosmographical significance, even as European time became secularized too, and the role accorded to New World in-

FIGURE 6.4

Imaginary picture of the crook-backed ox (buffalo) of America from a sixteenth-century engraving. From E. and J. Lehner, *How They Saw The New World*, p. 123. Published by Tudor Publishing Co., 1966. Reprinted by permission of Amiel Book Distributors Corp.

habitants and their lifestyles assumed different dimensions, changing from the broadly "sacralized" roles of symbolically inverted monsters, wild men, or barbarians, to the cynical ironies of the concept of the "Noble Savage" and the taxonomies of natural historians, both of which were more appropriate to the New World's change of status in an increasingly secularized and exploitative European world view (White 1976).

As part of the enlarged Christian cosmography of the pre-Enlightenment, however, the inhabitants of the geographically distant New World were accorded diverse interpretations just as medieval Europe had diverse "others" in its geographical hinterlands. In the initial days of discovery and exploration the ferocious lushness and climatic violence of the equatorial New World, the cold "white terror" of its north and the incredible and miraculous powers reportedly contained in America's natural products, aroused the wonder and amazement of the newcomers.[14] Similarly, its strange natives and curious animals were also

[14] Something of the extraordinary qualities with which this new cosmograph-

interpreted as fabulous or devilish anomalies or as supernatural
denizens of myths and legends (Amazons, giants who ate drag-
ons, ageless benefactors of fountains of youth, etc.; Quinn
1976:641; Hand 1976:47, 52; White 1976:125; Jones 1964:55–57,
61–70).

When interpretations turned simply to points of behavioral
contrast between natives and Europeans, the relative acceptance
that had existed between European wild men as anomalous inhabitants of the natural wilderness, and settled villagers and
townsmen as purveyors of civilized social life was extended,
sometimes even with an element of admiration, to the New
World to define relationships between native and European (e.g.,
early English views of North American Indians as backward but
receptive to peaceful contact and exchange). When interpretations turned to points of moral testing, natives who failed to at-
tain European standards of righteous and ordered Christian living could be regarded as beast-like or barbaric "children"
incapable of learning.

In more extreme cases, when moral excesses (idolatry, cannibalism, sexual promiscuity) were observed or when native reactions became more sanguinary, they were feared as powerful
agents of the Christian Devil (who, like Indians, flourished in the
"most remote parts" of the world) for whom extermination or at
least persistent combating of diabolical evil for the sake of Christian good was approved behavior (see Taussig 1980a:169–70;
Jones 1964:55–61; Pearce 1965:20–24 regarding European fears of
natives as products of the Devil; see also Rosaldo 1978 for an excellent parallel discussion of European attitudes towards natives
of the Philippines). It is noteworthy, however, that in pursuing
the perceived evils of the Devil the Spaniards also granted him his
due. "No doubt the Indians stood in awe of the Spaniards and
perhaps regarded them as quasi-divine. But the Spaniards, too,
were entranced by the power of the Indians' demons. In their re-
morseless extirpation of idolatry, as much as in *their resort to Indian*

---

ical realm was believed to be endowed can be glimpsed in the wonderful cures for
practically any and all diseases, particularly those previously declared incurable,
claimed by European physicians for the plants, animals, medicinal stones, herbs,
and trees of the New World (see Jones 1964:37–38).

magic for healing and divination, the Spanish bestowed a strange power on their subjects. In conquering the Indians they granted them the power of their supernatural foe, the devil" (Taussig 1980a:170, my emphasis; 1980b:229).[15]

As many writers have observed, the diverse images of New World Indians made it difficult for European observers and scholars to reach consensus regarding the nature of the New World inhabitants. Virtually the only point of commonality lay in the interpretation of Indians as anomalous and ambiguous beings— as men, but men *"without* God, *without* law, and *without* breeches" (Bucher 1981:144; White 1976: 125–26), i.e., men with either no god or with the devil, with either social chaos or natural order, and with a simple life without need for cultural artifice. Such a state could only be achieved outside the Christian oikoumene on cosmological frontiers spatially-temporally distant from the heartland. Eventually, as Europeans gradually became better acquainted with the New World, the rather ambiguous temporal domain associated with the West increasingly clarified and provided a means for consolidating behavioral anomalousness in the concept of primitivism, that is, in the idea that New World natives were men living as in an earlier era, one that was untilled and undeveloped and very like the time of Abraham, or was reflected in the Greco-Roman past. In arriving at this conclusion, the New World was finally settled fairly decisively in sacred time as an exemplar of an age of origins, and with this final cosmological setting passed onto the secular stage of the Age of Enlightenment where further intellectual permutations awaited (Marshall and Williams 1982:187–226; see note 12).

The eighteenth century, with its reinvention and re-creation of the significance of geographically distant peoples and places as essentially "non-peoples" and "non-places," as merely philosophically useful constructs for interpreting the reality of European life (e.g., the "Noble Savage" as analyzed by White 1976), did not en-

---

[15] One of the most intriguing reverse variations on this perspective is the Protestant interpretation of the Spanish Catholic impact on the New World as exemplative of a destructive diabolical temptation by papal "devils" of naive inhabitants comparable to the original temptation and consequent Edenic fall of original innocents (Bucher 1981; Boon 1982.38).

tirely negate the earlier cosmological assessment of the distant West as a blissful, ageless, pagan paradise on some fabled but elusive Fortunate Isle. As the eighteenth century expanded the extent of secularized overseas territory it simply pushed the fabled frontiers still farther away until the paradisiacal Isle was finally located in the still alien watery immensity of the Pacific world that lay beyond the difficult entrance through the Strait of Magellan (traditionally believed to be guarded by a race of giants, appropriately enough). Paradise was on Tahiti, or more accurately, paradise was fantasized in the public reaction to the published journal of Louis Antoine de Bougainville describing what he called *La Nouvelle Cythère* (the birthplace of the Greek goddess of love). Unfortunately, as expressed both in classical legend and in the mores of native Polynesia the paradise of the West was by definition non-Christian or pre-Christian. Therefore, this new "sacred" Western paradise lying beyond Christian cosmography was short-lived, and ultimately remained as elusive as the Blessed Isles themselves, for the sometimes unparadisiacal diversity in behavior and characteristics of different islanders—and the by-now established Christian missionary perspective on the unwholesome qualities of geographical distance in general—came to triumph in Polynesia, too (Daws 1974; Marshall and Williams 1982:258–96).

Traditional Christian cosmography also stopped short of black Africa, with the important exception of Ethiopia, one of several possible locations for the elusive kingdom of Prester John and/or the Garden of Eden. Ethiopia in this sense was cosmologically and geographically associated with Asia during the medieval centuries (when Ethiopia and India were often confused, and the geographical extent of Africa underestimated), and the characteristics of its inhabitants, being proximate to such glorious settings, were generally admired in the usual mix of marvels and monsters associated with distant magical locales (Wright 1925:302–304). The fine qualities of Ethiopians had been lauded earlier in classical times, too. In Homer they are mentioned in connection with a feast of the gods, who repaired south to the shores of the eastern ocean to enjoy their sacrifices. Herodotus, introducing an element of fabulous extremes, does so positively and describes certain Ethiopians as the tallest and handsomest men in the world blessed with longevity thanks to a health-giving fountain and whose land held abundant gold.[16]

The rest of sub-Saharan Africa, which was basically unknown, never received such plaudits, except as the source, somewhere, of the medieval El Dorado or River of Gold (Penrose 1952:13). On the contrary, according to Herodotus and other writers, here were monstrous beings of a different sort, troglodytes who ate reptiles, others who were ostrich-eaters or locust-fanciers, people with no heads or with feet like thongs, creatures with the bodies of men but living the life of beasts; in other words, the usual fantastic inhabitants of one of the most remote corners of the world that lay well beyond any civilized intercourse and proximate especially to the inhospitable torrid zone. To be sure, black Africans lived in Europe in both classical and medieval times as slaves or human curiosities, but their country and its indigenous inhabitants were unknown and remained part of the wilderness outside Christendom. It was a strange place, fearfully mystical, without Christian norms or society, irrevocably uncultured and uncultivated, particularly since Africans were black, not to mention naked, allegedly cannibalistic, and given to strange diets in their homelands (Marshall and Williams 1982:37; Oakes 1944:193).

Blackness, a color with a range of negative, even evil, associations in medieval thought (including death, the Devil, evil magic), had long evoked distaste, even revulsion, towards Africans (Marshall and Williams 1982:35–36). The Biblical account of Ham, the son of Noah, who was banished accursed into the wilderness, there to become the ancestor of the black race, unequivocally removed black-skinned Africans from the realms of the blessed. When Europeans finally began more sustained contact with the coasts of the Dark Continent they found little to ameliorate the preconceived picture: hellish heat, monstrous and incredible animals, and natives living in a seemingly godless (and, therefore, beastly) state (ibid., p. 34). They "found" a land that exemplified, on the one hand, the spiritual epitome of the Old Testament wilderness, a place totally devoid of God's grace and

[16] Other Ethiopians were accorded less complimentary treatment as curious and monstrous beings, reputations that lasted into the Middle Ages (Wright 1925).

blessing, and, on the other, a fabled land of deformed and exaggerated nonhuman marvels of the sort reserved for the lands beyond the ends of the known earth. Small wonder the primary interest of Europeans in black Africa for so long was as a source of "unhuman" labor (Oakes 1944; George 1958).

In the native view of the initial stages of the ultimate clash of cultures, Europeans materialized from intangible cosmographical and cosmological distance, from across the sea or out of the sky, supernaturally powerful, knowledgeable, surrounded by the material riches that evidenced their magical superiority. Arriving in this manner, they personified the divinity or spiritual aspect of human experience—ancestors or spirits of the dead or wise strangers who brought elements of the power of geographical distance to the native heartland. In the European perspective of the same experience, Europeans traveled from their own heartland to extraordinary cosmographical frontiers beyond the boundary of sacred Christendom, and indigenous peoples were encountered in situ as the denizens of such supernaturally charged realms. As such, natives generally came to personify neither ancestral spirits nor knowledgeable supermen (neither Prester John nor the Garden of Eden ever materialized, though prospects for a utopian paradise lingered), but the intangible and tangible qualities of monsters, wild men, or barbarians of the uncultured, uncivilized and devil-ridden medieval frontier wilderness. They were, therefore, considered closer (or identical) to demonic and animalistic anomalies of European cosmology than to its more beneficent spiritual beings.

In the initial stages of the conjunction of Europeans and natives, then, natives enhanced the humanity of the newcomers with supernatural attributes that they both revered and feared, while Europeans usually degraded the humanity of their hosts with supernatural attributes that they both despised and feared. The moment marked a major event, a literally cosmological event, in the sacred time of both groups, for both recognized the extraordinary power inherent in the other. For the natives, Europeans expressed an exceptional aura evidenced in their knowledge and wealth; for the Europeans, natives expressed the demonology of the pagan universe. Unfortunately, given such opposed interpretations, this meeting of cosmographical frontiers also marked the advent of the last era in traditional sacred time for both.

Merchants, Friars, and Other Heroes

During the Middle Ages, depending on the time and the circumstances, Europeans from all walks of life were willing, even eager, travelers even though journeys were always perilous undertakings. Practitioners of the *peregrinatio* consigned themselves to endless travel without specific earthly destination, earnest pilgrims streamed to numerous sacred shrines and to the Holy Land, and the years of the Crusades saw thousands on the move— nobles, townsmen, and peasantry alike. Motives were undoubtedly varied, and included a mix of personal piety, escapism or automatic "following the crowd," religious obligation, political prestige, desire for adventure and "to see the world," and possibly, for some, economic benefit.

The peregrinatio, pilgrimages and the Crusades, of course, were all at least formally religious in tone and purpose, and were conducted within the territorial borders or sacred precepts of Christendom which recognized Jerusalem and the Near East as holy centers. Each in its own way was a means of bringing the traveler closer to a sacred source, whether it be the final heavenly existence at the end of the peregrini's wanderings or a more immediate earthly setting at a holy shrine or at the Christian *axis mundi*. Such journeying was also conducted within a sacred or scriptural landscape of either the present or the past such that travelers' accounts, to the discomfort of later geographers, historians, and anthropologists, may accord far more space to holy sites visited and relics adored, to pious rituals conducted and states of grace enjoyed, than to the "reality" of daily life in the cities and countryside traversed.

Travel beyond the limits of Christendom was another matter, in degree if not in kind. For one thing, the setting was different. The Mediterranean world was a populous center surrounded by relative emptiness: by the ocean with its fabulous islands to the west; by extensive, indeed colossal, stretches of thinly inhabited

Central Asian steppes and desert to the East; and by the immensity (by current transportation modes) of the Sahara and the uncertain vagueness of whatever lay beyond the Sahara to the south (Chaunu 1979:215; Braudel 1972:171). The Christian world was viewed as a sacred heartland surrounded by wilderness harboring a supernatural landscape filled with pagans and demons. The mundane world of everyday life at home was contrasted with stories of the fabulous monsters, tremendous riches, and awesome potentates that existed "far away." Compared to the many who journeyed within Christendom, only a few of a special kind of traveler were willing to risk excessive physical hardships and dangers, the spiritual threat of evil spirits, and encounters both with the strangeness of foreign peoples and the sometimes erratic greatness of distant kings.

In the world of popular legend and sacred history such travelers were "ancestral heroes," either great conquerors such as Alexander, who by medieval times had also been accorded aspects of the supernatural himself, or great religious figures such as St. Thomas and St. Bartholomew (in India) or St. Brendan, or lesser religious figures such as the hermits and recluses who sought salvation in the wilderness or the pious monks who allegedly traveled to paradise and back or sought the place "where the earth joins the sky" (Wright 1925:263). In the "real world" of long-distance contacts they were physicians and merchants, holy hermits and friars, as well as men and women of lesser station (Rowbotham 1942:22). Religious figures and merchants probably often served common roles to some extent, particularly as diplomats. Both members of religious orders (such as John of Plano Carpini, William of Rubruck, John of Monte Corvino and a number of others) and ostensible merchants (such as the Polos and merchants from Genoa) were sent as papal ambassadors or royal political agents to the camps and courts of the Mongol Khans of central and east Asia (who tended to regard them in turn more as vassals paying homage) and served as high-level foreign advisers and learned "men from afar" to distant imperial courts, as did the Jesuit fathers three centuries later (Lopez 1943:165–66; Beazley 1901, 1906; Meyendorff 1926:118, note 2).

The high point of such long-distance adventuring was short-lived, occurring from the mid-thirteenth to mid-fourteenth centuries (*ca.* 1245–1345) when Europe and the East could effect direct contact as a result of the western extension of the Mongol "empire," and when traveling wise men ("priests, physicians, and learned men") were exempt from taxes along the overland routes carved out by Genghis Khan (Rowbotham 1942:22; Power 1926:152). After the dissolution of this political network and the disruption of travel, Europe reverted more and more to the exaggerated elements associated with distance, and the fables associated with the *Book of Sir John de Mandeville* began to outweigh in general popularity the direct observations recorded in legitimate travel accounts such as the *Travels of Marco Polo* or the *Descriptio Orientalium Partium* of Odoric of Pordenone, though the latter works still remained influential among educated elite (Chaunu 1979:78, Penrose 1952:16).

The travelers themselves, regardless of their specific identification as freelance missionaries, traders, or high-level couriers and diplomats, all had to become experts in long-distance travel. Thus, merchants were often also mariners and experts in both trade and seamanship, while overland travelers for their own survival undoubtedly had to become skilled in the arts of thirteenth-century caravan travel and "roughing it," coping with thieves, bad weather, and river crossings, "traveling over roads that were often no more than trails, sleeping in the open air, existing on cooked millet and melted snow . . ." (Rowbotham 1942:25, describing a trip by William of Rubruck; see also Chaunu 1979:61), not to mention traveling for extensive periods of time.[17]

As travelers, all probably combined elements of their diverse occupations to some extent. Friars had to obtain means to sustain themselves materially and in some cases carried rich gifts for Tartar hosts, while European merchants, though hardly given to much explicit proselytizing, carried ideological identification as Christian (or Jewish) traders in the polytheistic realms of the East. Friars and merchants traveled together for safety, sometimes even on the same mission, as did Friar John of Monte Cor-

[17] A Venetian describing Persia a few centuries later wrote, "one can travel through this land for four months without leaving it" (Braudel 1972:173).

vino and his companion, Peter of Lucalongo (a "great merchant" and "faithful Christian"), who were sent to the heads of state of the Tartar world. Both friars and merchants transported tangible valuables, including diplomatic letters, intangible ideas, information, and diplomatic intelligence. Both found shelter in Mongol post stops and in the lonely Christian mission outposts that dotted the overland routes to the East where resident friars served their calling by combating "the enmity of Nature and Man" under the most extreme conditions (not unlike heathen priests or shamans who sometimes personally battled evil in their own sacred wildernesses). Both offered mutual support in the cities of their final destination, and sometimes shared martyrdom (Lopez 1943:165; Power 1926:146).

Risks and hardships were great, survival by no means assured, customs were strange, probably especially so for minds prepared aforehand for the curious and the unusual, and time spent in such journeys was likely to be measured not just in months but in years. Years spent wandering and living in non-Christian distance among non-Christian pagans on missions that often were addressed to political-religious issues that, regardless of direct practicality (e.g., converting foreign potentates or obtaining allies for joint ventures against the spiritual evil and trade restrictions of Islamic countries of the Levant), were still perceived in terms of a cosmologically Christian world where good opposed evil and the True God battled the Enemy in his numerous guises. Such experiences, whether by pragmatic merchants or travel-hardened missionaries or friar-diplomats suggest another form of *peregrinatio*, of wandering "homeless" for months or years for the cause of Christian trade or the Christian God or his anointed royal representatives, wandering now not within Christendom but in its awesome and dangerous cosmological hinterland, where successful navigation was attributed by the faithful to God's guidance rather than man's skill (Beazley 1906:171) and whence many did not return.

On the other hand, to the extent that a definite earthly destination was usually involved, such as the court of a Mongol chief or the Great Khan himself, traveling traders and missionary diplomats sought a more tangible goal than did the Irish *peregrini*.

Yet, like Christian travelers within Christendom, they still seem to have journeyed within something of a "supernatural" landscape, for their letters and reports show a mixture of fact and fantasy. Thus Marco Polo could combine straightforward, if limited, observation with lyrical super-description of the precious gems, mythical horses, bounteous earth, and Alexandrine origins of the ruling house of the Oxus highlands (Beazley 1906:65), while John of Monte Corvino, describing the great cities and wretched conditions of India, reported also of his inability, after exhaustive inquiries, to find any evidence of monstrous races and terrestrial paradise (ibid., p. 166). Similarly, Odoric of Pordenone gave way, also while in India, to describing bats as big as doves, mice the size of dogs, and other comparable tales of the strange and the mysterious (ibid., pp. 261, 282–83). Accounts written by more fervent friars mixed myth and stereotype to an even more extreme degree (e.g., the writings of Ricold of Monte Croce, ibid., pp. 190–99).

Given the immensity of the tasks assigned and the geographical distances and physical stamina involved, together with the sacred-supernatural aspects of the prevailing cosmology, it is not surprising to find that the friar-diplomat John of Monte Corvino, a towering figure in Christian missionary efforts of the time, assessed his accomplishments in China by associating himself and his experiences with heroic travelers of the sacred past. He noted proudly (and accurately) that he was a pioneer in regions where Apostles or disciples of Apostles never came (Beazley 1906: 169; Fabian 1983:6). Similarly, it is not surprising to read that when the mission under John of Plano Carpini arrived back in Europe (Russia) after some eighteen months' absence they were greeted by the people of Kiev as persons returning from the dead, and to remember the incredulity with which the Venetians initially regarded Marco Polo when he suddenly arrived among them after many years' absence, dressed in strange and exotic costume, with hoards of jewels, recounting incredible adventures (Rowbotham 1942:21, 29).

It is also significant that, whereas a number of missionaries and friar-diplomats like John of Monte Corvino frequently left written reports of their personal and professional experiences from which we can glean some feeling for what was involved, merchants, though probably far more numerous than friars as long-distance travelers, generally were not nearly as communicative, in order presumably to protect business secrets and limit competition. Merchants not only wrote far fewer accounts of their travels but in some cases, particularly involving the Genoese (perhaps most active of the Italian city-states in developing long-distance trade), left out even such basic information as the final destination of their trips in the contracts drawn up before notaries (Lopez 1943:168). Secrecy with respect to what can be considered a kind of esoteric information, therefore, was also a factor in at least some long-distance contact in the Middle Ages, as it was in some of the later voyages of exploration (e.g., the early Portuguese voyages), and may have helped maintain an atmosphere of mystery and adventure toward distant lands, though secrecy in this context probably served as much to protect activity in distant lands as to support the prestige and mystique of the traveler-traders.

Europeans, as I have said, have at times been prone to be on the move. The broader motives underlying the peregrinations and pilgrimages of the medieval faithful—the restlessness and urge to wander, the desire to seek understanding and have experience of a wider world, to be free of local ties—were recognized by writers of the later Middle Ages in a comparable manner, i.e., as definitive of the uniquely human condition, as that which separates man from beast and directs him to seek qualities of the divine. For Dante's Ulysses, whose legendary journey has been metaphor for this essay, travel was a humanizing quest for knowledge and experience of the unknown, for men "were not born to live as beasts, but to follow virtue and knowledge." In Petrarch's letter to Andrea Dandolo, Doge of Venice, regarding his restless love of travel, he finds the classical, Homeric view of the perfect man to be "as a world-wanderer, everywhere learning something new." For himself, "to know more was always among the first of my desires and I seemed somehow to be overcoming ignorance by mere movement of mind and body." This restlessness was not unrelated to godliness. Just as the heavens, God's home, was in perpetual motion, so it was not strange that men should seek with an "innate longing" to see new places and change their homes; "those who sit forever in one spot experience a strange boredom in their repose." Yet another humanist, Coluccio Salutati, compared the hardiness of the sailors who took galleys back and forth between Italy and northern ports via the Atlantic to the endurance shown by earlier saints in their devotion to God. Writing in the mid-fifteenth century of the early Portuguese voyages into the central Atlantic, Giannozzo Manetti alludes to these trips as evidence of man's God-given intellectual power: God-given in that invention—the ability which has allowed man to create history and civilization from the raw materials given by God—is also a gift for man from God which, in effect, makes man a "second creator." A few decades later, Marsilio Ficino wrote of man's desire to "be everywhere," to be "content with no frontier," to run through all things "wherever they are in whatever times and places," to command everywhere and be praised everywhere, which is to say, man "strives to be as God everywhere" (all quotes from Trinkaus 1976).

In short, for this intellectual elite of the later Middle Ages and early Renaissance, as for church fathers before them, travel as part of a quest for knowledge or, as in the case of the sailors, even as part of more mundane survival, is, directly or indirectly, divinely inspired and associated with God-like or at least saint-like qualities. It is both an heroic activity and a Christian activity, requiring and expressing exceptional God-given gifts and abilities. Irish wanderers and earnest pilgrims would have agreed. So, too, would friar-diplomats and missionaries and perhaps merchants struggling through the immensity of central Asia or trusting to the vagaries of sea travel as holy saints and legendary classical heroes had before them. Ships' captains, navigators, and common sailors who ventured along the African coast or who sought the Orient via the Atlantic a few hundred years later definitely agreed.

Indeed, a sense of the heroic appears particularly strong in these "Age of Discovery" travels or at least is more openly expressed in the fact that travelers were eager to keep journals or write letters as records of adventure, in the content of these personal accounts, and in the reaction to exploration by humanist scholars of the

243

time (Hirsch 1965). An heroic sense appears in motive as much as in accomplishment, perhaps because of a change in means of accomplishment, particularly in mode of transportation (navigation), perhaps because of the unexpectedness of the peoples and places encountered in this tremendous spatial expansion of the European world. This unexpectedness required active investigation and intellectual identification in order to be placed in the European cosmological order, thereby literally casting explorers, missionaries, and chroniclers in the role of "second creators" alluded to in a more technical, navigational context by Manetti.

Let us consider navigation. Despite its history of gradual development, ocean navigation was nonetheless a new "invention" for travel, far newer than coastal sailing or pack asses or bone-crunching rides in various rough-wheeled conveyances. Ocean navigation involved nothing less than the exploration of the hitherto "closed" or "empty" edge of the medieval European world. As such it bespoke exceptional heroic skill and intellectual expertise, creative abilities that were recognized by pre-Enlightenment men (as by so many of the cultures they encountered) as God-given *and* God-expressive (Evans 1973:255). In addition, navigation and the sailors and naval captains who employed it to successfully brave the Ocean Sea and the Torrid Zone made the globe available to Europeans as never before. Navigators "open[ed] distances over the heavens and the seas of which we have never heard before, . . . show[ed] us peoples and nations of great interest to us because of their extraordinary customs . . . truly to man was opened his plane" (Vives, in a dedicatory letter to Joao III of Portugal in 1530, quoted in Hirsch 1965:42). Samuel Purchas, who in the early seventeenth century wrote of the glory of new discoveries from a very particular perspective (see below), celebrated the art of navigation as a God-given means (along with printing) for making the seas and earth available for European nations.

> God Almightie pittying this Frailtie, intending better things to the last and worst Ages of the World [for which he also sent his Son] hath given the Science of the Loadstone and As-tronomicall Rules and Instruments, applyed by Art to Nav-

FIGURE 6.5

The first printed picture of Christopher Columbus' caravel, *Nina*, from *Oceanica Classis*, Basle, 1493. From E. and J. Lehner, *How They Saw The New World*, p. 76. Published by Tudor Publishing Co., 1966. Reprinted by permission of Amiel Book Distributors Corp.

igation, that hee might give more ample Possession of the Sea and the Earth to the sonnes of Men. . . . Amongst all which helpes by humane industry, none (in my mind) have further prevailed than these two, the Arts of Arts, Printing and Navigation. . . . (quoted in Boon 1982:157)

As to the heroics of the "second creators" themselves, there seems to have been a stronger sense of an active search for new resources, whether material or spiritual (i.e., souls to be saved), although admittedly this may in part be a reflection of the greater quantity of extant literature and interest in events, then and now, than is available for earlier medieval travelers. Even so, there is an overt appreciation even by contemporary observers of the uniqueness and importance of this time, of the discoveries made, and of the qualities of those who actively participated in them.[18] "The discoverer . . . is proud of his achievement, which is credited to his great endurance, determination, and will power. On his homecoming he is rightly celebrated as a hero; he has gained a position for himself by himself" (Hirsch 1965:37).

Humanist scholars, who often knew the adventurers quite well, expressed a grand sense of association with earlier eras of heroic travels by heroic personages. Thus Henry the Navigator is effusively compared with Alexander the Great, indeed excels Alexander: "Thanks to his conquests, Alexander the Great covered the whole world, but the places and countries which he reached had been visited by many others before him; but your courage has taken you to countries of the world which, it seems, no-one had penetrated before you" (the Italian humanist, Poggio, in a letter to Henry, quoted in Chaunu 1979:201). The sixteenth-century Portuguese scholar Damião de Góis claimed that the overseas exploits "were a fit topic for a modern Homer who could derive his epics not from legend but from reality" (Hirsch 1965:43); further, the Italian humanist Buonamico, writing in 1539, exalted that nothing was more honorable to the age than the invention of the printing press and the discovery of the New World, two things that could be compared "not only with Antiquity, but immortality" (ibid).[19]

In a less obvious manner, and presumably with a different set of traditional heroes in mind, friars saw another chance for Christian service in heathen hinterlands. It is noteworthy that Columbus' efforts in Castile were strongly assisted by a Franciscan community whose brothers appear to have been taken by what

[18] Chaunu cautions us that the impact of European expansion at the time has been somewhat exaggerated by later historians and that these activities had greater impact on later ages than on the age in which it occurred (1979:viii, 205).

[19] With all respect to heroic travelers, it should be remembered that the Renaissance thinkers' emphasis on a rebirth and a surpassing of the learning and wisdom and general superiority of classical antiquity was very freely applied at the time (Kristeller 1966).

seemed to be a new opportunity to reopen West–East communication and establish alliance with now isolated Asian churches, convert masses of pagans, and effect the deliverance of holy Christian centers (Chaunu 1979:151, 282). Some fifty years later, Jesuit missionaries began over a century and a half of association with India and imperial courts of the Far East (and eventually the New World). Rowbotham, discussing Jesuit missions in the Far East, sees the expansion of their missionary activities, as well as earlier explorations of the era, essentially as a continuation of the crusading ardor of medieval sacred history. Speaking initially of the gradual progress of the Portuguese along the coast of Africa to the Indian ocean and points east, he comments,

> "These adventures into unknown seas were directed by men who had something of the spirit of the medieval knight. The search for new lands acquired some of the mystical ardor of the quest for the Grail. Columbus, in undertaking his voyage into the unknown, . . . had an enthusiastic belief in his divinely appointed mission to bring fresh souls to the knowledge of God and to the Holy Church. Henry the Navigator, by his crusading zeal, belonged to the Middle Ages, though his critical mind and practical genius linked him with the modern world. In his ardor for the cause of the Cross, he is a pre-Renaissance Saint Louis . . ." (Rowbotham 1942:39).[20]

In short, travel to geographically distant and symbolically charged extraordinary lands in pre-Enlightenment Europe was an extraordinary undertaking. Such an enterprise required personal fortitude and bravery and certainly set a man apart from his own home and society. Some of this distancing was created by the realities of the months and years required for travels, some undoubtedly by the unavoidable difficulty upon return of relating experiences and observations that could not be expressed in terms of everyday life at home. (When Marco Polo was urged by friends to tone down his narrative lest it seem too fanciful he replied that

---

[20] St. Louis, king of France in the thirteenth century, sent several missions to the Great Khan, including that of William of Rubruck.

FIGURE 6.6

The first printed picture of Columbus' landing in Hispaniola, from *Oceanica Classis*, Basle, 1493. From E. and J. Lehner, *How They Saw The New World*, p. 76. Published by Tudor Publishing Co., 1966. Reprinted by permission of Amiel Book Distributors Corp.

he hadn't described the half of what he had seen.) Part of the distancing was the company with which the traveler was likely to be identified, at least by implication, for he was ultimately in association with holy saints and legendary heroes—the recognized "official" category, as it were, for persons who ventured into strange, power-filled distance and came face to face with the evils and marvels located here.

Long-distance travel in traditional Europe continually created new generations of heroes who sought and acquired knowledge and experience either of traditional hinterlands of Christian cos-

248

mology or of newly found and "created" ones. In the more rarified intellectual opinion of humanistic scholars, such voyaging, by virtue of the use of God-given facilities and qualities that it entailed and by virtue of the existential challenges it posed, was also a direct expression of and challenge to the spiritual (intellectual, God-reflective, nonbestial) side of "human nature." It is unfortunate that the actual behavior of explorers and "discoverers" did not always evidence this sublimity, yet, to the extent that they believed their behavior represented the reaction of Christian heroes battling the evil of the demonic hinterland, in a certain sense, it did.[21]

Aristocracy and the Wider World

By extension, the qualities associated with long-distance travel and travelers conferred prestige on those who supported travelers' exploits or employed them as their agents and representatives. Long-distance travelers from Christian Europe came from diverse backgrounds and traveled for a variety of personal, economic, and political-ideological reasons, but the fruits of their exploits generally served most directly the needs and interests of the elite of church and state. Conversely, many long-distance expeditions could not have been carried out except with aristocratic support. Peasants and peddlers may have walked considerable

[21] The explorers of the Enlightenment were also accorded great fame and honor even though the intellectual and cosmological climate in which they lived was changing, for while the methods used to approach and interpret the world and its phenomena were being adjusted, attitudes towards those who took these methods into distant, still fabled, places, did not. Explorations in the Pacific, that last bastion of the paradise of the West, produced a "new type of national hero in the shape of naval explorers and itinerant scientists. Expeditions set off into the unknown, to return three years later laden with specimens from the South Seas, eager to publish descriptions, maps and views of the wondrous places visited and the peoples seen" (Marshall and Williams 1982:258). Captain Cook became the epitome of the methodical, intelligent naval explorer-cum-hero. Africa also produced its share of explorer-heroes for European and national acclaim. Wider dissemination of knowledge and recognition of overseas exploits as nationalistic enterprises further enhanced and expressed the quality of the heroic traditionally attributed to long-distance travelers into the unknown. Whether such voyagers were natural scientists or missionaries was irrelevant so long as some degree of mystique was maintained about the realms they reached.

distances as simple pilgrims, but popes and princes made possible, and necessary, the great voyages of land and sea of Medieval and Renaissance Europe.

The involvement of political-ideological elites in travels within and without Christendom offers some useful, even if very general, contrasts regarding travel itself as an elite activity. Within the bounds of the Christian world, elites traveled enthusiastically in the context of pilgrimage. They traveled for prestige and for public display of high status; probably, too, for genuine reasons of piety and for penances incurred by the greater sins to which the greater worldly involvement required of their high status made them prone. Generally speaking, elites either enjoyed or could be subjected to aspects of pilgrimage to more extreme degrees than common folk. For example, during the era of Irish peregrinatio "the sins of monks and those of the higher clergy were visited more often with penitential pilgrimages than those of any other class" (Sumption 1975:99). During the Middle Ages in general the graver sins of elites tended to be regarded as more scandalous because they were more "public" and were talked about more widely. Public sins, as opposed to "solemn" sins (similar offenses committed by ordinary laymen), were generally atoned for by pilgrimage, and since "the scandalous overtones were obviously stronger in cases involving clerics or noblemen, . . . it was above all these classes who were wont to be sent on long pilgrimages" (ibid).

Elites were also more likely to be more exposed to sin than were ordinary people, for the social responsibilities of the nobility forced on them "a worldly existence" and exposed them to the temptations of power. The nobility also was acutely aware of its special spiritual needs, and individual members responded in varying fashion in order to protect their eternal souls, some by ultimately renouncing the world by adopting monastic life ("pilgrims who became hermits and recluses were chiefly drawn from the noble and well-to-do"; ibid., p. 126); others by devotional exercises of which pilgrimage was foremost. In fact, the annual or biennial pilgrimage became a recognized mark of aristocratic piety. As Sumption has noted, it is not possible to make statistical analyses of the clientele of the great medieval shrines, but from what records are available the number of nobility visiting a shrine such as, for example, Canterbury in the twelfth century, appear to be out of all proportion to their numerical importance in the population at large (1975:122–23).

Pilgrimage could also be a most congenial means of expiating sin, a means that could be made compatible with one's elevated station in life in terms of opportunity for display. Aristocrats may have had to endure more pilgrimages, but many did so comfortably, even luxuriously. Traveling bishops and noblemen not infrequently were mistaken for kings by the splendor of their passage. Thus, Gunther, Bishop of Bamberg, who led several thousand persons on a mass pilgrimage to the Holy Land in 1064, traveled with other leaders in litters carried by liveried retainers, lived in tents hung with silk, ate splendid suppers off gold and silver plate carried on long trains of packhorses, and worried about being captured by Arabs who might think him a king in disguise (Sumption 1975:123).[22]

Pilgrimage, in short, allowed elites to express their high rank in all respects, both spiritual and temporal. They held more power than ordinary men, and thereby faced greater spiritual temptation, thereby committed graver crimes and sins, thereby atoned more publicly, and thereby exhibited their grandeur more publicly, too, many by displaying the elaborate trappings of travel, although others chose to emphasize the greater austerity that travel could inflict (Sumption 1975:101).[23]

In a very real sense, the elevated social status of elites correlated with farther dimensions of geographically and temporally sacred distance. Their greater involvement with the potency of high political and spiritual powers was neatly and concisely expressed by the greater requirement to travel greater distances to greater centers of sacredness (Rome, Jerusalem, Santiago); centers that also were associated with the great ancestral saints and apostolic he-

[22] Not surprisingly, the good bishop was attacked at every stage of the trip, lost much treasure, suffered heavy casualties, and did not have too much sympathy from some observers.

[23] For those so inclined, mortification of the flesh by walking was considered a most virtuous mode of penitential pilgrimage. Barefoot pilgrims were particularly esteemed (Sumption 1975:101, 127–28).

roes of their political-ideological world, whom some at least felt they would behold almost face to face when they reached the holy place (Sumption 1975:120). The frequent attendance of elites at distant sacred centers undoubtedly contributed to elite prestige even if it did not always effect greater wisdom or greater sanctity. In medieval Europe the attainment of positions of political-religious glory required parallel emphasis on the *ingloriousness* (sinfulness) forced by such high achievement, as if it were necessary to apply a brake of some sort to expressions of worldly grandeur and power that would otherwise rise to unacceptable heights or become too uncontrollable unless rechanneled into more manageable expressions of piety. Yet even enforced piety could increase personal prestige through the elaborateness with which it was individually expressed, and highly visible lengthy pilgrimages provided a perfect means.

If the act of pilgrimage to sacred centers expressed the qualities of high rank, it would not be surprising to find that some more lasting, tangible expression attesting to association of political-ideological elites with sacred centers and sacred heroes would be coveted by those in high office. The emphasis given to the acquisition of holy relics can be understood in this context. As was noted in Chapter 4, objects that had been in contact with a saint or his shrine (including cloth, paper, lamp oil, even dust from the ground) or bodily pieces of martyrs became enormously important as collectors' items, particularly among the elite. "Most princes of western Europe at all times expended a great deal of money and energy in enlarging their collections," many of which derived from Constantinople, where the emperors of Byzantium had built up an extraordinarily large and varied relic collection. According to Sumption, relics were regarded as objects of national pride by the general populace and as "guarantors of political prestige and spiritual authority," which "explain[s] much of the frenzied acquisitiveness of Latin rulers and their subjects throughout [the] period" (1975:29–30). Rivalries in relic collecting were akin to political rivalries: the Bishop of Norwich, upon the occasion of the deposition of a vase of the blood of Christ in Westminster Abbey (together with sealed authenticating documents), expounded on the proposition that possession of Christ's blood gave England a greater holy treasure than France, where Louis IX had recently acquired a fragment of the True Cross (Sumption 1975:30).

When it came to contacts and travel outside the realm of medieval Christendom, however, elites' motives and methods differed. As we have seen, the hardships attending distant travel and the delicate exploration of political alliances or the acquisition of precious material goods now were allocated to personal agents, representatives, or colleagues who were dispatched as need arose. Thus popes and princes could remain at home while friar-diplomats traveled in their stead and, in a parallel type of mercantile partnership, stay-at-home wealthy "capitalists" interested in distant trade provided financing for long-distance business activities by merchants who did the traveling but supplied little, if any, capital (Chaunu 1979:261, 80). In contrast with the grandeur of pilgrimage, this type of foreign travel was usually a painful way to reach a destination or achieve a goal. In itself it was useful neither for political prestige nor for personal display, and therefore was best left to cleric-ambassadors or merchants employed for the purpose. Whatever successes were eventually achieved by the end of the journey could be enjoyed "by appropriation" by those who had stayed safely and comfortably at home.

A comparable elite approach to long-distance travel beyond Europe can be seen in the early growth of ocean navigation and overseas contacts. The areas of involvement here are complex and worthy of a separate study, but, broadly speaking, elite activities in overseas exploration and expansion were subsumed within the basic point that ocean travel, like long-distance land travel but more so, was expensive in terms of money, skills, and personnel. Exceptional knowledge, ships, and crews were required, and access to such resources as well as prerogatives to deploy resources in such undertakings were available only to the wealthy and the high-born, to kings, aristocrats, and international merchants. Actual incentive to use money and men in this way, however, was not always readily evidenced by the aristocratic sector, and accounts (particularly of the earlier decades of overseas exploration) not infrequently reveal considerable hesitancy on the part of particular kings or other highly placed and influential notables to commit resources to such uncertain exploits (Penrose 1962).

Such hesitancy did not obtain in Portugal. In this respect, one of the most significant characteristics of Henry the Navigator and of the Portuguese ruling house of Avis was simply that Henry and his associates had the incentive to deploy resources in this way. Royal support had encouraged shipbuilding and development of a merchant marine in the fourteenth century. By Henry's time and thereafter many of the Portuguese nobility were city dwellers and many were lords of the most important ports and ship-owners in their own right as well as government office holders. "In Portugal the possibilities of maritime trade lured many noblemen to the Atlantic ports, especially to Lisbon, and the kings, themselves the country's first and richest merchants, set an example of noble participation in trade." (As merchants, the nobility, of course, dealt solely in wholesaling, which was not considered detrimental to noble status; Konetzke 1953–54:117; Prestage 1926:198; Beazley 1923:30; Pike 1972:22–32.)

Henry was a noble entrepreneur of this sort who combined persistent efforts to sail along the African coast with a still medieval set of motives: a combination of economic and political-ideological interests, including need for the material riches of Africa south of the Sahara (especially gold and pepper) and of the more distant lands of the Indian Ocean that ought to be reachable by sailing around Africa; interest in the diplomatic alliance between Christian countries that could be effected if Prester John could be contacted in Ethiopia; and possibilities for renewed contacts with Christian outposts in Ethiopia or India (Beazley 1923:193–42; Prestage 1926:202–204; Penrose 1952:34). All in all, Henry appears as a highly influential, highly informed, and highly intelligent "patron of the art" of navigational development, an excellent organizer and administrator who was able to assemble in one place (Sagrès) the necessary maps and charts, learned astronomers, cosmographers, physicians, and ships' captains. Although the prince himself stayed at home, he could finance from his various business enterprises their efforts to improve ship design and navigation and to sail the Atlantic (Konetzke 1953:118; Penrose 1952:35–37).

Henry's high-level scholarly hobby—the profession of a younger son excluded from the throne—was encouraged by his royal brothers and was eventually given further direct support by private noble investors. Their interest reflected many factors, including high-level concern with international trade and more immediate competition between the traditional Portuguese aristocracy and socially mobile merchants for power, privileges, and valuable resources (Chaunu 1979:307–308; Beazley 1923:117, 136; Prestage 1926:206–207).[24] As Chaunu has stated it, "[Henry] was much more a nobleman than a scholar or merchant; he symbolizes the interests of the nobility who . . . had been somewhat separated from power. . . . He had a taste for gold and other solid forms of wealth and he had great pride in the glory and prestige of his family" (Chaunu 1979:110). In addition, Henry's princely backing provided the beginnings of a form of state support for long-distance overseas ventures, a tactic that would eventually link the royal families and national prestige of the various European polities to long-distance exploits in a far more direct fashion than ever before.

In addition to whatever necessary resources might be acquired from afar,[25] contact with foreign places could also become symbolic of newly emerging monarchical-national prestige and power, the institutional complement of the heroics attributed to individual travelers and explorers. The emphasis in this symbolic construction, however, was not on the personal association of the ruler himself with distant lands-cum-foreign places as much as on the inclusion of new lands and seas within the expanding, ideologically legitimate, political universe that he symbolized. As applied to fifteenth-century monarchs of Henry's era, this widening of the known (Christian, European, Mediterranean) world was

[24] Also behind this support was the time-honored recognition by the crown that internal aristocratic competition and confrontations could be reduced if attentions were diverted to an external interest, while royal coffers could also benefit from an outside source of income. It was this latter concern that also probably prompted the official secrecy and suppression of information surrounding the African exploits (Prestage 1926:210–14; Chaunu 1979:97–104, 269–70, 307–308).

[25] The acquisition of more broadly useful resources from distant locales developed as ship tonnage increased, and eventually changed drastically the interpretation of the significance of geographically distant places in European perspective.

expressed by the inclusion of heretofore distant, "shadowy," and "chaotic" places within the "light" of the European orbit. "He [John II] added to the earth (*terrarum orbi*) a large number of new and distant islands; he in this way enlarged the world (orbem)" (from the speech of obedience of John II of Portugal to Pope Alexander VI, 1493, quoted in Chaunu 1979:223, 202). Not surprisingly, the power and prestige gained by this expansion could be evidenced directly by the acquisition of foreign exotics.[26] To take one of a number of possible examples, when King Manuel of Portugal (1495–1521) received a gift of elephants and rhinoceroses from India, "in his pride he not only paraded them in the streets of Lisbon, but sent some specimens to Rome to impress the pope with his far-reaching power" (Hirsch 1965:35).[27]

In the sixteenth century, the elaborate imperial (and anti-papal) symbolism associated with Elizabeth I of England included imagery of the Virgin Queen initiating a new (or reborn) golden age of peace and justice as divine, sacred, and supreme monarch of an expanded universal realm. According to John Dee, leading mathematician, astronomer, bibliophile, and the queen's learned astrologer, the realm that would maintain and increase the "Royall Maiesty and Imperiall Dignity of our Soverayn Lady Elizabeth" included lands and seas to which she could lay claim by virtue of the "Perfect Arte of Navigation" and a good navy (Yates 1947:46–

---

[26] "This is some monster of the isle with four legs. . . . If I can recover him, and keep him tame, and get to Naples with him, he's a present for any emperor that ever trod on neat's-leather" Shakespeare, *The Tempest*, Act II, Scene II. (Stephano, on first seeing the animalistic Caliban on the desert island).

[27] In medieval Europe and later centuries, collections of exotic rare and foreign animals were often maintained as private menageries of the nobility. The Emperor Charlemagne received an elephant and some monkeys from the Caliph of Baghdad. Henry I of England a few centuries later established a royal zoo, and continental rulers, as well as the pope, did likewise. One of the Medici families even kept a troop of "barbarians" who reputedly talked many different languages—a sort of human menagerie—and returning explorers of the Age of Discovery not infrequently brought back contingents of natives for general exhibition and the entertainment of royalty. In the sixteenth and seventeenth centuries, when collecting was all the rage, a miscellany of human artifacts and handicrafts from all over the world were included in the curio cabinets of the serious collector, "to confirm faith in the marvelous" (see *Encyclopaedia Britannica*, 11th and 14th editions, regarding "zoological gardens"; Hodgen 1964:111–17, 122–23, 156 note 21, 166; Evans 1973:chapter 7, regarding the underlying theory of collecting as a search for universal order in Medieval and Renaissance times).

FIGURE 6.7

King Manuel I of Portugal rides around the Cape of Good Hope. From Waldsee-
müller's *Carta marina*, Strasbourg, 1525. From F. Chiappelli, ed., *First Images of
America*, Vol. II, p. 626, figure 95. Published by University of California Press,
1976. Reprinted by permission of the publisher.

48). In other panegyrical lyrics, the advent of an age of voyaging and discovery is prophetic of the rise of universal empire and the golden age; maritime discovery and adventure extends the sacred empire to include new worlds of which the ancients knew nothing.[28] As Yates has expressed it, "the theme of nautical adventure and overseas expansion, purely nationalistic and aggressive though it may be in practice, has behind it for these sixteenth century minds some memory of empire in the ancient and religious sense. The discovery of new worlds raises the problem of the expansion of the concept of holy empire [under one imperial sovereign] to fit a world larger than that known to Virgil or to Dante" (Yates 1947:53).

In like fashion, Boon has discussed the symbolism of overseas travel as a legitimizing association for James I of England, as evidenced in the multivolume tomes of world travels prepared by Samuel Purchas, published in 1625. In this case, the emphasis lay in defining a world network of particular monarchies that included the "truly legitimate" rulers of Europe (i.e., England) and lords of great Eastern realms. A true king was defined by Purchas as one who was not bound to parliaments or special interest groups, but who dealt on a worldwide basis only with other great monarchs, and whose fame was equally universal. In Purchas' exuberant prose, the worthy monarch, James I, set at the center of the global stage, was hailed as the divinely wise sponsor of the art of navigation that gathered the riches of the world into a harmonious network of sea trade. The fame of his name, like that of Elizabeth, his predecessor, was spread far and wide, indeed, was "discovered" by explorers as "pre-existing" European contact in distant lands. This fame facilitated development of a global network of royal relationships that linked the splendidly exotic, semidivine and benevolent rulers of Eastern kingdoms (Sumatra, Java, Bali) with the equally glorious realm of James, a true Western monarch. (Boon further notes that while the Eastern kings

[28] The notion of Tudor unity and the Tudor *pax*, personified in Elizabeth I, was influenced by the larger European perspective of Hapsburg unity and a Hapsburg *pax* personified in Charles V, and behind both of these was the concept of Holy Roman Empire, "reaching out in ever-widening influence to include the whole globe, both the old and the new worlds" (Yates 1947:52, 55).

may not have been quite as Purchas portrayed them, so neither was James; 1982:154–68).

English kings and the more glorious aspects of distant contacts were still linked in the Enlightenment, a hundred years later. In his dedicatory address to King George III, James Bruce, who traveled the upper reaches of the Nile in the late eighteenth century, saw "the study and knowledge of the Globe" as the "principal and favorite pursuit of great princes" of all ages. But in contrast to the alleged greed and cruelty of some earlier conquerors, the discovery sponsored during his Majesty's glorious reign united humanity and science and employed educated and liberal men in "the noblest of all occupations, that of exploring the distant parts of the globe . . ." (Oakes 1944:78–79). Such contemporary heroes, Bruce went on to note, were men who, though equal in courage to the "navigators of the past," excelled them in the purity or beneficence of their motives. The paternalistic bearing of the white man's burden for the benefit of his lesser savage brethren surpassed the "fantastic notions of [personal] honour and emulation" held by earlier explorers (ibid.).

In short, with the beginning of the Age of Discovery, long-distance exploration and contacts with foreign lands and peoples ennobled kings and created heroes just as they had to some extent in earlier European history. Yet, in contrast to medieval travel in legendary distant lands, the initiation of successful ocean navigation and the "discovery" and "invention" of the New World (as well as the emergence of new nation-states), was seen by each succeeding century as marking the monarchs and adventurers of that age not only as noble and heroic as those of previous eras, but more so. Thus Bruce's explorer was more highly principled than were earlier navigators, just as contemporaries of the earlier navigators felt their exploits not only equalled those of the great heroes of antiquity, but excelled them.[29]

After the discovery of the New World long-distance travelers

[29] "The printing press and the discovery of the new world . . . could be compared not only with Antiquity, but immortality" (Buonamico 1539); "Alexander the Great covered the whole world, . . . but your [Henry the Navigator] courage has taken you [where] no-one had penetrated before you" (Poggio, mid-fifteenth century); see Hirsch (1965:43); Chaunu (1979:201).

(and by extension their aristocratic patrons) were no longer simply hazarding their painful, God-fearing way through exotic distances to far off lands long known and long regarded with a mix of fear and fantasy. In medieval centuries cosmological hinterlands, as the location of universal "origins" and apocalyptic endings, of paradisiacal good and satanic evils, and of great feats by ancient heroes and legendary saints, had long been granted much more of an aura of "immortality" than any of the travelers who ventured into them. Now it was travelers and their kings and princes who sought immortality as "second creators" of distant worlds which for them were newly established and newly regarded not only with fear and fantasy, but also with the confident superiority of men, who, now God-like as much as God-fearing, having conquered the ocean with their bravery, skills, and intelligence, believed they could conquer whatever else they encountered.[30]

[30] This attitude, of course, has been cited not only with respect to the conquest of new lands but as characteristic of Renaissance intellectual attitudes in general. In addition to navigation and printing, gunpowder and other achievements in the arts and sciences also impressed philosophers and humanists of the era with the potential for unheard of levels of achievement greater than even the revered ancestors (ancients) had attained (Kristeller 1966).

7

Conclusion

In traditional societies esoteric knowledge has long been the select purview of political-religious elites. As anthropologists we have generally understood esoteric knowledge to include matters of cosmic significance, including understanding of the origins of the universe and of human society, comprehension of the dynamics of the sacred powers that fuel the operation of the universe and all things and beings therein, and recognition of the diverse expressions of these powers in the sounds and odors, colors and consistencies, shapes and sizes of phenomena of the natural world. Such knowledge has also included the means to contact and control such powers for the benefit (or harm) of individuals or of society at large, and mastery of often awesomely large corpuses of lore as expressed in song, myth, ceremony, and secret or ritually distinctive formulas or languages. We have also understood that the locus of such esoteric understanding lay in the "other worlds" of experience entered by altered psychological states achieved by hallucinogenic trance, fever (Posey NDb), or extreme deprivation of various sorts, and in the specialized education in esoteric matters offered, often with some degree of secrecy, by political-religious elites to select neophytes.

The central argument of this essay has been twofold; first, that anthropological understanding of the locus of esoteric materials, the "other worlds" of political-religious exotic experience, should be expanded to include the realm of geographical distance and the peoples, places and things found therein; second, that knowledge of these domains has long formed an important part of the corpus of esoteric materials controlled by learned political-religious elites.

In order to develop these points, traditional concepts of geographical distance as expression of cosmologically significant space-time were reviewed in Chapter 2. In traditional cosmologies places and peoples located at a distance from a central heartland have been conceptualized as being increasingly different from or contrastive with the central *axis mundi*. The comparison is generally one of extremes. It may be expressed in terms of moral contrasts, whereby distant realms express either greater good or greater evil than is found at home. It may emphasize the presence of beneficial, orderly, "civilizing" qualities in the homeland and their absence in frontier wilderness or, alternatively, it may focus on the existence of harmful or uncontrolled or "natural" qualities in distant places versus their banishment from the heartland. The contrast may be expressed in increasing differentiation of cosmological time, as when geographical distance or direction correlates with earlier epochs of human existence and *thus with moral or behavioral conditions associated with earlier* forms of uncontrolled and "uncivilized" human behavior. Conversely, geographical distance as indicative of earlier epochs ("origins") may be expressed through association with the heroic deeds of founding ancestors or civilizing culture heroes, who brought social order and useful skills to the chaos of earlier existence. In some cases, contemporary travelers to or from such distant places may assume the guise of ancestors or heroes (or even of dangerous pre-civilized beings) while they combat the spiritual-physical dangers and obstacles signified by distance and by travel.

Chapter 3 considered in more detail various motives, attributes, and activities associated with specialists who have direct experience of geographically distant realms and who, like the places whence they come or where they go, are regarded as exceptional. Motives for travel were found to be diverse, to be directed toward self-realization as much as to socially relevant goals, and to be predominantly of a political, ideological, or intellectual nature. Curiosity and desire for adventure, the search for knowledge (including states of ritual grace and knowledge of other peoples' customs and rituals), pursuit of fame and prestige, freedom from social constraints, punishment for social failings, and acquisition of tangible and intangible valued goods are all commonly cited in the ethnographic literature. Implicit in this activity (and sometimes explicitly expressed by travelers) is the widespread belief that things, information, and experiences acquired from distant places, being strange and different, have great potency, great supernatural power, and, if attainable, increase the ideological power and political prestige of those who acquire them. Such attitudes underlie the activities of travelers and the influence accorded those who, as shaman-curers/scholars/priests/traders may arrive at a given locale as learned and experienced "wise strangers from afar." The same attitudes motivate political-religious elites or their agents to leave their home societies in order to acquire knowledge of foreign lands and peoples as part of their own education in esoteric matters or for their lords at home.

In light of the recognition and expertise accorded travelers as delvers into the unknown, the liminal nature of long-distance travel as a ritually distinctive "middle passage" experience, and the esoteric qualities associated with distant places and things, it was suggested that geographical long-distance travelers or specialists in traditional societies be associated in anthropological thought with already recognized categories of political-religious specialists (shamans, priests, high chiefs, kings), who are also expected to be especially familiar with esoteric strategic resources and with various other forms of distance. Indeed, in many cases, shamans, high-ranking lords, and other recognized political-religious specialists, being familiar with social, political, ideological, and ritual "distance" in general, may well be the most traveled and the most informed regarding matters of geographical distance, too. In other situations, foreign visitors, such as missionaries or learned merchant-scholar-diviners, may be usefully viewed in a comparable light, all the more so given their frequent roles as advisers, prognosticators, educators, and skilled craftsmen for ruling elites who value their "strangeness," and in this way acquire additional association with and knowledge of foreign matters.

Chapter 4 examined more closely the particular interests of indigenous leaders in concepts, things, and events associated with geographical distance. This concern reflected not only the fact that "foreign" things or peoples that are not identified and claimed by local social (kin) groups often automatically fall under chiefly control by *fiat*, but also elites' general involvement with or more privileged access to exceptional "outside" things and events of all sorts. "Exceptional" in this context can refer to a considerable range of phenomena that are far away or "out of sight" and are associated with distant domains, whether such domains are psychologically or geographically foreign, or are contacted by shamanic trance, oracular insights, physical travel to foreign lands, or by the reception of foreign visitors at home. All such exceptional matters will be imbued with some aspect or degree of sacredness, mystical power, or symbolic significance within the dynamic universe that political-religious elites are expected to comprehend and actively control.

Since elites' power itself is an "invisible mystery," overt evidencing and activating of their roles and abilities is essential, and it is particularly within this context that the association or involvement of elites with "distance" of all sorts becomes an important part of the validation or legitimation of their positions. Consequently, not only do we find situations in which rulers or culture hero ancestors are believed to be derived from an outside source, but potential or hopeful local leaders may seek support from outside personages believed to be unusually powerful or may themselves seek to experience direct contact with the outside in order to derive exceptional powers by "walking in the wilderness" or by visiting distant lands and foreign sacred centers.

Not only have leaders sought experience with distant phenomena but they have also taken great pride in the acquisition of sea shells, copper bells, and a wide range of curious relics and other material goods from places beyond their realms. Similarly, both great kings and lesser tribal leaders, who are often believed to be the most ardent keepers of conservative ancestral traditions, may in fact be the first to receive representatives of new foreign faiths and customs, to accept new charms and protective amulets, to adopt foreign modes of personal deportment, official dress and regalia, and to accept foreign advisers, or even new political ideologies and models of rule.

Chapters 5 and 6 explored the several hypotheses under consideration in light of the most extensive experience of geographical long-distance contact on record, that between Europeans and native peoples in the rest of the world. Focusing particularly on the early days of contact, it becomes readily apparent that in native eyes the first Europeans to appear were given the only identification that could be attributed to beings from a distance; i.e., they had to be ogres or demons or spirits or ancestors or gods because such were the types of animate beings that "inhabited" the distant spaces from which these newcomers apparently derived. As such, Europeans by definition had to be embodiments of supernatural powers for good or for harm. They were also viewed as "wise strangers" from afar, versed in the esoteric mysteries and magic of literacy and of other new and unusual crafts and skills; even able, with medicine and guns, to control life and death on a scale and by means heretofore unrealized. Association with such potent representatives of the powers of distance clearly was appropriate for and often avidly sought by native lords and leaders, whose own reputations could hardly fail to benefit from such acquaintance, or at least so it seemed at first.

For many native peoples the initial advent of Europeans, though often something of a shock and surprise, was nonetheless manageable. The newcomers were generally placed rather easily within existing cosmological frameworks with interpretations that attest to native understandings of the nature of things from afar. The ultimate failure of Europeans to fill such expectations in the desired manner largely reflected the simple fact that European cosmological interpretations of the nature of people from afar did not present an equally complementary framework for interaction, although in general traditional European interest in and exploration of distant phenomena were similar to non-European approaches to the same material.

Concepts of the nature of geographical distance, the qualities attributed to those who explore it, and the significance of such understanding, though reported piecemeal in the ethnographic literature, can be fitted, even if roughly, into a fairly comprehensible paradigm emphasizing a political-ideological dimension of leadership in traditional society that we as anthropologists should carefully consider. Anthropologists stand in the rather peculiar position of geographical long-distance experts who at least overtly express the intent to make the frontiers of the Western world increasingly understandable within the "secular," non-mystical, "scientific" context of our discipline as we have traditionally perceived it (but see Fabian 1983). In so doing we seem to have assumed that we should interpret the activities of geographical distance specialists in other times and places within similar "practical" or "secular" contexts. We have often done so, frequently by the almost ritual invocation of very pragmatic terms such as "trade" and "exchange" as glosses for long-distance activities.

Since the movement of goods has long been an aspect of long-distance contacts, it is certainly appropriate to seek to understand the nature of such associations by consideration of these items. But we must constantly take care to understand the full range of possible contexts and related meanings reflected in the movement of "prestige economy" goods in traditional societies (see Flannery 1968; Friedman and Rowlands 1978; Upham 1982:121–23). Bloch's admonishment that we seek understanding by considering underlying "facts of connection and interchange" provided by the wider contexts of experience is always worth remembering: "Do you expect really to know the great merchants of Renaissance Europe, vendors of cloth or spices, monopolists in copper, mercury, or alum, bankers of kings and the Emperor, by knowing their merchandise alone? Bear in mind that they were painted by Holbein, that they read Erasmus or Luther" (Block 1953:156).

In our own society (perhaps even within the anthropological community), greater acclaim is still attributed to those who present the distant geographical frontiers even of the secular world as strange and curious, though they are said now to be filled with "scientific" natural wonders rather than with "mystical" natural wonders. Nor is it surprising that in anthropology, where fieldwork has been described as a "mystic charter" for modern ethnography, the ethnographer may appear as hero, "returning from the field with the 'Golden Fleece of ethnographic knowledge' " (de Laguna 1985:166).

Mystical powers from far away can continue to be important in the modern Third World, too. Taussig has reported (1980b) that in southwest Colombia the apparent secularity of the post-colo-

nial mix of cultures and the rise of modern commodity production and capitalist development has led to an increase in and
broadening of the powers of traditional "wise men from afar"
among lower classes. It has also motivated local elites (rich peasants and hacienda owners) to activate distant shamanic contacts
(sometimes involving lengthy journeys) to seek immunity, by
consultation and yagé sessions, from economic problems attributed to ensorcellment by peons or poorer neighbors whom they
suspect of envious sorcery in response to the harsh economic contrasts of rich and poor in modern society. As Taussig points out,
peons have neither time nor resources for such protective trips. It
is the landlord who "has the money to buy superior magic to
keep [the class war] at bay and maintain the pattern and intensity
of labor exploitation" (1980b:256). This situation is hardly new.
Though specific circumstances may vary, elites have always been
the ones able to acquire superior powers from more potent places
to enhance their own positions and to direct toward political issues at large.

The travels of contemporary Colombian landlords may seem
far removed from the mythical peregrinations of Dante's Ulysses, whose voyage provided food for thought in the opening
pages of this essay. Yet, there are points of commonality. Both
expected to gain exceptional knowledge or power from acquaintance with distant places, Ulysses in order to fulfill Dante's sense
that the noblest meaning of human existence is a quest for wisdom, the landlords in order to maintain political superiority
within human society through the acquisition of superior knowledge from afar. Similarly, whether travel serves as metaphor for
ideals or services active political needs, it speaks of unusual things
beyond the here and now and generally beyond the means of ordinary folk. Like Colombian landlords and myriad other travelers of high rank in distant realms, Ulysses became a fearless voyager facing risk in the mystically unknown because he was also a
king.

In closing, a final caveat. In Dante's version of Ulysses' adventures, the sail into the unknown and the search for wisdom prove
fatal. This unfortunate conclusion brings to mind various myths
from both Western and non-Western societies in which the hu-

man search for an approximation of the perfection of the gods through ultimate knowledge and wisdom leads to catastrophic consequences. There is also, perhaps, appropriate warning for those who would probe too deeply into cosmic mysteries in the New American Bible version of Daniel 12:4 (cited in the King James version as an opening epigram to this volume), which equates the quest for knowledge with the erosion of good and the triumph of the darker side of the cosmic duality: "many shall fall away and evil shall increase." As Mande heroes know (Chapter 1), both travel and learning can be threatening as well as broadening. This, of course, is also why local men of wisdom sometimes may be less than totally cordial to strangers and why Homer's more domestic solution to Ulysses' plight is so appealing. The conflict is well expressed, too, in an anecdote told of Alexander the Great on meeting with sages of India:

> On the appearance of Alexander and his army, these venerable men stamped [the earth] with their feet and gave no other sign of interest. Alexander asked through interpreters what they meant by this odd behavior, and they replied: "King Alexander, every man can possess only so much of this earth's surface as this we are standing on. You are but human like the rest of us, save that you are always busy . . . traveling so many miles from your home, a nuisance to yourself and to others" (Arrian, quoted in Smith 1972:148).

References

Abrahams, Israel, 1911. *Jewish Life in the Middle Ages*. Philadelphia: Jewish Publication Society of America.

Adamu, Mahdi, 1978. *The Hausa Factor in West African History*. Ibadan: Oxford University Press Nigeria.

Alpers, Edward A., 1969. Trade, state, and society among the Yao in the nineteenth century. *Journal of African History* 10:405–20

Anderson, Gerald H., 1976. The Philippines: Reluctant beneficiary of the missionary impulse in Europe, in *First Images of America*, Vol. I, ed. Fredi Chiappelli. Berkeley: University of California Press, pp. 391–404.

Attenborough, David, 1976. *The Tribal Eye*. New York: Norton.

Babcock, William H., 1922. *Legendary Islands of the Atlantic*. New York: American Geographical Society.

Baldus, Herbert, 1974. Shamanism in the acculturation of a Tupi tribe of central Brazil, in *Native South America*, ed. Patricia J. Lyon. Boston: Little, Brown, pp. 385–90.

Barth, Fredrik, 1965. *Political Leadership Among Swat Pathans*. London School of Economics, Monographs on Social Anthropology, No. 19. New York: Humanities Press.

Baudet, Henri, 1965. *Paradise on Earth*. New Hanover: Yale University Press.

Beazley, C. Raymond, 1901. *The Dawn of Modern Geography*, Vol. II. London: Murray.

———. 1906. *The Dawn of Modern Geography*, Vol. III. Oxford: Clarendon Press.

———. 1923. *Prince Henry the Navigator*. London: Putnam's.

Becker, Ernest, 1975. *Escape from Evil*. New York: Free Press.

Becker, Howard, 1933. Early generalisations concerning population movement and culture contact: Prolegomena to a study of mental mobility: II. *The Sociological Review* 25:137–52.

Bentley, G. Carter, 1986. Indigenous states of Southeast Asia. *Annual Review of Anthropology* 15:275–305.

Berdan, Frances F., 1982a. *Principles of Regional and Long-Distance Trade in the Aztec Empire.* Unpublished paper presented at the 44th International Congress of Americanists, Manchester, UK.

———. 1982b. *The Aztecs of Central Mexico.* New York: Holt, Rinehart and Winston.

Bernheimer, Richard, 1952. *Wild Men in the Middle Ages.* Cambridge: Harvard University Press.

Bhardwaj, Surinder Mohan, 1973. *Hindu Places of Pilgrimage in India.* Berkeley: University of California Press.

Biernoff, David, 1978. Safe and dangerous places, in *Australian Aboriginal Concepts*, ed. L. R. Hiatt. New Jersey: Humanities Press.

Bird, Charles S. and Martha B. Kendall, 1980. The Mande hero, in *Explorations in African Systems of Thought*, ed. Ivan Karp and Charles S. Bird. Bloomington: Indiana University Press, pp. 13–26.

Bittman, Bente and Thelma D. Sullivan, 1978. The Pochteca, in *Mesoamerican Communication Routes and Cultural Contacts*, ed. Thomas A. Lee, Jr. and Carlos Navarrete. Provo, Utah: Brigham Young University, pp. 211–17.

Blackburn, Julia, 1979. *The White Men: The First Response of Aboriginal Peoples to the White Man.* New York: New York Times Books.

Bloch, Marc, 1953. *The Historian's Craft.* New York: Knopf.

Bloch, Maurice, 1968. Astrology and writing in Madagascar, in *Literacy in Traditional Societies*, ed. Jack Goody. London: Cambridge University Press, pp. 278–97.

Boon, James A., 1982. *Other Tribes, Other Scribes.* London: Cambridge University Press.

Bowen, Elenore S., 1964. *Return to Laughter.* Garden City, N.Y.: Doubleday.

Bradfield, Richard M., 1973. *A Natural History of Associations*, Vol. I. New York: International Universities Press.

Braudel, Fernand, 1972. *The Mediterranean and the Mediterranean World in the Age of Philip II*, Vol. I, trans. Sian Reynolds. New York: Harper & Row.

———. 1984. *The Perspective of the World. Civilization and Capitalism 15th–18th Century*, Vol. III, trans. Sian Reynolds. New York: Harper & Row.

Bridges, Roy C., 1970. John Hanning Speke: Negotiating a way to the Nile, in *Africa and Its Explorers: Motives, Methods and Impact*, ed. R. I. Rotberg. Cambridge: Harvard University Press, pp. 95–138.

Bronitsky, Gordon, 1982. Long distance trade: Rise and fall of an early medieval monopoly. *Virginia Social Science Journal* 17:26–33.

Broome, Richard, 1982. *Aboriginal Australians: Black Response to White Dominance 1788–1980.* Sydney: George Allen & Unwin.

Brotherston, Gordon and Dawn Ades, 1975. Mesoamerican description of space I: myths; stars and maps; and architecture. *Ibero-Amerikanisches Archiv* (n.s.) 1:279–305.

Brown, Norman O., 1947. *Hermes the Thief: The Evolution of a Myth.* New York: Vintage Books.

Brown, Peter, 1971. The rise and function of the holy man in late antiquity. *The Journal of Roman Studies* 61:80–101.

Brunton, Ron, 1975. Why do the Trobriands have chiefs? *Man* 10:544–58.

Bucher, Bernadette, 1981. *Icon and Conquest.* Chicago: University of Chicago Press.

Bucher, Hubert, 1980. *Spirits and Power.* Cape Town: Oxford University Press.

Burland, Cottie A., 1968. *The Exotic White Man.* Vienna: Verlag Anton Schroll.

Burridge, Kenelm O. L., 1969. *New Heaven, New Earth.* New York: Schocken.

———. 1975. The Melanesian manager, in *Studies in Social Anthropology,* ed. J.H.M. Beattie and R. G. Lienhardt. Oxford: Clarendon Press, pp. 86–104.

Butt, Audrey J., 1960. The birth of a religion. *Journal of the Royal Anthropological Institute* 90:66–106.

Buxton, Jean, 1973. *Religion and Healing in Mandari.* Oxford: Clarendon Press.

Campbell, Joseph, 1949. *The Hero with a Thousand Faces.* New York: Pantheon.

Carlstein, Tommy, Don Parkes, and Nigel Thrift, eds. 1978. *Making Sense of Time.* New York: John Wiley & Sons.

Carmack, Robert M., 1976. Ethnohistory of the Central Quiche: The community of Utatlan. *Archaeology and Ethnohistory of the Central Quiche,* ed. Dwight T. Wallace and Robert M. Carmack. Institute for Mesoamerican Studies, State University of New York at Albany. Publication No. 1, pp. 1–19.

Carrasco, David, 1982. *Quetzalcoatl and the Irony of Empire.* Chicago: University of Chicago Press.

Casson, Lionel, 1974. *Travel in the Ancient World.* Toronto: Hakkert.

Chaffetz, David, 1981. *A Journey Through Afghanistan: A Memorial.* Chicago: Regnery Gateway.

Chang, K. C., 1983. *Art, Myth and Ritual. The Path to Political Authority in Ancient China*. Cambridge: Harvard University Press.

Chapin, Mac, 1970. *Pab Igala. Historias de la Tradición Kuna*. Universidad de Panama, Centro de Investigaciones Antropologicas.

Charles-Edwards, T. M., 1976. The social background to Irish *Peregrinatio. Celtica* 11:43–59.

Chaunu, Pierre, 1979. *European Expansion in the Later Middle Ages*, ed. Katharine Bertram. Amsterdam: North-Holland.

Ch'en, Ta-tuan, 1968. Investiture of Liu-Ch'iu kings in the Ch'ing period, in *The Chinese World Order*, ed. John K. Fairbank. Cambridge: Harvard University Press, pp. 135–64.

Chiappelli, Fredi, ed., 1976. *First Images of America*, Vol. II. Berkeley: University of California Press.

Christian, William A. Jr., 1972. *Person and God in a Spanish Valley*. New York: Seminar Press.

Christie, A., 1964. The political use of imported religion. *Archives de Sociologie des Religion* 9:53–62.

Clendinnen, Inga, 1980. Landscape and world view: The survival of Yucatec Maya culture under Spanish conquest. *Comparative Studies in Society and History* 22:374–93.

Coedès, G., 1968. *The Indianized States of Southeast Asia*, ed. W. F. Vella. Honolulu: East–West Center Press.

Cohen, Abner, 1971. Cultural strategies in the organization of trading diasporas, in *The Development of Indigenous Trade and Markets in West Africa*, ed. C. Meillassoux. London: Oxford University Press, pp. 266–80.

Collins, Roger, 1983. Theodebert I, 'Rex Magnus Francorum', in *Ideal and Reality in Frankish and Anglo-Saxon Society*, ed. Patrick Wormald. Oxford: Blackwell, pp. 7–33.

Colson, Audrey Butt, 1973. Inter-tribal trade in the Guiana Highlands. *Antropologia* 34:1–69.

Columbus, Christopher, 1960. *The Journal of Christopher Columbus*, trans. Cecil Jane. New York: Clarkson N. Potter.

Curtin, Philip D., 1971. Pre-colonial trading networks and traders: The Diakhanke, in *The Development of Indigenous Trade and Markets in West Africa*, ed. C. Meillassoux. London: Oxford University Press, pp. 228–39.

———. 1984. *Cross-cultural Trade in World History*. London: Cambridge University Press.

Daniel, E. Valentine, 1984. *Fluid Signs*. Berkeley: University of California Press.

Dante Alighieri, 1966. *The Divine Comedy, I, Hell*, trans. Louis Biancolli. New York: Washington Square Press.

David-Neel, Alexandra, 1953. Running lamas, in *Primitive Heritage*, ed. Margaret Mead and Nicolas Calas. New York: Random House, pp. 407–12.

Davidson, Judith R., 1979. *The Spondylus Shell in Chimu Cosmology*. Paper presented at the annual meeting of the American Society for Ethnohistory, Albany, New York.

Davidson, William V., 1974. *Historical Geography of the Bay Islands, Honduras*. Birmingham: Southern University Press.

Daws, Gavan, 1974. Looking at islanders: European ways of thinking about Polynesians in the eighteenth and nineteenth centuries, in *Topics in Culture Learning*, Vol. 2, ed. Richard V. Brislin, East–West Culture Learning Institute. Honolulu: East–West Center Press, pp. 51–56.

de Laguna, Frederica, 1972. *Under Mount Saint Elias: The History and Culture of the Yakutat Tlingit*. Smithsonian Contributions to Anthropology, Vol. 7, Pt. 1. Washington, D.C.: Smithsonian Institution Press.

———. 1985. Review of *Observers Observed: Essays on Ethnographic Fieldwork. History of Anthropology*, Vol. I, ed. George Stocking, Jr. *Ethnohistory* 32:165–68.

de Landa, Friar Diego, 1978. *Yucatan Before and After the Conquest*, trans. William Gates. New York: Dover.

Dennis, Philip A. and Michael D. Olien, 1984. Kingship among the Miskito. *American Ethnologist* 11:718–36.

Detienne, Marcel, 1977. *The Gardens of Adonis: Spices in Greek Mythology*, trans. Janet Lloyd. New Jersey: Humanities Press.

Deutsch, Karl W. and Walter Isard, 1961. A note on a generalized concept of effective distance. *Behavioral Science* 6:308–11.

Diez Canseco, Maria de Rostworowski, 1977. Coastal fishermen, merchants, and artisans in pre-Hispanic Peru, in *The Sea in the Pre-Columbian World*, ed. Elizabeth Benson. Washington, D.C.: Dumbarton Oaks Research Library and Collections, pp. 167–86.

Downs, Roger M. and David Stea, 1973. *Image and Environment: Cognitive Mapping and Spatial Behavior*. Chicago: Aldine.

Duignan, Peter, 1958. Early Jesuit missionaries: A suggestion for further study. *American Anthropologist* 60:725–32.

Durán, Fray Diego, 1971. *Book of the Gods and Rites and the Ancient Calendar*, trans. and ed. Fernando Horcasitas and Doris Heyden. Norman: University of Oklahoma Press.

Durkheim, Emile, 1915. *The Elementary Forms of the Religious Life*, trans. J. W. Swain. London: George Allen and Unwin.

Dyson, Stephen L., 1985. *The Creation of the Roman Frontier*. Princeton: Princeton University Press.

Eberhard, Wolfram, 1965. *Conquerors and Rulers*, 2d revised ed. Leiden: Brill.

Edwards, Adrian C., 1962. *The Ovimbundu under Two Sovereignties*. London: Oxford University Press.

Eliade, Mircea, 1958. *Patterns in Comparative Religion*. New York: Sheed and Ward.

———. 1962. *The Forge and the Crucible*. New York: Harper & Row.

———. 1963. *Myth and Reality*. New York: Harper & Row.

———. 1969. *Images and Symbols*. New York: Sheed and Ward.

Elkin, A. P., 1977. *Aboriginal Men of High Degree*, 2d ed. New York: St. Martin's Press.

Elliott, John H., 1976. Renaissance Europe and America: A blunted impact? in *First Images of America*, Vol. 1, ed. Fredi Chiappelli. Berkeley: University of California Press, pp. 11–26.

Evans, R.J.W., 1973. *Rudolf II and His World*. Oxford: Clarendon Press.

Evans, Joan, 1922. *Magical Jewels of the Middle Ages and the Renaissance, Particularly in England*. Oxford: Clarendon Press.

Evans, Raymond and Jan Walker, 1977. "These strangers, where are they going?" Aboriginal–European relations in the Fraser Island and Wide Bay region 1770–1905. University of Queensland Anthropology Museum *Occasional Papers in Anthropology* 8:39–105.

Evans-Pritchard, E. E., 1937. *Witchcraft, Oracles and Magic among the Azande*. Oxford: Clarendon Press.

———. 1949. *The Sanusi of Cyrenaica*. Oxford: Clarendon Press.

———. 1956. *Nuer Religion*. Oxford: Clarendon Press.

Fabian, Johannes, 1983. *Time and the Other*. New York: Columbia University Press.

Fairbank, John K., ed., 1968. A preliminary framework, in *The Chinese World Order*. Cambridge, Mass.: Harvard University Press, pp. 1–19.

Fairbank, John K. and S. Y. Têng, 1941. On the Ch'ing tributary system. *Harvard Journal of Asiatic Studies* 6:135–246.

Feldman, Lawrence H., 1971. *A Tumpline Economy. Production and Distribution Systems of Early Central-East Guatemala*. PhD Thesis, Pennsylvania State University.

Feldman, Robert A., 1978. Technology of Peruvian metallurgy, in *Peru's Golden Treasures*, ed. Michael E. Moseley. Chicago: Field Museum of Natural History, pp. 69–73.

REFERENCES

Ferdon, Edwin N., 1981. *Early Tahiti as the Explorers Saw It, 1767–1797*. Tucson: University of Arizona Press.

Fernandez, James W., 1982. *Bwiti: An Ethnography of the Religious Imagination in Africa*. Princeton: Princeton University Press.

Fernandez de Oviedo y Valdes, Gonzalo, 1852–53. *Historia general y natural de las Indias*. Vols. 2–3. Madrid: La Real Academia de la Historia.

Fitzgerald, C. P., 1961. *China*. New York: Praeger.

Flannery, Kent V., 1968. The Olmec and the valley of Oaxaca: A model for inter-regional interaction in formative times, in *Dumbarton Oaks Conference on the Olmec*, ed. Elizabeth Benson, Washington, D.C.: Dumbarton Oaks Research Library and Collection, pp. 79–117.

Ford, Richard I., 1972. Barter, gift or violence: An analysis of Tewa intertribal exchange, in *Social Exchange and Interaction*, ed. Edwin N. Wilmsen. Ann Arbor: University of Michigan Press, pp. 21–45.

Foreman, Carolyn T., 1943. *Indians Abroad, 1493–1938*. Norman: University of Oklahoma Press.

Forge, Anthony, 1967. The Abelam artist, in *Social Organization: Essays Presented to Raymond Firth*, ed. Maurice Freedman. Chicago: Aldine, pp. 65–84.

Fowler, Loretta, 1982. *Arapahoe Politics, 1851–1978*. Lincoln: University of Nebraska Press.

Fraser, Douglas, 1968. *Village Planning in the Primitive World*. New York: Braziller.

Fraser, Douglas, and Herbert M. Cole, eds., 1972 *African Art and Leadership*. Madison: University of Wisconsin Press.

Frazer, Sir James G., 1922. *The Golden Bough*, Part II. *Taboo and the Perils of the Soul*. London: Macmillan.

Friedman, J., and M. J. Rowlands, eds., 1978. *The Evolution of Social Systems*. Pittsburgh: University of Pittsburgh Press.

Fülöp-Miller, Rene, 1930. *The Power and Secret of the Jesuits*. New York: Viking.

Ganz, David, 1983. Bureaucratic shorthand and Merovingian learning, in *Ideal and Reality in Frankish and Anglo-Saxon Society*, ed. Patrick Wormald. Oxford: Blackwell, pp. 58–75.

Gardner, Peter M., 1982. Ascribed austerity: A tribal path to purity. *Man* 17:462–69.

Geertz, Clifford, 1980. *Negara. The Theatre State in Nineteenth-Century Bali*. Princeton: Princeton University Press.

George, Katherine, 1958. The civilized West looks at primitive Africa, 1400–1800: A study in ethnocentrism. *Isis* 49:62–72.

Giddens, Anthony, 1979. *Central Problems in Social Theory.* Berkeley: University of California Press.

Gladwin, Thomas, 1970. *East is a Big Bird.* Cambridge: Harvard University Press.

Goldman, Irving, 1940. Cosmological beliefs of the Cubeo Indians. *Journal of American Folklore* 53:292–97.

———. 1970. *Ancient Polynesian Society.* Chicago: University of Chicago Press.

———. 1977. Time, space and descent: The Cubeo example. *Social Time and Social Space in Lowland South American Societies.* Joanna Overing-Kaplan, organizer. Actes XLII Congrès International des Americanistes, Vol. II, Paris, pp. 175–84.

Goldstein, Thomas, 1965. Geography in fifteenth-century Florence, in *Merchants and Scholars,* ed. John Parker. Minneapolis: University of Minnesota Press, pp. 11–27.

———. 1976. Impulses of Italian renaissance culture behind the age of discoveries, in *First Images of America,* Vol. I, ed. Fredi Chiappelli. Berkeley: University of California Press, pp. 27–36.

Goodenough, Ward H., 1986. Sky world and this world: The place of Kachaw in Micronesian cosmology. *American Anthropologist* 88:551–68.

Goody, Jack, 1968. Restricted literacy in Northern Ghana, in *Literacy in Traditional Societies,* ed. Jack Goody. London: Cambridge University Press, pp. 199–241.

Gossen, Gary H., 1974. *Chamulas in the World of the Sun.* Cambridge: Harvard University Press.

———. 1975. Animal souls and human destiny in Chamula. *Man* 10:448–61.

Granet, Marcel, 1958. *Chinese Civilization.* K. E. Innes and M. R. Brailsford, trans. Cleveland: World Publishing.

Gregor, Thomas, 1977. *Mehinaku.* Chicago: University of Chicago Press.

Gullick, C.J.M.R., 1981. Pilgrimage, cults and holy places. *Journal of the Durham University Anthropological Society* 6:1–13.

Hallowell, A. Irving, 1955. Cultural factors in spatial orientation, in *Culture and Experience,* ed. A. Hallowell. Philadelphia: University of Pennsylvania Press, pp. 134–202.

Hamell, George R., 1981. *The Magic of Glass Beads—Trade Beads as Crystals.* Unpublished manuscript.

———. 1982. *Trading in Metaphors: The Magic of Beads.* Unpublished manuscript.

Hand, Wayland D., 1976. The effect of the discovery on ethnological and folklore studies in Europe, in *First Images of America*, Vol. I, ed. Fredi Chiappelli. Berkeley: University of California Press, pp. 45–56.

Handy, E. S. Craighill, et al., 1965. *Ancient Hawaiian Civilization*, rev. ed. Rutland, Vt.: Tuttle.

Harding, Thomas G., 1967. *Voyagers of the Vitiaz Straits*. Seattle: University of Washington Press.

Harner, Michael, 1973. *The Jivaro*. New York: Anchor Press–Doubleday.

Hasan, Yusuf Fadl, 1966. The penetration of Islam in the Eastern Sudan, in *Islam in Tropical Africa*, ed. I. M. Lewis. London: Oxford University Press, pp. 144–59.

Heizer, Robert F., 1947. Francis Drake and the California Indians, 1579. *University of California Publications in American Archaeology and Ethnology* 42:251–79.

Helms, Mary W., 1979. *Ancient Panama: Chiefs in Search of Power*. Austin: University of Texas Press.

———. 1981. Precious metals and politics: Style and ideology in the intermediate area and Peru. *Journal of Latin American Lore* 7:215–38.

———. 1986a. Art styles and interaction spheres in Central America and the Caribbean: Polished black wood in the Greater Antilles. *Journal of Latin American Lore* 12:25–44.

———. 1986b. Of kings and contexts: Ethnohistorical interpretations of Miskito political structure and function. *American Ethnologist* 13:506–23.

Heyden, Doris, 1981. Caves, gods, and myths: World-view and planning in Teotihuacan, in *Mesoamerican Sites and World-Views*, ed. Elizabeth P. Benson. Dumbarton Oaks Research Library and Collections, Washington, D.C., pp. 1–27.

Hickerson, Harold, 1973. Fur trade colonialism and the North American Indians. *Journal of Ethnic Studies* 1:15–44.

Hill, W. W., 1948. Navaho trading and trading ritual: A Study of cultural dynamics. *Southwestern Journal of Anthropology* 4:371–96.

Hirsch, Elizabeth F., 1965. The discoveries and the humanists, in *Merchants and Scholars*, ed. John Parker. Minneapolis: University of Minnesota Press, pp. 35–45.

Hogden, Margaret T., 1964. *Early Anthropology in the Sixteenth and Seventeenth Centuries*. Philadelphia: University of Pennsylvania Press.

Holloman, Regina E., 1969. *Developmental Change in San Blas*. PhD Dissertation, Northwestern University.

Howe, James, 1974. *Village political organization among the San Blas Cuna.* PhD Dissertation, University of Pennsylvania.

―――. 1986 *The Kuna Gathering: Contemporary Village Politics in Panama.* Austin: University of Texas Press.

Hugh-Jones, Christine, 1977. Skin and soul: The round and the straight. Social time and social space in Pira-Parana society. *Social Time and Social Space in Lowland South American Societies.* Joanna Overing-Kaplan, organizer. Actes XLII Congrès International des Americanistes, Vol. II, Paris, pp. 185–204.

―――. 1979 *From the Milk River: Spatial and Temporal Processes in Northwest Amazonia.* London: Cambridge University Press.

Hugh-Jones, Stephen, 1982. The Pleiades and Scorpius in Barasana cosmology, in *Ethnoastronomy and Archaeoastronomy in the American Tropics,* ed. Anthony F. Aveni and Gary Urton. New York: New York Academy of Sciences, pp. 183–202.

Hunt, Eva, 1977. *The Transformation of the Hummingbird.* Ithaca: Cornell University Press.

Hunwick, J. O., 1966. Religion and state in the Songhay empire, 1464–1591, in *Islam in Tropical Africa,* ed. I. M. Lewis. London: Oxford University Press, pp. 296–317.

Isaac, Erich, 1965. *Religious Geography and the Geography of Religion: Man and the Earth.* University of Colorado Studies, Series in Earth Sciences No. 3:1–14.

Isbell, Billie Jean, 1978. *To Defend Ourselves: Ecology and Ritual in an Andean Village.* Austin: University of Texas Press.

Jaenen, Cornelius J., 1982. "Les Sauvages Ameriquains": Persistence into the 18th century of traditional French concepts and constructs for comprehending Amerindians. *Ethnohistory* 29:43–56.

Johnson, Hildegard B., 1976. New geographical horizons: Concepts, in *First Images of America,* Vol. II, ed. Fredi Chiappelli. Berkeley: University of California Press, pp. 615–34.

Jones, Howard M., 1964. *O Strange New World.* New York: Viking Press.

Jones, W. R., 1971. The image of the barbarian in Medieval Europe. *Comparative Studies in Society and History* 13:376–407.

Kaeppler, Adrienne, 1978. Exchange patterns in goods and spouses: Fiji, Tonga and Samoa. *Mankind* 11:246–52.

Kendall, Alan, 1970. *Medieval Pilgrims.* New York: Putnam.

Kent, R. K., 1969. Madagascar and Africa III. The Anteimoro: A theocracy in southeastern Madagascar. *Journal of African History* 10:45–65.

———. 1970. *Early Kingdoms in Madagascar 1500–1700*. New York: Holt, Rinehart and Winston.

Keyes, Charles F., 1975. Buddhist pilgrimage centers and the twelve-year cycle: Northern Thai moral orders in space and time. *History of Religions* 15:71–89.

Kimble, George H. T., 1938. *Geography in the Middle Ages*. London: Methuen.

Kipling, Rudyard, 1963. *In the Vernacular: The English in India*. Garden City, N.Y.: Anchor.

Kirby, W. F., trans. 1907. *Kalevala, the Land of the Heroes*, Vol. I. London: Dent.

Kolaja, Jiri, 1969. *Social System and Time and Space*. Pittsburgh, Pa.: Duquesne University Press.

Konetzke, Richard, 1953–54. Entrepreneurial activities of Spanish and Portuguese noblemen in medieval times. *Explorations in Entrepreneurial History* 6:115–20

Kottak, Conrad P., 1972. A cultural adaptive approach to Malagasy political organization, in *Social Exchange and Interaction*, ed. Edwin N. Wilmsen. Ann Arbor: University of Michigan Press, pp. 107–28.

———. 1980. *The Past in the Present*. Ann Arbor: University of Michigan Press.

Kramer, Fritz W., 1970. *Literature Among the Cuna Indians*. *Etnologiska Studier* 30. Göteborg, Sweden.

Krige, E. Jensen and J. D. Krige, 1943. *The Realm of a Rain-Queen*. London: Oxford University Press.

Kristeller, Paul O., 1966. Philosophy and humanism in Renaissance perspective, in *The Renaissance Image of Man and the World*, ed. Bernard O'Kelley. Ohio State University Press, pp. 29–51.

La Lone, Darrell E., 1977. *Trade and Commerce in Inca Peru*. Paper presented at the 76th annual meeting of the American Anthropological Association, Houston.

Lathrap, Donald W., 1973. The antiquity and importance of long-distance trade relationships in the moist tropics of pre-Columbian South America. *World Archaeology* 5:170–86.

Lattimore, Owen D., 1968. The frontier in history, in *Theory in Anthropology*, ed. Robert A. Manners and David Kaplan. Chicago: Aldine, pp. 374–86.

Launay, Robert, 1982. *Traders without Trade*. London: Cambridge University Press.

Lawless, Robert, 1975. Effects of population growth and environmental changes on divination practices in northern Luzon. *Journal of Anthropological Research* 31:18–33.

Lawrence, Peter, 1964. *Road Belong Cargo*. Manchester: Manchester University Press.

Leach, Edmund R., 1961. Two essays concerning the symbolic representation of time, in *Rethinking Anthropology*, ed. E. R. Leach. London: Athlone Press, University of London, pp. 124–36.

Leach, Jerry W. and Edmund R. Leach, eds., 1983. *The Kula: New Perspectives on Massim Exchange*. London: Cambridge University Press.

Lechtman, Heather, 1979. Issues in Andean metallurgy, in *Pre-Columbian Metallurgy of South America*, ed. Elizabeth P. Benson. Washington, D.C.: Dumbarton Oaks Research Library and Collections, pp. 1–40.

Lehman, F. K., 1979. Who are the Karen, and if so, why? Karen ethnohistory and a formal theory of ethnicity, in *Ethnic Adaptation and Identity*, ed. Charles F. Keyes. Philadelphia: Institute for the Study of Human Issues, pp. 215–54.

Lehner, Ernest and Johanna Lehner, 1966. *How They Saw the New World*. New York: Tudor.

León-Portilla, Miguel, 1963. *Aztec Thought and Culture*, trans. Jack E. Davis. Norman: University of Oklahoma Press.

———. 1969. *Pre-Columbian Literatures of Mexico*. Norman: University of Oklahoma Press.

———. 1973. *Time and Reality in the Thought of the Maya*, trans. Charles L. Boiles and Fernando Horcasitas. Boston: Beacon Press.

Lévi-Strauss, Claude, 1967. The social and psychological aspects of chieftainship in a primitive tribe: The Nambikuara of northwestern Mato Grosso, in *Comparative Political Systems*, ed. Ronald Cohen and John Middleton. Garden City, N.Y.: The Natural History Press, pp. 45–62.

Levtzion, Nehemia, 1973. *Ancient Ghana and Mali*. London: Methuen.

Lewis, I. M. 1966. Introduction to *Islam in Tropical Africa*, ed. I. M. Lewis. London: Oxford University Press, pp. 4–126.

Lienhardt, Godfrey, 1954. The Shilluk of the Upper Nile, in *African Worlds*, ed. Daryll Forde. London: Oxford University Press, pp. 138–63.

———. 1961. *Divinity and Experience*. Oxford: Clarendon Press.

Lindstrom, Lamont, 1984. Doctor, lawyer, wiseman, priest: Big-men and knowledge in Melanesia. *Man* 19:291–309.

Lips, Julius E., 1937. *The Savage Hits Back*. New Haven: Yale University Press.

Lopez, Robert S., 1943. European merchants in the medieval Indies: The evidence of commercial documents. *Journal of Economic History* 3:164–84.

———. 1945. Silk industry in the Byzantine Empire. *Speculum* 20:1–42.

Lot, Ferdinand, 1931. *The End of the Ancient World and the Beginnings of the Middle Ages*. New York: Knopf.

Lovejoy, Arthur O., 1948. *Essays in the History of Ideas*. Baltimore: Johns Hopkins University Press.

Loven, Sven, 1935. *Origins of the Tainan Culture, West Indies*. Göteborg: Elanders.

Malinowski, Bronislaw, 1922. *Argonauts of the Western Pacific*. New York: E. P. Dutton.

Mannoni, O., 1964. *Prospero and Caliban*. New York: Praeger.

Manuel, Frank E. and Fritzie P. Manuel, 1971. Sketch for a natural history of paradise, in *Myth, Symbol and Culture*, ed. Clifford Geertz. New York: Norton, pp. 83–128.

Marlowe, David H., 1979. In the mosaic: The cognitive and structural aspects of Karen–other relationships, in *Ethnic Adaptation and Identity*, ed. Charles F. Keyes. Philadelphia: Institute for the Study of Human Issues, pp. 165–214.

Marshall, P. J. and Glyndwr Williams, 1982. *The Great Map of Mankind*. Cambridge: Harvard University Press.

Mason, J. Alden, 1957. *The Ancient Civilizations of Peru*. Harmondsworth, UK: Penguin.

Mathew, Gervase, 1975. The dating and the significance of the Periplus of the Erythrean Sea, in *East Africa and the Orient*, ed. H. Neville Chittick and Robert J. Rotberg. New York: Africana Publishing, pp. 147–64.

Mattingly, Harold, 1957. *Roman Imperial Civilization*. New York: St. Martin's Press.

McAuley, James, 1960. We are men—What are you? *Quadrant* (Sydney, Australia) 15:73–79.

McCarthy, F. D., 1939. "Trade" in Aboriginal Australia, and "trade" relationships with Torres Strait, New Guinea and Malaya. *Oceania* 9:405–38 and 10:80–105, 171–95.

McKinley, Robert, 1976. Human and proud of it: A structural treatment of headhunting rites and the social definition of enemies, in *Studies in Borneo Societies: Social Process and Anthropological Explanation*, ed. G. N. Appell. Center for Southeast Asian Studies, Northern Illinois University, pp. 92–145.

Meek, C. K., 1969. *A Sudanese Kingdom*. New York: Negro Universities Press.

REFERENCES

Meyendorff, Baron A. F., 1926. Trade and communication in Eastern Europe, A.D. 800–1200, in *Travel and Travelers of the Middle Ages*, ed. Arthur Percival Newton. New York: Knopf, pp. 104–23.

Middleton, John, 1960. *Lugbara Religion*. London: Oxford University Press.

Miller, Christopher L. and George R. Hamell, 1986. A new perspective on Indian–White contact: Cultural symbols and colonial trade. *Journal of American History* 73:311–28.

Miller, J. Innes, 1969. *The Spice Trade of the Roman empire*. Oxford: Clarendon Press.

Mingana, Alfonso, 1925. The early spread of christianity in Central Asia and the Far East: A new document. *Bulletin of the John Rylands Library* 9:297–371.

Mirsky, Jeannette, 1964. *The Great Chinese Travelers*. Chicago: University of Chicago Press.

Mishkin, Bernard, 1940. Cosmological ideas among the Indians of the Southern Andes. *Journal of American Folklore* 53:225–41.

Moerman, Michael, 1975. Chiangkham's trade in the "old days," in *Change and Persistence in Thai Society*, ed. G. William Skinner and A. Thomas Kirsch. Ithaca: Cornell University Press, pp. 151–71.

Montague, Susan P., 1980. Kula and Trobriand cosmology. *Journal of Anthropology* 2:70–94.

Morphy, Howard, 1978. Rights in paintings and rights in women: A consideration of some of the basic problems posed by the asymmetry of the "Murngin system," in *Trade and Exchange in Oceania and Australia*, ed. Jim Specht and J. Peter White. *Mankind* 11:208–19.

Mulvaney, D. J., 1976. 'The chain of connection': The material evidence, in *Tribes and Boundaries in Australia*, ed. Nicolas Peterson. Australia Institute of Aboriginal Studies. New Jersey: Humanities Press, pp. 72–94.

Munn, Nancy, 1977. The spatiotemporal transformations of Gawa canoes. *Journal de la Société des Oceanistes* 33:39–54.

———. 1983. Gawan Kula: Spatiotemporal control and the symbolism of influence, in *The Kula, New Perspectives on Massim Exchange*, ed. Jerry W. Leach and Edmund R. Leach. London: Cambridge University Press, pp. 277–308.

Murphy, William P., 1981. The rhetorical management of dangerous knowledge in Kpelle brokerage. *American Ethnologist* 8:667–85.

Myerhoff, Barbara G., 1978. Return to Wirikuta: Ritual reversal and symbolic continuity on the peyote hunt of the Huichol Indians, in *The*

282

Reversible World, ed. Barbara A. Babcock. Ithaca: Cornell University Press, pp. 225–39.

Nash, June, 1972. The devil in Bolivia's nationalized tin mines. *Science and Society* 36:221–33.

Netherly, Patricia J., 1980. *Exchange in the Lambayeque and Chimu States.* Paper presented at the annual meeting of the American Anthropological Association, Washington, D.C.

Netting, Robert McC., 1972. Sacred power and centralization: Aspects of political adaptation in Africa, in *Population Growth: Anthropological Implications*, ed. Brian Spooner. Cambridge: Massachusetts Institute of Technology, pp. 219–44.

Newton, Arthur P., 1926. "Travelers' tales" of wonder and imagination, in *Travel and Travellers of the Middle Ages*, ed. A. P. Newton. New York: Knopf, pp. 159–73.

Nordenskiöld, Erland, 1929. The relationship between art, religion and magic among the Cuna and Choco Indians. *Journal de la Société des Americanistes*, n.s. 21:141–58.

———. 1938. *An Historical and Ethnological Survey of the Cuna Indians.* Comparative Ethnographic Studies No. 10, Göteborg, Sweden.

Nordholt, H. G. Schulte, 1971. *The Political System of the Atoni of Timor.* Verhandelingen van het Koninklijk Instituut voor Taal-, Land- en Volkenkunde. The Hague: Martinus Nijhoff.

Noveck, Simon, ed., 1959. *Great Jewish Personalities in Ancient and Medieval Times.* Washington, D.C.: B'nai B'rith Department of Adult Jewish Education.

Oakes, Katherine B., 1944. *Social Theory in the Early Literature of Voyage and Exploration in Africa.* PhD Dissertation, University of California.

Oberem, Udo, 1974. Trade and trade goods in the Ecuadorian montaña, in *Native South Americans, Ethnology of the Least Known Continent*, ed. Patricia J. Lyon. Boston: Little, Brown, pp. 346–57.

O'Gorman, Edmundo, 1961. *The Invention of America.* Bloomington: Indiana University Press.

Olien, Michael D., 1983. The Miskito kings and the line of succession. *Journal of Anthropological Research* 39:198–241.

Ong, Walter J., 1982. *Orality and Literacy.* London: Methuen.

Ortiz, Alfonso, 1969. *The Tewa World.* Chicago: University of Chicago Press.

Ottenberg, Simon, 1958. Ibo oracles and intergroup relations. *Southwestern Journal of Anthropology* 14:295–315.

Overing-Kaplan, Joanna, organizer, 1977. *Social Time and Social Space in Lowland South American Societies.* Actes XLII Congrès International des Americanistes, Vol. II. Paris: International Society of Americanists.

Packard, Randall M., 1980. Social change and the history of misfortune among the Bashu of eastern Zaire, in *Explorations in African Systems of Thought*, ed. Ivan Karp and Charles S. Bird. Bloomington: Indiana University Press.

Pagden, Anthony, 1982. *The Fall of Natural Man*. London: Cambridge University Press.

Park, George K., 1966. Kinga priests: The politics of pestilence, in *Political Anthropology*, ed. Marc J. Swartz, Victor W. Turner, and Arthur Tuden. Chicago: Aldine, pp. 229–37.

Patterson, Thomas C., 1983. *Pachacamac—the Andean oracle under Inca Rule*. Unpublished manuscript.

Pearce, Roy H., 1965. *The Savages of America*, revised edn. Baltimore: Johns Hopkins University Press.

Penrose, Boies, 1952. *Travel and Discovery in the Renaissance, 1420–1620*. Cambridge: Harvard University Press.

———. 1962. *Tudor and Early Stuart Voyaging*. Charlottesville: University Press of Virginia.

Pike, Ruth, 1972. *Aristocrats and Traders*. Ithaca: Cornell University Press.

Pinxten, Rik, Ingred van Dooren, and Frank Harvey, 1983. *Anthropology of Space*. Philadelphia: University of Pennsylvania Press.

Pocock, D. F., 1975. North and south in the Book of Genesis, in *Studies in Social Anthropology*, ed. J.H.M. Beattie and R. G. Lienhardt. Oxford: Clarendon Press, pp. 273–84.

Polanyi, Karl, 1975. Traders and trade, in *Ancient Civilization and Trade*, ed. Jeremy Sabloff and C. C. Lamberg-Karlovsky. Albuquerque: University of New Mexico Press, pp. 133–54.

Posey, Darrell A., 1979. *A Non-lineal Universe and the Struggle for Survival*. Unpublished manuscript.

———. NDa. *The Kayapó Origin of Night*. Unpublished manuscript.

———. NDb. *The Journey to Become a Shaman: A Narrative of Sacred Transition of the Kayapó Indians of Brazil*. Unpublished manuscript.

Power, Eileen, 1926. The opening of the land routes to Cathay, in *Travel and Travellers of the Middle Ages*, ed. Arthur P. Newton. New York: Knopf, pp. 124–58.

Prestage, Edgar, 1926. The search for the sea route to India, in *Travel and Travellers of the Middle Ages*, ed. Arthur Percival Newton. New York: Knopf, pp. 195–216.

Quinn, David B., 1976. New geographical horizons: Literature, in *First*

Images of America, Vol. II, ed. Fredi Chiappelli. Berkeley: University of California Press, pp. 635–58.

Rabineau, Phyllis, 1975. Artists and leaders: The social context of creativity in a tropical forest culture, in *The Cashinahua of Eastern Peru*, ed. Kenneth M. Kensinger, et al. Brown University, Haffenreffer Museum of Anthropology, pp. 87–109.

Ramsay, Raymond H., 1972. *No Longer on the Map*. New York: Viking.

Rappaport, Joanne, 1983. *Sacred Space, Frontiers and Politics in Southern Highland Colombia*. Paper presented at the annual meeting of the American Anthropological Association, Chicago.

Rasmussen, Knud, 1931. *The Netsilik Eskimos: Social Life and Spiritual Culture*. Report of the Fifth Thule Expedition 1921–24. Vol. 8, No. 1–2. Copenhagen: Gyldendalske Boghandel, Nordisk Forlag.

Read, Kenneth E., 1958. A "cargo" situation in the Markham Valley, New Guinea. *Southwestern Journal of Anthropology* 14:273–94.

Reay, Marie, 1967. Present-day politics in the New Guinea Highlands, in *Comparative Political Systems* ed. R. Cohen and John Middleton. New York: Natural History Press, pp. 193–215.

Rees, Alwyn and Brinley Rees, 1961. *Celtic Heritage*. London: Thames and Hudson.

Reichard, Gladys A., 1963. *Navaho Religion*. New York: Pantheon.

Reichel-Dolmatoff, Gerardo, 1981. Things of beauty replete with meaning—metals and crystals in Colombian Indian cosmology, in *Sweat of the Sun, Tears of the Moon: Gold and Emerald Treasures of Colombia*, ed. Peter Furst, et al. Los Angeles: Terra Magazine Pub. and Natural History Museum, pp. 17–33.

Reynolds, Henry. 1978. 'Before the instant of contact': Some evidence from nineteenth-century Queensland. *Aboriginal History* 2:63–68.

Ribeiro, Rene, 1970. Brazilian messianic movements, in *Millennial Dreams in Action*, ed. Sylvia L. Thrupp. New York: Schocken, pp. 55–69.

Rice, Don S. and Daniel Foley, 1983. *The Accession of Maya Kings: Regeneration, Transformation and Political Power*. Paper presented at the annual meeting of the American Anthropological Society, Chicago, Ill.

Rigby, P.J.A., 1966. Sociological factors in the contact of the Gogo of central Tanzania with Islam, in *Islam in Tropical Africa*, ed. I. M. Lewis. London: Oxford University Press, pp. 268–95.

Roe, Peter G., 1982. *The Cosmic Zygote*. New Brunswick, N.J.: Rutgers University Press.

Rogers, Edward S., 1965. Leadership among the Indians of eastern subarctic Canada. *Anthropologica* n.d. 7:263–84.

Rosaldo, Renato I., Jr., 1978. The rhetoric of control: Ilongots viewed as natural bandits and wild Indians, in *The Reversible World*, ed. Barbara A. Babcock. Ithaca: Cornell University Press, pp. 240–57.

Roscher, Wilhelm, 1944. The status of the Jews in the Middle Ages considered from the standpoint of commercial policy. *Historia Judaica* 6:13–26.

Rotberg, Robert I., 1970. Introduction to *Africa and Its Explorers*, ed. Robert I. Rotberg. Cambridge: Harvard University Press, pp. 1–12.

Rousseau, Philip, 1978. *Ascetics, Authority, and the Church in the Age of Jerome and Cassian*. London: Oxford Unversity Press.

Rowbotham, Arnold H., 1942. *Missionary and Mandarin. The Jesuits at the Court of China*. Berkeley: University of California Press.

Roys, Ralph L., 1972. *The Indian Background of Colonial Yucatan*. Norman: University of Oklahoma Press.

Ruby, Robert H. and John A. Brown, 1975. *The Chinook Indians*. Norman: University of Oklahoma Press.

Sahagún, Fray Bernardino de, 1957. *General History of the Things of New Spain*. Book 4: *The Soothsayers*, and Book 5: *The Omens*, trans. Charles E. Dibble and Arthur J. O. Anderson. Santa Fe, N.M.: School of American Research and the University of Utah.

———. 1959. *General History of the Things of New Spain*. Book 9: *The Merchants*, trans. Charles E. Dibble and Arthur J. O. Anderson. Santa Fe, N.M.: School of American Research and the University of Utah.

Sahlins, Marshall, 1981. *Historical Metaphors and Mythical Realities*. Ann Arbor: University of Michigan Press.

Salisbury, Neal, 1982. *Manitou and Providence*. New York: Oxford University Press.

Salmond, Anne, 1975. "Mana makes the man": A look at Maori oratory and politics, in *Political Language and Oratory in Traditional Society*, ed. Maurice Bloch. London: Academic Press, pp. 45–63.

Salomon, Frank, 1981. Killing the Yumbo: A ritual drama of northern Quito, in *Cultural Transformations and Ethnicity in Modern Ecuador*, ed. Norman E. Whitten, Jr. Urbana: University of Illinois Press, pp. 162–208.

———. 1986. *Native Lords of Quito in the Age of the Incas*. London: Cambridge University Press.

Sanders, Ronald, 1978. *Lost Tribes and Promised Lands*. Boston: Little, Brown.

Sauer, Carl O., 1969. *The Early Spanish Main*. Berkeley: University of California Press.

Sawyer, P. H., 1977. Kings and merchants, in *Early Medieval Kingship*, ed. P. H. Sawyer and I. N. Wood. Leeds, UK: University of Leeds Press, pp. 139–60.

Schafer, Edward H., 1963. *The Golden Peaches of Samarkand*. Berkeley: University of California Press.

———. 1967 *The Vermilion Bird*. Berkeley: University of California Press.

Schapera, I., 1956. *Government and Politics in Tribal Societies*. London: Watts.

Schneider, Jane, 1977. Was there a pre-capitalist world system? *Peasant Studies* 6:20–29.

Schoff, Wilfred H., trans. and annotator. 1974. *The Periplus of The Erythraean Sea*, 2d ed. New Delhi: Oriental Books Reprint Corp.

Scholes, France V. and Ralph L. Roys, 1968. *The Maya Chontal Indians of Acalan-Tixchel*. Norman: University of Oklahoma Press.

Scoditti, Giancarlo M. G., with Jerry W. Leach, 1983. Kula on Kitava, in *The Kula: New Perspectives on Massim Exchange*, ed. Jerry W. Leach and Edmund Leach. London: Cambridge University Press, pp. 249–76.

Seeger, Anthony, 1977. Fixed points on area circles: The temporal processual aspects of Suya space and society. *Social Time and Social Space in Lowland South American Societies*. Joanna Overing-Kaplan, organizer. Actes XLII Congrès International des Americanistes, Vol. II, Paris, pp. 341–60.

———. 1981. *Nature and Society in Central Brazil*. Cambridge: Harvard University Press.

Shennan, Stephen, 1982. Exchange and ranking: The role of amber in the earlier Bronze Age of Europe, in *Ranking, Resource and Exchange*, ed. Colin Renfrew and Stephen Shennan. London: Cambridge University Press, pp. 33–44.

Sherzer, Joel, 1983. *Kuna Ways of Speaking*. Austin: University of Texas Press.

Skinner, Elliott P., 1963. Strangers in West African societies. *Africa* 33:307–20.

Smith, Jonathan Z., 1969. Earth and gods. *Journal of Religion* 49:103–27.

———. 1972 The wobbling pivot. *Journal of Religion* 52:134–49.

Snow, Philip and Stephanie Waine, 1979. *The People from the Horizon*. New York: Phaidon.

Sorokin, Pitirim A., 1943. *Sociocultural Causality, Space, Time*. Durham: Duke University Press.

Soustelle, Jacques, 1970. *Daily Life of the Aztecs*. Stanford: Stanford University Press.

Southall, Aidan W., 1953. *Alur Society*. Cambridge, UK: Heffer.

Southall, Aidan W., 1979. White strangers and their religion in East Africa and Madagascar, in *Strangers in African Societies*, ed. W. Shack and E. P. Skinner. Berkeley: University of California Press, pp. 211–26.

Spence, Jonathan D., 1984. *The Memory Palace of Matteo Ricci*. New York: Viking.

Stancliffe, Clare, 1983. Kings who opted out, in *Ideal and Reality in Frankish and Anglo-Saxon Society*, ed. P. Wormald. Oxford: Blackwell, pp. 154–76.

Stein, Burton, 1965. Coromandel trade in medieval India, in *Merchants and Scholars*, ed. John Parker. Minneapolis: University of Minnesota Press, pp. 49–61.

Stevenson, R. C., 1966. Some aspects of the spread of Islam in the Nuba Mountains, in *Islam in Tropical Africa*, ed. I. M. Lewis. London: Oxford University Press, pp. 208–32.

Stover, Leon E., 1974. *The Cultural Ecology of Chinese Civilization*. New York: New American Library.

Strayer, Robert, 1976. Mission history in Africa: New perspectives on an encounter. *African Studies Review* 19:1–15.

Strehlow, T.G.H., 1947. *Aranda Traditions*. Melbourne University Press (New York: Johnson Reprint Corp.)

Sumption, Jonathan, 1975. *Pilgrimage: An Image of Mediaeval Religion*. Totowa, N.J.: Rowman and Littlefield.

Sundström, Lars, 1974. *The Exchange Economy of Pre-Colonial Tropical Africa*. New York: St. Martin's Press.

Tambiah, S. J., 1983. On flying witches and flying canoes: The coding of male and female values, in *The Kula: New Perspectives on Massim Exchange*, ed. Jerry W. Leach and Edmund Leach. London: Cambridge University Press, pp. 171–200.

Taussig, Michael T., 1980a. *The Devil and Commodity Fetishism in South America*. Chapel Hill: University of North Carolina Press.

———. 1980b. Folk healing and the structure of conquest in southwest Colombia. *Journal of Latin American Lore* 6:217–78.

Tedlock, Barbara, 1982. *Time and the Highland Maya*. Albuquerque: University of New Mexico Press.

Tedlock, Barbara and Dennis Tedlock, 1985. Text and textile: Language and technology in the arts of the Quiche Maya. *Journal of Anthropological Research* 41:121–46.

Tefft, Stanton K., ed. 1980. *Secrecy*. New York: Human Sciences Press.

Thapar, Romila, 1966. *A History of India*, Vol. 1. Harmondsworth, UK: Penguin.

————. 1971. The image of the barbarian in early India. *Comparative Studies in Society and History* 13:408–36.

Thompson, J. Eric S., 1970. *Maya History and Religion*. Norman: University of Oklahoma Press.

Thornton, Robert J., 1980. *Space, Time and Culture among the Iraqw of Tanzania*. New York: Academic Press.

Tindale, Norman B., 1978. Notes on a few Australian Aboriginal concepts, in *Australian Aboriginal Concepts*, ed. L. R. Hiatt. New Jersey: Humanities Press, pp. 156–63.

Toby, Ronald P., 1984. *State and Diplomacy in Early Modern Japan*. Princeton: Princeton University Press.

Townsend, Richard F., 1979. *State and Cosmos in the Art of Tenochtitlan*. Studies in Pre-Columbian Art and Archaeology, No. 20. Washington, D.C.: Dumbarton Oaks Research Library and Collections.

Traube, Elizabeth, 1984. *Authoritative Knowledge in an East Timorese Society*. Paper presented at the annual meeting of the American Anthropological Association.

Trimingham, J. Spencer, 1959. *Islam in West Africa*. Oxford: Clarendon Press.

Trinkaus, Charles, 1976. Renaissance and discovery, in *First Images of America*, Vol. I, ed. Fredi Chiappelli. Berkeley: University of California Press, pp. 3–10.

Tuan, Yi-Fu, 1977. *Space and Place: The Perspective of Experience*. Minneapolis: University of Minnesota Press.

Turner, Victor, 1972. The center out there: Pilgrim's goal. *History of Religions* 12:191–230.

Turner, Victor and Edith Turner, 1978. *Image and Pilgrimage in Christian Culture*. New York: Columbia University Press.

Uberoi, J. P. Singh, 1971. *Politics of the Kula Ring*. Manchester, UK: Manchester University Press.

Upham, Steadman, 1982. *Politics and Power*. New York: Academic Press.

Urton, Gary, 1981. *At the Crossroads of the Earth and the Sky*. Austin: University of Texas Press.

Van Gennep, Arnold, 1960. *The Rites of Passage*. Chicago: University of Chicago Press.

Villas Boas, Orlando and Claudio Villas Boas, 1970. *Xingu: The Indians, Their Myths*. New York: Farrar, Strauss and Giroux.

Vogt, Evon Z., 1981. Some aspects of the sacred geography of highland Chiapas, in *Mesoamerican Sites and World-Views*, ed. Elizabeth P. Benson. Washington, D.C.: Dumbarton Oaks Research Library and Collection, pp. 119–42.

Wagley, Charles, 1977. Time and the Tapirapé. *Social Time and Social Space in Lowland South American Societies*. Joanna Overing-Kaplan, organizer. Actes du XLII Congrès International des Americanistes, Paris, pp. 369–78.

Wagner, Gunter, 1954. The Abaluyia of Kavirondo, in *African Worlds*, ed. Daryll Forde. London: Oxford University Press, pp. 27–54.

Wallace-Hadrill, J. M., 1966. *The Barbarian West, 400–1000*. London: Hutchinson University Library.

———. 1971. *Early Germanic Kingship in England and on the Continent*. Oxford: Clarendon Press.

———. 1975. *Early Medieval History*. Oxford: Blackwell.

Wassen, S. Henry, 1940. An analogy between a South American and Oceanic myth motif and Negro influence in Darien. *Etnologiska Studier* 10:69–79.

———. 1972. A medicine-man's implements and plants in a Tiahuanacoid tomb in highland Bolivia. *Etnologiska Studier* 32:8–114.

Watson, O. Michael, 1970. *Proxemic Behavior: A Cross-Cultural Study*. The Hague: Mouton.

Weber, Max, 1946. The Chinese literati. *From Max Weber: Essays in Sociology*, trans. & ed. H. H. Gerth and C. Wright Mills. New York: Oxford University Press, pp. 416–44.

Webster, Elsie M., 1984. *The Moon Man*. Berkeley: University of California Press.

Weckmann-Muñoz, Luis, 1976. The Alexandrine bulls of 1493: Pseudo-Asiatic documents, in *First Images of America*, Vol. I, ed. Fredi Chiappelli. Berkeley: University of California Press, pp. 201–10.

Weiner, Annette B., 1976. *Women of Value, Men of Renown*. Austin: University of Texas Press.

Werner, Dennis, 1981. Are some people more equal than others? Status inequality among the Mekranoti Indians of central Brazil. *Journal of Anthropological Research* 37:360–73.

Wheatley, Paul, 1961. *The Golden Khersonese*. Kuala Lumpur: University of Malaya Press.

———. 1971. *The Pivot of the Four Quarters*. Chicago: Aldine.

———. 1975a. Analecta Sino-Africana Recensa, in *East Africa and the Orient*, ed. H. Neville Chittick and Robert I. Rotberg. New York: Africana Publishing Co., pp. 76–114.

———. 1975b. Satyānrta in Suvarnadvīpa: From reciprocity to redistribution in ancient Southeast Asia, in *Ancient Civilization and Trade*, ed.

Jeremy Sabloff and C. C. Lamberg-Karlofsky. Albuquerque: University of New Mexico Press, pp. 227–65.

Wheeler, Gerald C., 1910. *The Tribe and Intertribal Relations in Australia.* London: Murray.

Wheeler, Sir Mortimer, 1955. *Rome Beyond the Imperial Frontiers.* New York: Philosophical Library.

White, Hayden, 1972. The forms of wildness: Archaeology of an idea, in *The Wild Man Within*, ed. Edward Dudley and Maximillian E. Novak. Pittsburgh: University of Pittsburgh Press, pp. 3–38.

———. 1976. The noble savage theme as fetish, in *First Images of America*, Vol. I, ed. Fredi Chiappelli. Berkeley: University of California Press, pp. 121–34.

Whitten, Norman E., Jr., 1976. *Sacha Runa.* Urbana: University of Illinois Press.

Wilbert, Johannes, 1977. Navigators of the winter sun, in *The Sea in the Pre-Columbian World*, ed. Elizabeth P. Benson. Washington, D.C.: Dumbarton Oaks Research Library and Collections, pp. 17–44.

———. 1979. Geography and telluric lore of the Orinoco delta. *Journal of Latin American Lore* 5:129–50.

Wilks, Ivor, 1966. The position of Muslims in metropolitan Ashanti in the early nineteenth century, in *Islam in Tropical Africa*, ed. I. M. Lewis. London: Oxford University Press, pp. 318–41.

———. 1968. The transmission of Islamic learning in the western Sudan, in *Literacy in Traditional Societies*, ed. Jack Goody. London: Cambridge University Press, pp. 162–94.

Williams, Francis E., 1977. Trading voyages from the Gulf of Papua, in *"The Vailala Madness" and Other Essays*, ed. Erik Schwimmer. Honolulu: University Press of Hawaii, pp. 48–72.

Williams, George H., 1962. *Wilderness and Paradise in Christian Thought.* New York: Harper & Brothers.

Williamson, Robert W., 1933a. *Religious and Cosmic Beliefs of Central Polynesia*, Vol. 1. New York: AMS Press.

———. 1933b. *Religious and Cosmic Beliefs of Central Polynesia*, Vol. 2. London: Cambridge University Press.

Wilson, Godfrey, 1939. *The Constitution of Ngonde.* Rhodes–Livingston Papers, No. 3. Livingston, Northern Rhodesia.

Wilson, Monica, 1958. *The Peoples of the Nyasa–Tanganyika Corridor.* University of Cape Town, School of African Studies.

———. 1977. *For Men and Elders.* New York: Africana Publishing Co.

———. 1979. Strangers in Africa: Reflections on Nyakyusa, Nguni, and

Sotho evidence, in *Strangers in African Societies*, ed. W. Shack and E. Skinner. Berkeley: University of California Press, pp. 51–66.

Wolff, Kurt H., trans. & ed., 1950. *The Sociology of Georg Simmel*. Glencoe, Ill.: Free Press.

Wood, Michael, 1983. The making of King Aethelstan's empire: An English Charlemagne? in *Ideal and Reality in Frankish and Anglo-Saxon Society*, ed. Patrick Wormald. Oxford: Blackwell, pp. 250–72.

Woodburn, James, 1979. Minimal politics: The political organization of the Hadza of north Tanzania. *Politics in Leadership*, ed. W. Shack and R. Cohen. Oxford: Clarendon Press. pp. 244–66.

Wright, John K., 1925. *The Geographical Lore of the Time of the Crusades*. New York: American Geographical Society.

Wrigley, G. M., 1917. The traveling doctors of the Andes: The Callahuayas of Bolivia. *Geographical Review* 4:183–96.

Yates, Frances A., 1947. Queen Elizabeth as Astraea. *Journal of the Warburg and Courtauld Institutes* 10:27–82.

Yu, Ying-shih, 1967. *Trade and Expansion in Han China*. Berkeley: University of California Press.

Zuidema, R. Tom, 1964. *The Ceque System of Cuzco*. Leiden: Brill.

———. 1982. Bureaucracy and systematic knowledge in Andean civilization, in *The Inca and Aztec States, 1400–1800*, ed. George A. Collier, Renato I. Rosaldo, and John D. Wirth. New York: Academic Press, pp. 419–58.

Index

distance, characteristics of (*cont.*)
154–56; geographical and supernatural, 4–5, 30; Hermes as god of, 112–13; and knowledge, 74–75, 155; as obstacle, 58–61; as political resource, 49; political significance of, 58–59; and power, 69–72; and ritual, 30–31; and space-time, 38–45; and speed, 61–64; symbolism of, 38–45, 167; value of goods therefrom, 52–53; vertical and horizontal, 21, 26–28, 44–45

distance specialists, in centralized society, 170; in egalitarian society, 170

distant contacts, as evidence of ability, 152–54

Dyula, 44, 67 n. 1, 95–97

education, foreign, and elites, 157–60

Elema, 46, 84

Eliade, Mircea, 9, 60, 114

elites, adopt European customs, 195–97, 207–208; association with foreigners, 167; and avoidance of distance, 168; and distance, 81–82, 131–32, 149, 162–64, 166–67, 251–52, 255–59, 263–64; and distant goods, 120–21, 123–24; and distant power centers, 137–48; and esoteric knowledge, 5, 151, 163–64, 261; extent of knowledge, 161–62; and foreign education, 157–60; and honor, 167 n. 17; and knowledge rivalry, 108–109; legitimation by European support, 199–200; political use of distance, 75; protect strangers, 149–50; seek European power, 192–98, 200–202; and travel, 85–86, 98, 152–53, 167, 250–60, 267; travel to European centers, 198–201, 203–204; and types of distance, 168–69; and zoos, 164–65. *See also* Chapter 4

Elizabeth I, 256–58

Eskimo, Netsilik, 151–52, 176, 186, 188–89, 203

esoteric knowledge, 261; in centralized society, 170; content of, 12; and distant lands, 16–17, 159–60; in egalitarian society, 170; and foreigners, 94–97, 139–42, 146–47; and leaders, 11–12, 15, 163–64; and rivalry, 95, 108–109; and travel, 155

European Jewry, 150

Europeans, attitudes towards natives, 211, 229–33, 236, 265; as cosmological event, 205; as craftsmen, 182–83; as curers, 174–75; as demons and spirits, 174; elite association with travel, 250–60; as knowledgeable, 180–81; material goods have supernatural powers, 205–208; and mortality, 187; as people with power, 173, 181–85, 188–91, 194–95; as returned ancestors, 173–76, 179–80; as supernaturals, 176–80; and wealth, 176, 180–81, 186, 202–203

fame, and distance and power, 154–56

Fang, 186

fieldworkers, 266

Fipa, 134–35

foreign peoples, characteristics of, 51–52, 56, 98, 103–106

foreign places, characteristics of, 50–51; political manipulation by elites, 51–53

frankincense, 127–28

Gawa Islanders, 24–25

George III, 259

Germanic tribes, 144, 158

gold mining, 117

goods, material, 122; associated with foreign lands, 52–53, 75, 113–14, 164–65, 170, 252–53, 262–63; characteristics of, 113–14; and geographical distance, 118–29; and power, 119–29, 205; value of, 118–29

navigation, and European travel, 244–45

Nestorian Christians, 103–105

New England, 119–20

New World, in space-time, 224–26. *See also* Medieval Europe, cosmography

Ngonde, 13

Nias Islanders, 37

Nilotic groups, 133

Nyakyusa-Ngonde, 135, 181

Nyasa corridor groups, 135

oracles, 30–31, 43, 75, 87 n. 11

Orient, in medieval European cosmography, 213–17, 220–23, 230

Paez, 44

Paliyan, 56

paradise, in European cosmography, 213, 217–20, 225–26, 233–34

peddlers, 167 n. 17

pepper, 128

Philippines, 179 n. 3

pilgrimage, 31–32, 47–48, 53–57, 60–61, 70–77, 100, 137, 139, 146, 150, 162, 200, 237, 240, 242, 250–52

pochteca, 75, 88–95, 122–23, 157

Polanyi, Karl, 167 n. 17

Polynesia, 27–28, 43 n 11, 175–76, 234

power, and distance, 69–72

Prester, John, 216–17, 234

Pueblo Indians, 168. *See also* Tewa

Quiche, 43

Quichua, 41, 70, 165–66

Quetzalcoatl, 116, 137 n. 4, 176–77

relics, 145–47, 252–53

rivalry among men of knowledge, 17–18

Roman Empire, 127–28, 144

ruling lineages and outside origins, 134–37

salt-making, 85 n. 9, 117

Samoa, 150–51

Sangu, 135

Sanusiya of Cyrenaica, 101–103

secrecy, 13–16, 84, 242

secret names, 84

shamans, 47 n. 13, 69–71, 80–81, 114–15, 133–34, 165, 170, 200

Shan, 161

Shilluk, 11, 117, 183

Shipibo, 24, 41 n. 10

Shona, 116

Simmel, George, 173

smiths, 117

Southeast Asia, headhunters of, 47 n. 13; and Indian influence, 141–43

space, geographical, 8–9

space-time and ancestors, 43–45; characteristics of, 10–11; cosmological conceptions of, 4, 33–35; geographical distance and, 38–43; in European cosmology, 223–25, 233

Sudanic states, 137–38

Suya, 24 n. 3

Swat Pathan, 15, 61

Tahiti, 149, 197

Tapirape, 187

Tegali, 136

Tewa, 29 n. 6

Thailand, 31–32, 35, 68

Tibet, 62, 73–74

Tlingit, 11–12, 27, 75–76, 120, 157, 176

Tonga, 150–51

trade, 5, 68, 129–30, 142, 152–53, 167 n. 17, 241–42, 266

trade goods, and supernatural associations, 205–207

travel, characteristics of, 16–17, 81–82, 88–89; as evidence of ability, 152–53; financing of, 67 n. 1, 96–97; as initiation rite, 86, 88–91, and knowledge, 68–70, 72–75, 78, 242–43; and leadership, 83, 98, 167; mo-

Library of Congress Cataloging-in-Publication Data

Helms, Mary W.
Ulysses' sail.

Bibliography: p.
Includes index.
1. Acculturation. 2. Intercultural communication. 3. Voyages and travels—
Religious aspects. 4. Social distance. 5. Power (Social sciences) I. Title.
GN366.H44 1988   304.2   87–14038
ISBN 0–691–09435–7 (alk. paper)   ISBN 0–691–02840–0 (pbk.)

Lightning Source UK Ltd.
Milton Keynes UK
UKHW02f1955150518
322629UK00003B/302/P